LONG
BALLS,
NO
STRIKES

Also by Joe Morgan and Richard Lally
Baseball for Dummies

LONG BALLS, NO STRIKES

What Baseball Must Do to Keep the Good Times Rolling

JOE MORGAN

with

RICHARD LALLY

Crown Publishers • New York

Published by Crown Publishers, 201 East 50th Street, New York, New York 10022.
Member of the Crown Publishing Group.

Random House, Inc. New York, Toronto,
London, Sydney, Auckland
www.randomhouse.com

CROWN is a trademark and the Crown colophon
is a registered trademark of Random House, Inc.

Printed in the United States of America

Design by Leonard Henderson

Library of Congress Cataloging-in-Publication Data
Morgan, Joe, 1943–
Long balls, no strikes : what baseball must do to keep the good times
rolling / by Joe Morgan. — 1st ed.
    1. Baseball—United States.   2. Baseball players—Salaries,
etc.—United States.   3. Baseball—Social aspects—United States.
    4. Baseball—United States—Finance.   I. Title.
GV863.A1 M64 1999
796.357'64'0973—dc21
99-33098

ISBN 0-609-60524-0

10 9 8 7 6 5 4 3 2 1

First Edition

From Joe:

*To my wonderful family, for their support when I was a player
and their love that keeps me motivated today*

From Richard:

*To Eve, for everything you are
and all that you will be*

Contents

Authors' Acknowledgments

From Joe: The most important people in the world are my family and friends. I want to thank the world's greatest parents, Ollie and Leonard, for always showing me the right way; my wonderful wife, Theresa, a great mother and a lovely lady (if James Brown is known as the "hardest working man in show business," then Theresa is the James Brown of mothers); our daughters: "Kid" Kelly, who will change the world as we know it, and "Angel" Ashley, who will help make the world a better place; my daughters: Lisa, who is very caring just like her mother, and Angela, who is as focused as her dad; my granddaughter, Jasmine; and my fabulous brothers and sisters, Linda, Glenda, David, Jimmy, and Patricia.

People come and people go, but friends are forever. I've been blessed with friends whom I know I can always count on, people like Mike Alesia, Tom Reich, Enos Cabell, Tim Busch, Joe Forrest, Jim Tracey, Hugh Tama, Bill Patterson, and Denny Polse. Their families are my family. I also want to express my thanks to Gloria Morgan (a special lady), Shirley Nelson, Jack Clark, and Corey Busch for making the trip to Cincinnati to see my number retired.

I'll always have a warm place in my heart for the other seven members of the "Original Eight" who made the first of twenty-four golfing trips with me to Hawaii: NBA great Bill Russell, former Raiders All-Pro Clem Daniels, Jim Hadnot, Ben Modisatte, Miles McAfee, Jim McCray, and George Elliott. Guys, thanks from The Pro. And I want to take a moment to celebrate the memories of absent friends: "Swede" Johnson of Denver, Colorado, a man who knew how to enjoy life to the fullest; Bob Connolly, my first friend in Cincinnati; Jim Hadnot, a great ABA basketball player from Oakland and an even finer man; Skip Korb, another Cincinnatian, who shared many great moments with me; and Louis Nippert, the owner of the Cincinnati Reds during the 1970s. I think of them often.

Thank you to my executive assistant, Lolita Aulston, who used to work for me—now she runs the office! I always thought that Doc Holliday was the fastest gun in the West, but he pales in comparison to my collaborator, Richard "Quick Draw" Lally. Val Kilmer is my favorite cinematic Doc Holliday; Richard is my favorite writer. Now I'll let him thank all the other people who helped us with this book. Believe it or not, this is my fourth tome. However, from *Baseball My Way* to *Joe Morgan, a Life in Baseball* to *Baseball for Dummies*, I've always had this book in the back of my mind.

From Richard: After doing two books with Joe Morgan, I have some idea how it feels to be Davey Concepcion. No one could ask for a better double-play partner. He's the only person in North America who has seen *Tombstone* more often than I, which tells you he's a man with exquisite taste in westerns. I am proud to be his collaborator, prouder still to be his friend. Joe's assistant, Lolita Aulston, provided her usual invaluable service as our liaison. Our editor, Peter Fornatale, was both eagle-eyed and passionate. Mark Reiter, our agent at IMG/Bach Literary, was always there with a soothing word when needed. Mark's assistant, Michelle Yung, kept all of us organized. A special thanks to Steve Ross, Crown's estimable editorial director, who masterminded this project. I don't have a research staff, but whenever I needed to check a fact or get an opinion on some unmanageable copy, I was always able to turn to one of my Gang of Usual Suspects: Billy Altman, Bill Shannon, Bill Daughtry, John Collett, and Jordan Sprechman, as well as Monique Norrie of ESPN, who gave us duty beyond the call when she dubbed all of Joe's 1998 broadcasts—we truly had an All-Star cast lending their insights to this project. Bob Costas, Jon Miller, Frank Robinson, Marvin Miller, Tom Reich, Len Coleman, Don Fehr, David Cone, Dusty Baker, Pete Pascarelli, John Hart, Mike Veeck, Andrew Levy, Jerry Colangelo, and Baseball Commissioner Bud Selig could not have been more generous with their time.

I also want to thank those friends and relatives who have supported me with their affection and encouragement throughout my career. I love each and every one of them: my brothers Joseph and Sean, for whom I could never be a good enough writer to properly express my love; my father, Richard, who once suggested the most imaginative use of a piece of baseball equipment that I've ever heard (after listening to a Pat Buchanan rant he said, "Every time I hear this guy talk, I want to go outside and beat myself to death with a baseball bat"); my late mother, Anne, who loved the Brooklyn Dodgers and taught me to cherish baseball; my future sister-in-law, Jamie, who has enough courage to become part of the wackiest family since the Barrymores; my aunt Kathy, who possesses that rare combination of sweetness and strength; the late Brother Leo Richard and his Clan of the Cave, including Dr. Patrick Murphy,

Authors' Acknowledgments

Dr. Robert Englud, Gerald Bowden, Father Edward Doran, Brother James Norton, Brother Regis, Pat Collins, and Jim Mulvey—no youngster detained by fear could ever find a nobler group of men to guide him through the darkness; my blood brother, Al Lombardo, who has always been at my side in the trenches whenever I needed him most, and his wife, Cathy; Joyce Altman, who, as always, has been patient enough to endure my talking baseball for endless hours on the phone with her husband, Billy; the Budny family: Alecks, Michaela, Paulina, and my best pal, Rasmus, also known as the incredible "Mr. Mookie"; the electrifying Maria Di Simone, my violet-eyed angel; Victor Kiam, who taught me to give everything my best effort, and his wife, Ellen; Richard Erlanger, the world's most dangerous Red Sox fan, and his wife, Jessie, who loves him anyway; Charles Ludlow, a true bud; Alan Flusser, who transformed my life forever by introducing me to Buddhism, and his wife, Maralice; Karl Durr, my favorite field marshal, and his forever lovely bride, Margrid; W. Michael Gillespie, a wordsmith who travels incognito as a marketing genius; Ray DeStephens and Brother Dan O'Riordan; Chris Dougherty; Barbara Bauer, my first mentor and muse; Robert Moss, who has always been generous with his guidance; James Spedaleri, a friend for life; President Daisaku Ikeda and the SGI (with congratulations to Orlando Cepeda, the first SGI member to make baseball's Hall of Fame); Ed and Vivian Neuwirth, Arthur Fitting, Todd Randolph, Jim Gerard, Delores Hughes, and my entire Abingdon Square District family; and Vesna and Joey, Jean and Mark, and the rest of my crew at Q Bistro in Forest Hills. Without their curried red snapper, seared tuna, and fine assortment of red wines to maintain my strength, I wouldn't have made it to deadline.

LONG BALLS, NO STRIKES

Baseball Comes Back:
70, 66, and Other Wonders

The summer of 1998. This was the year baseball came out of its coma. It was a sweet grand slam of a season when two prodigious sluggers, St. Louis Cardinals first baseman Mark McGwire and Chicago Cubs rightfielder Sammy Sosa, pushed their sport back to the forefront of the American consciousness. Fans, who had felt betrayed by the work stoppage of 1994, flocked back to the ballpark like true believers drawn to Brother Love's Traveling Salvation Show.

Home runs fueled the revival. Every morning, people across the country would check the box scores to discover whether Mark or Sammy (or Junior Griffey or Greg Vaughn) had clobbered yet another "Big Fly." Devotees, casual fans, even lapsed baseball followers caught the fervor. We all surrendered to the spell of this race toward excellence. And the long balls were only part of the story. We were also drawn to the personalities who made 1998 a season of legend: Big Mac, Sammy, Junior, Roger Clemens, Kerry Wood, and the entire Yankee team all exuded character and class.

They carried themselves like genuine heroes, men we could feel comfortable rooting for.

That hadn't been the case in recent seasons. Baseball's labor wars between the players and owners had soured fans on the game; they saw only villains on both sides of the dispute. Players like Albert Belle and Barry Bonds were considered antiheroes who won ballgames without winning public affection. Despite the extraordinary numbers they put up season after season, people often booed them wherever they played. And Albert and Barry, both of whom I like, weren't their only targets. Fans perceived many players to be cold, surly, and arrogant, unworthy of their accolades or embrace.

Throughout last year's magic summer, no one booed Sammy or Mark. They were gracious, humble, and accessible. Fans in enemy ballparks gave them standing ovations even while they were clubbing their team's brains into mush. I'd never seen anything like it. Neither had Mike Veeck, the senior vice-president of the Tampa Bay Devil Rays, though he had heard of a similar phenomenon. As the son of legendary baseball entrepreneur Bill Veeck, Mike is steeped enough in baseball lore to compare the McGwire-Sosa home-run duel to another healing event. "My father," he told us, "was certain that I would never understand the impact Babe Ruth made on baseball in 1920 when he hit twice as many home runs as anyone else had ever done before. With those homers, the Babe single-handedly dragged baseball out of the doldrums caused by the White Sox when they fixed the 1919 World Series, the Black Sox scandal.

"Well, it turns out it was one of the few times Dad was wrong. Now I can understand Babe's impact because I just watched

McGwire and Sosa pick baseball up on their shoulders and carry it to a new level. Society needs heroics, and these guys provided that. They were so decent, the way they pulled for each other, that by the time it was over, they were no longer just ballplayers. McGwire and Sosa had become different ways to spell joy."

Joey Gmerek, a die-hard Mets loyalist, who manages such high-profile rock bands as The Fixx and Splender, may have been speaking for all fans with his equally thoughtful explanation for the allure of these magnificent sluggers when he said, "It's all about innocence. There are few people in this country who didn't have their first pitch thrown to them by their dads. It's a rite of passage, like the wafer in Holy Communion, a baptism, or a bar mitzvah. That catch becomes a connection to our fathers and to ourselves, to every child who ever threw a ball.

"That's what McGwire and Sosa brought us back to last season. You know, if Bill Clinton had shown up when McGwire hit that record-breaking home run, I really believe the crowd would have booed. Clinton would have been an intruder on our memories and dreams. He's a character from the tabloids, which give us nothing but stories of defeat and disappointment. McGwire and Sosa gave us a chance to celebrate genuine accomplishment. We needed that."

Baseball needed them, and they needed each other. I'm convinced that while Mark might have broken Maris's record on his own, he would not have hit 70 if Sammy hadn't pursued him. Seventy. Let's savor that. I mean, that number is in another galaxy. You can't go that far without someone driving you. As a former player, I was most impressed by the way McGwire and Sosa raced passed each home-run milestone without pausing. You often see players fall into mini-slumps when they close in on a record. McGwire and Sosa rarely slowed down. When they were on the field, neither seemed to feel the pressure of Maris's 61.

How, I wondered throughout their magical season, could they be so immune? Pressure in baseball is continual. I don't care if a player is in a pennant race or twenty games off the lead in September, he always feels the pressure of performance. Most players want to play their best in every game. It's a matter of pride. When you add the weight of a record, the pressure can become crippling.

I remember when I was creeping up on the major-league mark for most consecutive games with one or more runs batted in (I didn't make it). Before each game, I felt a little extra tension because I didn't know if I would even get a chance to drive in a run that day. You try to put the record out of your mind and just go about your business, but the media won't let you. Reporters want to know what you had for breakfast, how you prepared for the opposing pitcher, what you plan to do after the game. It gets so that every time you go to the bathroom, you check under the seat to see if someone is waiting there with a microphone or a notepad. That searing spotlight can make for one self-conscious ballplayer. Instead of concentrating on team goals, you begin fretting over individual achievement. That's when you try to do too much, to hit the three-run homer with only one man on base.

Sosa performed under less of this pressure than McGwire did. Sammy had never before hit more than forty home runs in a season. He came from out of nowhere to challenge Maris. Even when he smacked his fiftieth home run on August 23, few expected him to go the distance. McGwire had hit 52 homers in

1996, 58 in '97. Fans thought him preordained to pass Maris. Even Sosa kept telling the press that Mark would win their race, that he was "The Man." Until you've been there, you can't imagine how trying it is to perform against such lofty expectations.

Sammy enjoyed one other advantage over Big Mac. He and his Cub teammates spent the summer fighting for a post-season berth. Reaching the World Series was Sosa's primary objective. So he had the division and wild-card races to distract him from all the home-run hoopla. Sammy couldn't afford to allow his hunt for the record to take him away from his natural game. And he didn't. I saw many occasions, even late in the season, when he would slap a 2–0 pitch to right field to put his club ahead; most sluggers would have tried jerking the ball out of the park in that situation. McGwire's Cardinals were pretty much out of contention by the All-Star break. He didn't have any pennants to chase, only a number. That made it tougher for him.

Both of them, however, had it easier than Roger Maris did.

When the Yankee rightfielder broke Babe Ruth's home-run mark by hitting 61 in 1961, he was practically a national pariah. Most fans didn't think Maris was good enough to break the most famous record in sports. Even Yankee zealots pulled against him. To them, Maris was an interloper, some guy who had come to New York in a trade with Kansas City. What were his pinstripe bona fides? If anyone was going to pass the Babe, they wanted it to be Mickey Mantle, who had come up through the farm system already christened as the latest Yankee demigod.

The crowd's hostility had to hinder Roger, because fan support can make such a positive difference. Players can feed off the fan's applause as they step into the batter's box. It increases their concentration by giving them something to focus against. But when the fans are against you, as they were against Maris, it can undermine your performance.

I saw firsthand evidence of this when I played with the Philadelphia Phillies in 1983. Mike Schmidt was our third baseman; he probably had greater physical ability than any player I've ever shared a clubhouse with. He could hit for average, had tremendous power, was a fast, smart base runner, a good base stealer, and a Gold Glover at third. Mike could even bunt when the occasion demanded it. But you never saw a superstar with less confidence.

I believe it stemmed from his love-hate relationship with the Phillie fans. Let me give you an example of how fickle they could be toward their team's biggest star. In one late-September game at the height of the 1983 pennant race, Mike struck out two or three times with runners on. The Phillie fans booed him unmercifully. In the ninth inning, with our team down by a run, he homered to tie the game. Of course, the crowd responded with a standing ovation. The next day he hit another home run in the first inning. Another standing O. Then he struck out again and the boos started raining down once more.

This emotional roller coaster ate at Mike. He was so wary of fan reaction, he curtailed his pregame warm-ups. Schmidt would take batting practice with the rest of us, then finish his workout in the runway behind the dugout. It was strange. While taking grounders at second, I'd suddenly hear this loud bang. It was Mike loosening his arm by throwing the ball against the clubhouse door. He wouldn't set foot on the field until he absolutely needed to. That had to hurt his game. I know he was a three-time

MVP and Hall of Famer. Still, I think he would have been an even greater player if the hometown fans had been on his side.

Neither Mark nor Sammy had to deal with fan animosity. Mark did get temporarily distracted when the press practically moved in with him. He's normally a sweet-tempered man, but right after the All-Star break, I noticed a change in him. He was acting, well, cranky. Mark would snap at reporters or grumble about how they never left him alone. When one reporter commented on how Big Mac had really aired it out on one pitch, McGwire, who prides himself on his all-around hitting skills, bristled, "I never try to air it out!" During another interview he complained, "All anyone wants to talk about is home runs. That's not the purpose of why I play this game. It's got to be a piece of the pie; getting this team to the playoffs is what it's all about." The media crush finally appeared to be rattling him.

Here is where Sammy helped McGwire the most. During a Cubs-Cardinals series in early August, Mark saw how Sammy was having a ball with the race. Sosa knew this was a once-in-a-lifetime experience and he was reveling in it; he was a one-man baseball party. The two friendly rivals talked a lot over that weekend. Whatever Sammy told him, it returned the smile to McGwire's face. He was once again handling the reporters' often repetitious questions with his usual good humor and grace. The only complaints you heard came from the pitchers he assaulted night after night, because after that Mark went into cruise control. The nearer he got to the record, the easier he made it look. He closed the deal in September with the finishing kick of a fine thoroughbred: 15 home runs and a .329 batting average.

I saw him hit number 62 on television on September 8. Steven Spielberg couldn't have directed a better climax to the chase. McGwire hit it in St. Louis in front of a stadium packed with his adoring fans, including the Maris family. The opponents that evening? Who else but Sammy Sosa, who entered the game with 58 dingers, and the Chicago Cubs. At 341 feet, give or take an inch, the record-buster may have been the shortest homer Mark smacked all summer, but I doubt he hit many balls any harder. If it hadn't shot over Busch Stadium's left-field wall, it would have gone through it.

The scene that followed couldn't have been more heartrending. McGwire trotted around the bases, basking in the applause of the delirious multitude. After crossing home plate, he lifted his 11-year old son, the Cardinals' honorary bat boy for most of the Maris chase, in a loving bear hug. Sosa came trotting in from right field to congratulate the new home-run king. Then Mark made one of the most powerful gestures I've ever seen on a baseball field. He leaped into the stands to gather the widow and children of Roger Maris, the man he had just expunged from the record books, in his massive arms. What perfection! In that moment, McGwire wasn't just embracing the Maris family, he was embracing all of us. We were his family, the family of baseball.

As it turned out, that evening really was more a tease than a climax. Just when we thought it was over, Sammy and Mark kept us coming back for more. Sosa would get hot and pass Mark, but never for more than a day or two. Those two great athletes kept at each other until they established slugging standards that only six months earlier were beyond our wildest imaginings: 70 and 66. They didn't just pass the record, they shattered it. In their wake, we were left exhilarated by the wonder of it all, yet saddened by the sudden knowledge that nothing would ever seem impossible again.

And if we needed further proof of that, there were the Yankees, whose season of near perfection reminded us that baseball is more than just a game of individual achievement, that winning requires a collaborative effort. Unlike the great Yankee teams of the past, who often seemed as cold and arrogant as they were efficient, these Bronx Bombers were a likable, harmonious group who checked their egos at the clubhouse door. They didn't preen or trash talk on their way to a record-setting 114 regular season victories, but instead handled themselves with a quiet professionalism that should serve as a model to all major-league teams. In any other season, they would have been *the* story. Instead, they had to take second billing to baseball's new home-run heroes. But second wasn't bad in a year filled with amazing stories. Nineteen ninety-eight would have been a magical season if only for the remarkable feats of McGwire, Sosa, and that team from the Bronx. But what pushed it into the realm of the mythical were a series of events—some good, some bad, some ugly—that left indelible marks on the game. Among them:

Kerry Wood (Chicago Cubs) Strikes Out 20 Houston Astros (May 6): And while he was at it, he didn't walk anyone, which I find mind-boggling. That compelling mix of blinding speed and pinpoint control electrified all of baseball. Fans love power pitchers; there's something romantic about one man dominating an entire lineup of big-league hitters. Wood's big right arm gave the 1998 season a spectacular early push; all those K's had people talking for weeks. His feat brought baseball from the back pages to the front pages of the national newspapers, which was exactly what the sport needed.

Kerry's performance also lifted one of the National League's storied franchises out of its decade-long doldrums. Suddenly the Chicago Cubs were no longer about losing; Wood joined Sammy Sosa in convincing the franchise that it could once again contend. Kerry not only won ballgames; he also won over fans everywhere with his attractive combination of presence and modesty. After tying the major-league single-game strikeout record, he declined to appear on David Letterman's *Late Show* or Jay Leno's *Tonight Show*. "That's just not me," he explained. "I'm not very good at it." When reporters compared him to the great strikeout artists of baseball history, Woods hushed the hype by declaring, "Don't compare me to Nolan Ryan, Roger Clemens, Steve Carlton, and Tom Seaver. I'm not in that class. They are all Hall of Famers who had long careers. I just had one great day." If his elbow holds up, he's going to have a lot more.

David Wells (New York Yankees) Pitches a Perfect Game Against the Minnesota Twins (May 17): First, this was a career-making game for one of baseball's great characters. Rotund, tattooed, and often as profane as the bikers who helped raise him, Wells has been known more for his eccentricity than his ability. That changed once he etched his masterpiece. We suddenly saw a different, more confident Wells. He seemed to gain a new appreciation for his immense talents.

His performance was significant for the Yankees because it gave them another reliable starter at a time when staff ace David Cone was still trying to come back from an arm injury. With Andy

Pettite slumping and Hideki Irabu an uncertain commodity, New York needed someone to anchor the rotation. Wells became their rock. His perfect game convinced the entire team that it was something special.

Finally, it was great for baseball. Welles pitched his no-no before a sold-out Yankee Stadium crowd on Beanie Baby Day. Many of the attendees had never been to a ballgame before; they were there only for the promotion. As a bonus, they got to witness a highly charged drama with a colorful maverick of a figure commanding center stage. Imagine how many new fans were made that afternoon.

Major-League Owners Formally Elect Bud Selig Commissioner: Baseball had been without an official commissioner ever since the owners fired Fay Vincent back in 1993. As chairman of baseball's Executive Council, Bud had served as de facto commissioner for the preceding five years. He kept denying that he wanted the job permanently; don't you believe it. Bud is an expert when it comes to cultivating relationships and building consensus. I think he was buying time while he gathered enough votes to take the chair by acclamation. At one point, many National League owners opposed his candidacy. Dodger boss Peter O'Malley, among others, felt that Selig's ownership of the Milwaukee Brewers represented a clear conflict of interest. (Selig has since signed over the Brewers to his daughter. Now *there's* an arm's-length transaction.)

Selig's selection ended what had become a high farce. For five years, major-league owners swore that they were committed to finding a commissioner. Actually, they were just going through the motions. Sure, the Executive Council named Colorado Rockies owner Jerry McMorris to head a search committee, but what came of it? McMorris uncovered several viable candidates for the position, including former U.S. Senator George Mitchell. None of them received serious consideration.

Don't blame McMorris for that. He made a genuine effort to find a commissioner. The council bamboozled McMorris into thinking they wanted him to succeed. When the owners announced during the All-Star Game that Bud had accepted the job, my NBC broadcasting partner Bob Costas quipped, "Gee, I hope they don't disband McMorris's search party. Now they can send them out looking for Amelia Earhart."

During the McMorris hunt, many journalists wrote that the absence of a commissioner was eroding baseball's credibility with its fans. I never got that. If Elmer Fudd were the commissioner, I don't think the fans would notice or care. I think it's good, however, that we finally have an official commissioner because we finally have someone who is accountable. If you have a gripe or a suggestion, you have someplace to go. When the Executive Council failed to take action on an issue, it could spread the blame around. Now baseball's buck stops with Bud.

Do I mind that the commissioner was also a team owner? I agree with Peter O'Malley that there's a conflict of interest. Some people may say that at least it's not hypocritical. Over the last fifty years, nearly all the commissioners have represented the owners' interests rather than the players. Why not put it out in the open? I do, however, believe Selig comes to the office with one serious disadvantage. Fans will always remember him as the man who canceled the 1994 World Series. The owners should have found someone who didn't carry that baggage.

So just what *is* Amelia Earhart up to these days?

The O'Malley Family Sells the Dodgers to Rupert Murdoch: I was sad to see Peter O'Malley leave the game. More than any other owner, Peter appreciated baseball's roots and history; his family was the sport's last link to its Golden Age of the 1950s. Peter lent baseball stability, dignity, and conscience. He had a record of supporting many initiatives that were good for baseball, even if they were disadvantageous to his team.

Murdoch takes baseball into unknown territory. The Dodgers represent programming for his Fox Sports Network. Which means the Dodger management doesn't have to check the bottom line on every decision. Even if the team itself were to finish in the red, an unlikely event, Murdoch's network could still realize a profit from the money it makes from the Dodgers' television sponsors. This means Los Angeles can outspend the other clubs by a wide margin. As Rupert ups the ante, small market teams will find it that much tougher to compete. The owners of those less well-heeled franchises may become more desperate to generate fan interest and dollars. That could lead to a lot of bad decisions. We're already hearing how some club want to expand the playoffs by four more slots. That's the first step toward transforming baseball into hockey, which is still a second-tier sport in this country partially because its regular season is virtually meaningless. There has also been talk of putting all the low-end clubs in one league so that they all have a shot at the post-season. Think of that, an entire league dedicated to preserving mediocrity. Sounds to me like the Philistines are already inside the gate.

Kevin Brown Signs Seven-Year, $105 Million Contract with the Dodgers: See what I mean? Los Angeles's general manager, Kevin Malone, didn't care what it took to put this ace pitcher in

Dodger blue; he outbid everyone by a wide margin. No other club has admitted to offering the righthander more than $10 million a year.

While I think the players should make as much money as they can, this deal is bad for the Dodgers. Brown is 34 years old. Odds are that Los Angeles will get only three or four good years for their $105 million. So what do the Seattle Mariners now have to fork over to retain 29-year-old Ken Griffey Jr. and 23-year-old Alex Rodriguez? A superstar who plays every day has far greater value than any top-flight pitcher. Griffey has already spurned a Brown-like offer from Seattle. This tells us that Kevin's contract didn't just raise the salary bar; it obliterated it.

When the Dodgers signed Brown, manager Davey Johnson justified the expenditure by rhapsodizing on all the plusses the right-hander would bring to the clubhouse. What pitcher was he talking about? I guess it's possible that Brown will be a role model if the Dodger position is that you can never have enough surly players on your roster. Brown has never been anyone's first choice as the ideal teammate. When he was with the Marlins, Kevin threw a tantrum when someone hit a ground ball past his short-stop for a base hit. It seems Mr. Brown thought the shortstop was playing out of position. So he blew up on the mound. That is an absolute no-no. No player should ever show up his teammates in public. The next series, the Marlins held a clubhouse meeting to go over the opposing lineups. They meticulously reviewed where each hitter should be played, based on their charts and scouting reports. At the meeting's conclusion, Marlins manager Jim Ley-land, stood up and called for everyone's attention. Pointing toward Brown, Leyland said, "And when that ass over there is pitching, just play wherever he wants you to." This is the guy who's going to be the Los Angeles version of Nelson Mandela? Who's kidding whom?

Barry Bonds (San Francisco Giants) Creates the 400-400 Club (August 24): When Barry hit a solo homer during the Giants' 10–5 win over Florida, he became the first player in baseball history to top the 400 mark in career home runs and steals. His accomplishment reminded us that baseball is still a multifaceted game. It also certified Barry as the finest player of his generation.

Roger Clemens (Toronto Blue Jays) Wins His Fifth Cy Young Award: Another player who shows us how it's supposed to be done. In a time when pitchers baby their arms with pitch counts and short-inning stints, Roger Clemens demonstrated what it means to be a bona fide mound monster. At 36, he took the ball every fifth day, pitched nearly eight innings per start, and led the American League in wins (20), strikeouts (271), and ERA (2.65). That trifecta made him only the fourth pitcher ever to win consecutive pitching Triple Crowns.

Cal Ripken (Baltimore Orioles) Ends His 2,362-Game Playing Streak (September 20): The streak had gone sour for Cal. He wasn't playing up to his usual high standard; critics were screaming that he was hurting the Orioles by refusing to take a day off. Ripken's bat had slowed while his range in the field had nearly vanished. Yet still he played on.

I've always had ambiguous feelings about Cal's streak. On the one hand, I admired his work ethic. On the other, I thought the consecutive-games-played streak represented one of baseball's more meaningless records. Why? Because it has nothing to do with winning. Ballplayers need rest. A 162-game season is too long and grueling—mentally as well as physically—for anyone to compete in every game, year in, year out. Ripken's résumé carries a history of rough Septembers. In 1989, when the Orioles shocked all of baseball by finishing only two games out of first place with what was largely a no-name cast, Ripken's game fell apart when his team needed him most. He batted .198 in his final 100 at-bats with only 3 home runs and 15 RBI. Had Cal rested, his energy probably wouldn't have faded so badly and his club, which had finished dead last only the year before, might have pulled off one of the great upsets of this century. Frank Robinson always thought Ripken had it in him to be a 50-home-run guy. I think the streak kept him from reaching his full potential. Eventually, Cal's streak took on a life of its own. It became selfish and obsessive. Ripken often said that whether he played or not was up to the manager, but that was disingenuous. Everyone knew that only Ripken could take himself out of the lineup. Cal and his streak had become Baltimore icons. Skippers didn't dare bench him even when it was obvious the O's would be better if he just took an occasional day off. No player should ever be allowed to place individual achievement above team goals.

However, I must admit that Cal chose a fine way to end the streak. Without any fanfare, he told his manager, Ray Miller, that he wanted to sit out that evening's game against the New York Yankees. As soon as the Yankees realized that Ripken's name wasn't in the lineup, they rose as one to applaud the man and his accomplishment. No matter how you felt about the streak, this spontaneous, heartfelt gesture was one of the sweetest moments in baseball's sublime summer.

Sublime, but not quite perfect. In 1998, Ripken, McGwire, Sosa, Clemens, and the rest of their colleagues gave us enough blissful memories to fill a hundred scrapbooks. I've loved baseball for as long as I can remember, and was heartened by the renaissance they spurred. But I don't think we should fool ourselves. The game still has its problems. If they're not addressed, this comeback may be short lived. Although overall attendance rose, it still hasn't returned to its prestrike levels. An amazing fourteen of the thirty major-league clubs suffered declines at the box office. Television ratings for the World Series were the lowest in the event's history. And in poll after poll, baseball continued to rank behind professional football and basketball in overall popularity.

Those figures tell me there is still a lot of work to be done. What happened last season was unscripted, unplanned. There is no guarantee that the elements that made the "Summer of the Big Fly" so special can be replicated. Baseball is back, but it's not all the way back. Nineteen ninety-eight gave everyone connected to the game something to build on. How we utilize this opportunity will determine whether baseball can reclaim its title as the National Pastime, or will become a sport that has passed its time.

With that in mind, I've written this book to throw my two cents' worth into the debate on how baseball can keep the good times rolling. In these pages you'll find my suggestions—suggestions and nothing more—for improving what is already a great game. I may get a little tough at times, but it's always with the idea of growing the sport rather than tearing it down. My mission isn't to see baseball merely survive; I want it to flourish. The game *is* troubled, but it is also laden with unlimited possibilities. If the owners and players grab the opportunity that 1998 gift wrapped and handed to them, we may be entering a new Golden Age, a time when people everywhere are once again thrilled to hear what I still consider to be one of the most beautiful phrases in the English language: Play ball!

If we can just get it right, those words will be ringing out forever.

2

Taking Care of Labor Pains

T he best of times, the worst of times, Dickens would have loved every minute of it. There were four sluggers chasing Roger Maris and his magic 61. The Yankees didn't have a single superstar in their lineup, yet they were clearly the best team in baseball. Home runs were flying out of major-league stadiums in record numbers. This unprecedented power display kept the turnstiles spinning as many teams set attendance records. Though ERAs around the majors soared, Roger Clemens, Tom Glavine, Greg Maddux, David Cone, Randy Johnson, and other mound luminaries were still able to neutralize even the most muscular of offenses. It was a season not of stars but of supernovas so bright they made the sun seem superfluous.

Yes, there's no doubt about it: 1994 could have been 1998.

Unfortunately, what looked like one of the greatest baseball seasons ever ended prematurely when the players called a general strike on August 11. This walkout occurred after the baseball owners voted to implement a revenue-sharing plan predicated on a salary cap designed to limit player earnings. Luca Brasi, leading an armed squadron of hit men from the Corleone family, could not have persuaded Players' Association president Don Fehr to accept that proposal—especially since Fehr and the players believed they held enormous leverage in any late-season labor dispute.

That leverage was green. By the time they walked out, most of the players had already received nearly 75 percent of their salaries for the season. The union had also squirreled away a considerable strike fund. But no team could realize a profit unless the 1994 schedule, including the post-season, was played to completion. The union was therefore certain that the owners would never allow anything to jeopardize the playoffs and the World Series. After all, the television revenues generated by those events represent baseball's largest profit center.

Now, the baseball owners would have you believe that they are more sportsmen than businessmen. And it is true that money is the last thing they ever think about—just before they fall asleep at night. Knowing this, the players reasoned that the mere threat of losing all that TV cash would move even the most recalcitrant owner off the salary-cap proposal and back to the bargaining table.

The players got it wrong. They hadn't reckoned with the owners' hidden agenda. "This was not about money," says former Players' Association president Marvin Miller, "it was about power and control. The owners wanted a salary cap to limit wages *and* free-agent movement. Many of them—particularly the hardliners—were also eager to break the union. They thought a protracted strike would cause fissures throughout the membership."

A high-stakes game of chicken was under way, one in which neither side deviated from its course by so much as a step. Though a federal mediator tried to bring the two parties to an accord, they remained intransigent. Even the President of the United States couldn't persuade the players to take the field again while the two sides bargained in good faith. There were a few false starts toward settlement, but after a while you didn't even hear rumors about a possible compromise. Then, on September 14, the unthinkable occurred. Bud Selig, president of the Milwaukee Brewers and acting head of baseball's Executive Council, officially canceled the remainder of the 1994 season, including the playoffs and World Series.

Though temperatures were relatively balmy throughout most of the country, it was the frostiest baseball winter in memory. There were no trades, free-agent signings, or other transactions to stoke the embers of any Hot Stove League. Eventually the two sides did settle, though not before the first three weeks of the 1995 season were lost. In the end, there was no salary cap; the owners instead instituted a revenue-sharing plan built around a "luxury tax." Teams with the highest payrolls had to donate a percentage of their players' salaries to a common pool for redistribution to the poorer clubs. This tax had little noticeable effect on the players' wages, which continued to rapidly escalate.

But the work stoppage and subsequent cancellation of the 1994 post-season had an enormous negative impact on the game itself. Attendance plunged throughout the major leagues in 1995. The sale of licensed goods such as T-shirts, caps, and posters bearing major-league logos or player likenesses declined dramatically. TV ratings plummeted.

Worst of all, baseball lost priceless esteem with its fans. Their annoyance with what they regarded as a pissing contest between multimillionaires forced them to take a closer look at the game they once revered. They discovered a rash of warts. Suddenly, baseball seemed slow and out of touch. It lacked the NFL's pyrotechnic violence or the NBA's flashdance bravado. The National Pastime was beginning to look like a museum piece. Many even predicted that its status would soon be relegated to that of a second-tier sport.

They didn't consider baseball's resilience. The game started reviving during a dramatic 1995 post-season and gradually built up to the 1998 renaissance. "Baseball is back," the media proclaimed. And indeed it was. But deep beneath the summer's reverie, there is and remains a sense of foreboding. Many of the issues that mutilated the 1994 season while driving the game toward critical mass are still in play.

In baseball's labor wars, there has never been a genuine armistice, but only a series of uneasy cease-fires. The Basic Agreement between the owners and players expires in 2000, though the players can, and probably will, extend it to 2001. No matter when the two sides commence negotiating, it is likely, based on what we are already hearing, that the owners will come to the table bent on capping salaries as teams do in the National Basketball Association. That stance can only invite calamity since—and you can take this to the bank—baseball players will never accept a wage ceiling. If the hard-liners among the owners persuade their colleagues to share their line in the sand, another work stoppage is inevitable.

This must be avoided at all costs; it's doubtful that the game can survive another lengthy walkout. So the first thing the players and owners must do to ensure baseball's long-term prosperity is to negotiate a lasting peace. It's a task that could prove to be as difficult as it is necessary. Let's face it, Gandhi would have found bringing these two lifelong adversaries to conciliation a daunting challenge.

Past negotiations between the two sides have been, almost without exception, acrimonious. The owners continually try to erase those gains made by the players at the arbitration and bargaining tables over the last 25 years. The players resist all encroachments on their current position and, with good reason, mistrust nearly anything the owners claim. Doesn't exactly sound like the makings of a beautiful friendship, does it? Fans often asked me why the players and owners just can't get along. I can't say for sure, but I think player animosity toward management is inscribed in our DNA. You see, there's quite a bit of history here.

Before the players won free agency in a landmark arbitration case, something called the reserve clause tied us to an organization for life. Once a team signed a player, it literally owned him. Just imagine that. You had no say in where you could work until the day you retired. There were millions of other people laboring under the same onerous terms, but most of them were living on the wrong side of a wall in Germany, or in a Chinese commune.

That reserve clause gave the owners a whip they would crack without the slightest compunction. Salary negotiations, if you could call them that, couldn't have been more one-sided. If a player didn't like his team's final offer, his only recourse was to sit out the season. You couldn't seek employment with another club, and salary arbitration wasn't available back then. With conditions like these, it's no wonder that baseball wages remained stagnant for a long time while team profits soared. In 1947, the minimum salary in baseball was $5,000; 20 years later, after some of the worst inflation in this country's history, it was all the way up to $6,000.

Despite holding every advantage during salary negotiations, general managers would often use any means to coerce players into accepting their low-ball offers. Here's just one example of how far they would go: In 1966, Bob Locker of the Chicago White Sox was among the best relievers in the American League. The right-hander won nine games, saved twelve others (when saves were much more difficult to earn than they are today), and posted a glittering ERA of 2.40. In 95 innings, Locker allowed only 73 hits; he struck out 70 while walking a mere 23. Big numbers, the kind that cried out for a big raise.

Locker, a second-year player, asked the White Sox for $18,000. The general manager countered by offering $16,000. He justified the smaller sum by revealing that Phil Regan, the Dodger relief ace who had enjoyed an undeniably better season (14–1, 1.62 ERA, and a league-leading 21 saves) than Locker, had just signed for only $23,000. At least that's the number the general manager swore he had gotten from the Dodger brass. How, the executive wondered, could the sophomore Locker expect the White Sox to pay him an amount only $5,000 less than the more accomplished Regan, an eight-year veteran, was getting? Locker accepted his boss's rationale and signed for the lower figure. Some time later he discovered that Los Angeles had, in fact, agreed to give Regan $36,500 a year.

Now, some of you might call what the Chicago general manager had done lying. But back then, he and his colleagues called it negotiating. "Before there was a union," Marvin Miller recalls, "stories like that were common. I know of general managers who would produce contracts during negotiations purportedly signed by players that showed them making salaries much lower than they were actually earning. These were dummy documents, forgeries if you will, all used to convince the player his salary demands were out of line.

"Regan must have done some negotiating job to get his contract, because the Dodgers were not above playing hardball with their players. Let me tell you a story about them. One of the first things we tried to negotiate was an increase in baseball's minimum salary. I expected management to argue that increasing that minimum would be expensive because if you raised the floor, salaries would go up for everybody.

"To deal with their arguments intelligently, I needed to know something about the players' salary structure. Getting the information from management at that point was out of the question. I doubted they would give us the numbers, and doubted we could trust their accuracy even if they did. So we had the player representative on each team ask his teammates to write their salaries on a slip of paper to be forwarded to us.

"I wanted this information kept anonymous because many players had been brainwashed by management never to discuss their earnings with one another. They had been indoctrinated with what I called the bank clerk's mentality. A story commonly told in banking was that when a clerk approached a manager for a raise, the manager might grant it, but only on the condition the clerk told no one about it because 'you're making so much more than anyone else, if they find out we'll have to raise everyone and it will wipe us out.' Of course, it would turn out that even with the raise, the clerk was still the lowest-paid employee in the department. That's how it was in baseball. Management had access to all information pertaining to salaries; the players had none. This gave the general managers an enormous advantage.

"Our plan worked beautifully. I didn't need to know who was earning what. We just wanted a snapshot of the structure, which this provided. However, a few weeks into the process, Ron Fairly of the Dodgers stormed into my office, absolutely furious. He told me that when he had negotiated his most recent contract, Dodger general manager Buzzy Bavasi had told him his demands were out of line. Bavasi claimed the terms he was offering would make Fairly the fourth highest paid player on the Dodgers, right behind L.A.'s three biggest stars, Sandy Koufax, Don Drysdale, and Maury Wills. Well, that was about where Fairly should have been. He accepted that argument and signed. But after reviewing the slips, he discovered he wasn't the fourth highest paid; he wasn't even in the top ten. Fairly was barely twelfth. And Ron was probably the Dodgers' all-around hitter. That sort of thing happened all the time."

After Marvin agreed to head our union in 1967, the owners challenged the players on almost every issue. These battles were never really about money; they were over control. In 1972 the owners locked us out for the final weeks of spring training and the opening week of the regular season over a relatively trivial matter. As Marvin remembers, "It was the pension and health plan. All that we wanted the owners to do was meet the skyrocketing health-care costs. Now, mind you, we weren't asking for an upgrade in benefits. We just needed additional money to cover the then current plan. On the pension side, we asked for a simple cost-of-living increase to keep pace with inflation. To our amazement, the owners' representatives refused to give us anything on either point. When we asked why they were being so stubborn, they said, 'We've gone far enough. We're going to halt this thing you call progress.' That's when I knew they had another agenda. They wanted to lock us out, to frighten the players into leaving the union."

Players who doubled as union reps were often traded or released. Some general managers would rid their rosters of you if you merely hired an agent to negotiate your contract. Or they would ignore your representative. I know of one GM who threatened to throw an agent from his window rather than negotiate with him. (The agent, who was not a man to be bullied, dropped his briefcase to the floor and said, "Let's get it on. Right now!" That ended the intimidation tactics in a hurry.)

Fear was a management weapon. For years, the owners had successfully indoctrinated us and the public to believe we were lucky to making a living while playing a game. We did have a union back then, whose chief adviser was a fellow named Cannon. He was get this an owner appointee. Which means we were always coming to the plate with an umpire picked by the opposing side. Whenever a player questioned something the owners did, Cannon would tell us, "Boys, we have to remember the owners don't see baseball as a business. The only reason they own your teams is out of their love for the game. They're not making any money here. So if you rock the boat, they'll just go home, and that will be the end of baseball." We were so brainwashed that most of us believed him. So we never pushed too hard for our fair share of the revenue pie.

Until the late 1960s, many players had to hold second jobs to augment their salaries. We're not just talking about fringe talents, either. Phil Rizzuto worked in a men's clothing store during an off-season in which he won the MVP award. Others took positions in brokerages and car dealerships, and some even worked as laborers. Meanwhile, the owners kept piling up the cash.

Management kept pleading poverty but never agreed to open its books. We discovered later that nearly every team—including those that claimed bottom lines etched in red—was keeping a lion's share of revenues in often hidden profits. As Marvin, who had worked in several other industries before joining the players, observed, "The players were the most exploited group of workers I'd ever seen, and I use that characterization advisedly. The margin between what they were paid and what they were worth was probably far greater than that of the poor grape pickers."

Players had to battle for every dollar. "One year," agent Tom Reich remembers, "I negotiated with Pittsburgh for a pitcher who had just won 13 games, one of the club's biggest winners. I busted my behind all winter to move him from $13,000 a year to $22,000. It was a constant war. Since a club owned you in perpetuity, you had virtually no weapons to fight back with. And this wasn't just about money and control. It was also about health. If you were a pitcher with a sore arm, clubs could keep running you out there, particularly if you weren't a star. They'd force you to pitch through the pain. What did they care if your career ended? If you weren't a big name, they had relatively little money invested in you. Once your arm fell off, they'd replace you with someone else."

All that started to change as soon as Marvin formed us into a real union. He set the perfect tone. Ours was an open shop.

Unlike many other unions or guilds, we had no provisions forcing players to join. In the first year, only two players sat out; one of them signed up the following season, and the other retired to become a coach. Since 1968, every player who was allowed to join us has done so (replacement players whom the owners hired during the last work stoppage are the exceptions).

Once we were united, we began winning every time the owners opposed us in a labor dispute. As our wages and other benefits climbed, we gradually won various rights, including salary arbitration and limited trade vetoes. The big megillah, of course, was free agency. When an independent arbitrator ruled in 1976 that the owners could enforce the reserve clause for only one year—the famous Messerschmidt-McNally decision, named after the two pitchers who challenged the clause—much of the power in baseball shifted to the players. Now we could determine where we would play, provided we had at least six years of major-league service (a term negotiated between the union and management). Our salaries were based on free-market conditions rather than on management edicts.

Marvin's successor, Donald Fehr, made sure our winning streak continued. The owners tried to gut free agency in 1981 by unilaterally instituting a free-agent compensation system requiring every team that signed a player to give the club that lost him a player of comparable ability. Instead of being a genuine free agent, you became part of a trade. We knew this would have curtailed our employment options severely. So we struck for a third of the season, returning to the field only after we were assured that free agency would remain intact. Management came away from that work stoppage with practically nothing.

The owners have never forgotten the drubbing they absorbed that season. Ever since, they have tried to turn back the clock. In 1987 and 1988 the owners colluded to ensure that few free agents received bids higher than the offers tendered by their own teams. Suddenly, such stars as perennial 20-game winner Jack Morris couldn't find any takers for their services. When the union filed a grievance, an arbitrator found against the owners while awarding the players treble damages.

Perhaps now you can understand why there has been so much bad blood between baseball's labor and management. Based on past experience, the players have little reason to trust the owners, who continue to cry poor mouth while refusing to let anyone examine their ledgers. And the owners must be collectively suffering from the worst case of low self-esteem in history. That's understandable; I don't think Sicily has been conquered as often as these guys.

Therefore, many of the owners need to get a little of their own back. They want a greater share of power, which they can only get by limiting salaries and player movement. That's why the owners are forever talking about the vast revenue disparity between the small-market and big-market teams. They claim it destroys competitive balance since the poorer franchises cannot afford to stock their rosters with as much talent as the richer clubs.

On the face of it, this seems a reasonable argument. In 1998, no team with a payroll below $48 million made it into the post-season. Teams like the Minnesota Twins, Kansas City Royals, Montreal Expos, and Pittsburgh Pirates open spring training every year knowing they have little if any chance to qualify for the playoffs. Whenever the owners lament the plight of so-called small-market teams, those four franchises are trotted out as examples. They have become the poster children for baseball's "have and have not" syndrome. But let's take a close look at these teams. Money, or the lack of it, has certainly been a problem for each of these organizations. However, they are also plagued by issues that a salary cap cannot remedy.

For instance, Montreal just isn't a baseball town. It has never fully embraced the Expos, even when they were one of the most competitive franchises in baseball. The team hasn't topped 2 million in attendance since 1973. Montrealers do love sports. But if you're an athlete and you're not skating, they just aren't interested. This organization deserves better. It has the best manager in baseball, and a crackerjack front office that keeps its minor-league system stocked with talent. A salary cap wouldn't save this club, but a new address might. If the Expos moved to a city that hungers for baseball, they would be a sensation.

Minnesota has experienced box-office doldrums for a good part of this decade, but from 1987 to 1992 it was a baseball powerhouse. Despite being a so-called small-market team, the Twins won two World Series during that period and contended regularly. And just look at these attendance figures:

1987	2,081,976
1988	3,030,672
1989	2,277,438
1990	1,751,584
1991	2,293,842
1992	2,482,428
1993	2,046,673

Obviously, fans came out when the Twins were winning. Attendance fell off when the team's record nosedived in 1993. However, economics weren't this club's undoing; Minnesota hasn't lost a significant player to free agency since 1979. Its front office has always been able to retain such star players as Kirby Puckett, Kent Hrbek, and Jeff Reardon. The Twins started losing because their roster got old all at once and the team didn't have enough minor-league talent to take up the slack.

The good news is that its six-year slump may be nearing an end. Minnesota has a flourishing minor-league system that is just about to send a truckload of promising young players to the big leagues. I think we have to give this green talent a chance to develop. Should they transform the Twins into a contender, I don't see any reason why the fans shouldn't come back in force. And if Minnesota starts pulling in 2.5 to 3 million fans again, will anybody be able to call it a small-market team?

Unlike the Twins, the Pirates have been a relatively poor draw even when they were winning championships with Roberto Clemente and Willie Stargell in the seventies, and divisional titles with Barry Bonds and Bobby Bonilla in the eighties. Fans gave those fine teams lukewarm support. Attendance has dropped even further as the Pirates' record plunged below .500. This is a club that is genuinely operating under a financial crunch. It has lost many of its best stars—people like Bonds, Bonilla, and Cy Young Award winner Doug Drabek—to free agency, and has lacked the funds to replace them.

If I were a player, though, I wouldn't accept a salary cap to subsidize Pittsburgh's failure, because this is no longer a particularly well-run franchise. It has a handful of young, potential impact players such as catcher Jason Kendall, rightfielder Jose Guillen, and pitcher Francisco Cordova. The Pirates have few blue-chip prospects on their 40-man roster, however, and their front office doesn't have a game plan that makes any sense. For example, during the 1998 off-season, Pittsburgh offered free-agent leftfielder B. J. Surhoff a four-year, $17 million contract.

Surhoff is talented, but he's not a superstar that you can build a franchise around. He's a 20-homer, 80-RBI guy, the sort of player who certainly can help push the wagon, but cannot pull it on his own. B.J. brings a lot of value to a contender; compared with the average leftfielder, he might give a team an extra two or three wins over the course of a season. That can make a big difference to the Orioles, the club he eventually signed with. (Despite the franchise's recent woes, well-heeled Baltimore has an excellent shot at playing in the post-season every year.)

Those few extra victories mean little to a last-place club like Pittsburgh, however, because it's doubtful they will be enough to lift them out of the cellar. At 35, B.J. probably won't be on the Pirates' roster when they finally start winning again. So unless you're going to sign a few more players to help Surhoff—something the Pirates can't afford to do—what does he bring to the team that is worth $17 million? Pittsburgh would have been better off investing that cash in their moribund farm system.

Several months after Surhoff spurned their offer, Pittsburgh tried to trade National League stolen-base champion Tony Womack and outfielder Al Martin to the Arizona Diamondbacks for leftfielder Bernard Gilkey. Gilkey is sort of a B. J. Surhoff with speed, another solid but unspectacular 34-year-old player who will make a minimal impact on Pittsburgh's position in the standings. Why were the Pirates even willing to trade Womack, one of their two or three best players? Because they were afraid that after two productive seasons, Womack was about to become too pricey for them. So they tried to deal him for a player *whose salary was twice as high.* Does that sound like a plan to anyone?

Fortunately, when the transaction hit a snag, the Pirates were forced to accept a straight one-on-one swap of Womack for one of the Diamondbacks' elite minor-league prospects—which is exactly the trade a rebuilding franchise like Pittsburgh should have sought in the first place. Money alone isn't going to turn around a clueless team with an uninspired fan base.

Kansas City has quietly been baseball's biggest mess for years. When Ewing Kaufmann owned it, the Royals were one of the best organizations in baseball. From 1976 to 1985 it won six division titles, two American League championships, and one World Series. No large-market team of the last twenty years can match that record. But since Kaufmann's death, this franchise has become the gang that cannot shoot straight. The Kansas City front office has no idea what it wants its team to be. One season it launches a youth movement. When that doesn't take in a year or two—and what youth movement could succeed under that time constraint—it tries to win with veterans. And when they can't win in a hurry, the team starts another youth drive. One year they are going to win with speed and defense; the next year power is the key. I don't care how much cash you have, you just can't have such a short attention span and expect to run a successful major-league franchise.

Poor management is not confined to the less moneyed franchises. Whenever management starts belting out the blues over spiraling player salaries, I always remind people that despite free agency, the owners still control their payrolls. I've yet to hear of a single player or his agent who negotiated a contract while holding a Smith & Wesson to an owner's head. Many teams aren't getting full value for the money they spend, because the men running them lack baseball acumen.

What can you say about somebody like Jerry Reinsdorf, the owner of the Chicago White Sox? During the 1994 player strike, Reinsdorf was one of the hard-liners crying about the lack of fiscal responsibility in baseball. Eighteen months after the work stoppage ended, however, Reinsdorf gave free-agent slugger Albert Belle a contract that raised the salary bar by more than 30 percent. Who twisted his arm to do that? Then, over the next two seasons, Reinsdorf had to let Belle and most of his best players go when the team's box-office receipts couldn't keep pace with their salaries.

H. Wayne Huzienga shelled out millions to buy a World Series title for his Florida Marlins in 1997, then decimated the team the following season because he could no longer afford its payroll. The payoff for any championship occurs the year *after* it is won, when season-ticket sales traditionally skyrocket. Huzienga didn't even give his club a chance to cash in on that bonanza. Jerry Colangelo bought the Arizona Diamondbacks, a National League expansion team, in 1998. His was supposed to be the cutting-edge franchise that changed the way baseball did business. It sure did that. Arizona revolutionized the concept of overpaying for talent. Nearly everyone in baseball agrees that Colangelo was taken to the cleaners when he gave Jay Bell, a 32-year-old shortstop who had lost both his range and his bat speed, a five-year contract for a little over $35 million. No other team was offering Bell nearly so hefty a pact. And only one year after Bell signed with the Diamondbacks, manager Buck Showalter had to move him to second base because he no longer covered enough ground at short.

After the Dodgers signed pitcher Kevin Brown to a seven-year, $105 million deal, word got out that Los Angeles had outbid itself for Brown's services three times. The Dodgers kept upping the ante, even though all of the pitcher's other suitors had dropped out of the auction. Baseball owners constantly make financial misjudgments like these, then complain to the union that they can't compete unless the players agree to limit how much teams can pay them.

Which is sort of like Jeffrey Dahmer pleading with the police, "Stop me before I kill again."

Look, I'm perfectly willing to admit that the owners do have a problem. No matter how brilliant their front offices may be, clubs without hefty financial resources have a difficult time staying above .500. You can't expect the Expos, with their $12 million payroll, to pose much of a threat to Rupert Murdoch's Dodger Blue Baby, with its payroll of $85 million. But according to most owners, the only way to level this lopsided playing field is to institute a salary cap such as the one that currently exists in the NBA.

This is pure canard. Few owners genuinely care about competitive balance. If they did, they have the means to redress this issue without asking their employees to do a thing. Most of the owners' stated concerns would vanish if they could simply agree on a comprehensive revenue-sharing plan. The owners should require every franchise to contribute all of its revenues—including the money from those lucrative television deals that create much of the revenue disparity between large-market and small-market teams—into a common pool that will be equally divided among the thirty teams.

Under this system, the New York Yankees will have no more money to spend on talent than the Philadelphia Phillies. Cash flow will no longer determine which clubs remain competitive. Baseball savvy will become the new coin of the realm. Teams that scout well and buy smart will outperform teams that don't. Player salaries will stabilize, since no single club will have the wherewithal to drive up the bidding. The owners will no longer need to limit player movement or wages, which means a major obstacle to labor peace will finally be removed. Franchise values will skyrocket, since every team will operate in the black.

I'm sure critics of this simple albeit radical proposal will say it destroys incentive. Why should a team spend more than the absolute minimum on salaries if it is guaranteed a profit every season? The owners can prevent franchises from grabbing a free ride by requiring each of them to devote a set percentage of revenues to payroll. Clubs could choose to exceed that amount. Hey, it's their money. They can spend it any way they want. But their payrolls wouldn't be allowed to dip below a minimum. The owners could also introduce a mechanism that would make it easier to buy back and move franchises whose chronic poor attendance or sub-par television packages are a financial drag. Or it could dissolve those clubs and redistribute their players in a special draft.

As I see it, there is at least one possible glitch in this arrangement. An owner like Rupert Murdoch, who has nearly unlimited resources to draw upon, may dip into his personal coffers while attempting to buy a championship for Los Angeles. Such a move could once again upset competitive balance. Unlike most of his colleagues, Murdoch views the Dodgers as programming; he can absorb any of his team's financial losses while making it back on the TV side. I don't see any way the owners can legislate against such an occurrence unless the players agree to a salary cap of some kind, either on payroll or individual earnings. It may have to come to that. But before asking the union for assistance, teams must demonstrate that they can act out of a common interest and that their supposed concern over the fate of small-market teams isn't just a lot of smoke-blowing. The owners shouldn't expect the players to enter into any kind of partnership with them until they prove that they can be partners with themselves.

3

Let the Thieves Run Wild!

Buck, Bill, say it ain't so!

Arizona Diamondbacks manager Buck Showalter has always expressed a faint disdain for base-stealing. He feels it is an overused, overrated offensive tactic because, in his opinion, the cost of a caught stealing far outweighs the value of a stolen bag. Bill James, baseball's statistical maven and creator of *The Baseball Abstract,* has long concurred with Showalter's view. When James evaluates a player's productivity, he credits less weight to the stolen base than to any other offensive statistic.

And so, apparently, do a lot of managers and players. Since 1988, stolen bases have fallen 23 percent while stolen-base attempts have dropped by more than 30 percent. According to Stats Inc., the stolen-base rate dropped to 1.35 steals per game in 1998, a 23-year low. For a retired base thief like myself, these numbers couldn't be more alarming. I feel the way Willie Sutton would if he learned that every stickup man in America had sworn off robbing banks.

It's no coincidence that base-stealing has waned during an era when major-leaguers are smacking home runs in record numbers. Longball is now the name of the game. It has gotten so that almost any hitter in any lineup can go deep on any pitch. While batters have turned up the power, their managers have turned down the thievery. Skippers like Showalter prefer their base runners to stay safely anchored to their bags so that they can maximize each home run's output.

We've got to reverse this trend now. Baseball pays a heavy price when it clamps its burglars in leg irons. Though it's true you can win a lot of games with three-run homers, you can also lose a lot of games sitting around waiting for them. As speed becomes less of a factor in baseball, players not only stop swiping bags, they usually stop bunting and playing the hit-and-run. These low-caliber but effective offensive weapons lend baseball its rich nuance. When they fall into disuse, the game becomes one-dimensional, constricted, and less exciting. Offenses become predictable and easier to check.

When that occurs, the game is diminished. Baseball at its best is a sport of continual anticipation. Every at-bat should be fraught with possibilities. Whether you're in the stands or following the game from your living room, pondering the various options available to both sides keeps you riveted to the action on the diamond. Wondering what might happen draws you to the edge of your seat every bit as much as what actually does happen.

If the game becomes nothing more than one batter after another swinging for the fences, fans might find the thrill of the big bang exhilarating for a time. But eventually they'll be numbed to all the cannon fire. What will keep them watching then?

If it's runs fans are hungry for, we shouldn't shackle our base thieves. Speed enhances offense. When teams stop running, the clubs with the best pitching staffs become even more formidable. That's why the Atlanta Braves win so many games. They have the finest starting rotation in baseball, a staff of Cy Young Award winners. It's difficult to homer against pitchers of such quality. A one-dimensional offense just won't cut it when you're up against some mound stud who's having one of his better days. You'll usually need a full grab bag of weapons to score on him.

Just look at Braves ace Greg Maddux. He either induces batters to beat the ball into the ground or strikes them out. He hasn't walked a hitter since the Coolidge administration, and you'd need a rocket launcher to elevate one of his pitches beyond the outfield.

So how do you beat him? Apply unrelenting pressure by putting in motion the few base runners he allows. Maddux doesn't hold runners well. His pick-off move is below average, partly because he focuses on the batter so intently (outside of Roger Clemens, no pitcher in baseball can match Maddux's concentration). Greg has programmed himself to defeat the home run, but he's vulnerable to the stolen base. So if teams don't send their runners scurrying while he is on the mound, they are inviting Maddux into a comfort zone; they are playing right into his hands.

You can short-circuit a team's power; it will suffer slumps. Speed, though, never sleeps. While with the Philadelphia Phillies, I once trudged through a brutal 0-for-34 streak. Yet I still reached base often enough via walks to help my teammates win games with my legs. I didn't have to hit to put up numbers on the scoreboard. Lineups featuring speed can manufacture runs even when the opposing pitcher is dominating.

We've all seen how the home-run fever that is so virulent today can hurt players. When Chuck Knoblauch starred for Minnesota, he was one of the American League's premier offensive catalysts. His on-base percentage the last few years was over .420—that's Rickey Henderson country—and he had become one of baseball's more prolific base stealers.

But after joining the Yankees in 1998, Knoblauch got off to a horrendous start at the bat and in the field (suddenly this sure-handed Gold Glover couldn't make a true throw to first base). I think he was feeling the pressure of playing for a new team in the nation's media capital. Despite his frustrations at the plate, however, Knoblauch started hitting home runs at what was, for him, an unprecedented rate.

Sorry, Martha Stewart, but this was not a good thing. Knoblauch, a hard-nosed, blue-collar player I've long admired, is at his best when he's driving the ball through the infield or pelting line drives all over the outfield. His home-run-happy, fly-ball swing took something away from his offense. Sure, he set a career high in home runs with 17, but his on-base percentage and stolen-base totals tumbled. Knoblauch's 31 steals represented his lowest output since his rookie season. Even his slugging percentage shrank, despite the home runs. That tells you that Knoblauch was lofting the ball for much of the season rather than driving it. His homers came at the expense of other extra-base hits.

The Yankees don't pay Chuck to launch moon shots; they have Tino Martinez, Bernie Williams, Chili Davis, and Paul O'Neill to do that. New York pays Knoblauch to get on base with hits and walks, then use his speed to play mind games with the opposition. When he ceased doing that, he became a diminished player. Chuck should forget about hitting big flies and resurrect the playing style he used so effectively in Minnesota. If he does, and New York's offense performs as it did in 1998, Yankee Stadium is going to resemble the set of *Nightmare on Elm Street* for a lot of American League pitchers.

I'm sure Knoblauch's manager, Joe Torre, will encourage Chuck to start sprinting again. Torre appreciates how speed can open up a team's defense. Most managers are like Buck Showalter, however. They ignore the running game's hidden benefits. Just the threat of a stolen base can often be as potent a weapon as the steal itself. For example, let's imagine that New York Mets left-fielder Rickey Henderson, the all-time stolen-base king, has just singled with no one out in a tie game against Kevin Brown and the Los Angeles Dodger ace. Brown, the possessor of one of baseball's quicker pick-off moves, can't allow Henderson to carry the potential go-ahead run into scoring position unchallenged. He will try keeping Henderson close to the bag by making numerous throws to his first baseman. The longer Henderson's lead, the more throws he will attract.

Brown's best pick-off throws—coming off what he would call his "A-move"—are going to have some mustard on them. Though they lack the velocity of his pitches to the plate, those pick-off attempts will indeed exact a toll on a pitcher's arm. Every time Rickey elicits a Brown toss to first, he's removing another bullet from the pitcher's chambers—which means Brown could lose speed or movement on his ball sooner than usual. The Mets may very well be able to tag him for some late-inning runs or drive him from the game in favor of a fresher but less talented arm.

Base stealers are particularly noisome for hurlers whose managers adhere to strict pitch counts. Pitchers like right-hander Joey Hamilton of the Toronto Blue Jays have great stuff for 90 to 95 pitches, then abruptly lose all their heat. Each pick-off throw brings their meters closer to empty. The beauty of all this is that the base stealer doesn't actually have to *do* anything to tire a pitcher's arm; he just has to look as though he's thinking about running to inflict some damage.

When a speedster reaches first, the first baseman must stay close to the bag to accept his pitcher's pick-off attempts. This opens up a hole for the hitter on the right side of the infield. Base stealers can also induce pitchers to change their patterns. It is more difficult for a catcher to throw out a runner on a breaking pitch than on a fastball. Pitchers are therefore likely to throw fastballs in the presence of a base-stealing threat—a decided advantage for the hitter at the plate.

How much can that help a big-league batter? When Yankee first baseman Don Mattingly was in his prime and batting third in a stacked Yankee lineup, he was as terrifying a hitter as you'd ever hope to see with men on base. Donnie Baseball would bat around .350 with power in those situations. But when Mattingly batted second behind Rickey Henderson, something the first baseman occasionally did to revive a sluggish bat, he went from All-Star to All-World—a .400 hitter who slugged nearly .700. It was that steady diet of Henderson-inspired fastballs that got Donnie so fat.

Base stealers in particular, and speed in general, disassemble defenses. Sparky Anderson always told me, "When you have speed, you can drive the other team nuts. And the actual stolen base is only part of it. Faked steals, the hit-and-run, continually going from first to third, anything that injects movement into the game, is a plus for your side. When you do that, it is hard for the opposition to get set defensively. I always liked playing against teams that could only slug; take away their long balls and you had them. But teams that are always on the go can beat you so many different ways." Which is why our Cincinnati teams ran early and often when Sparky was in charge. It's also why it was so tough for any pitcher to shut us down.

Before we continue, we need to understand the difference between genuine base stealers and guys who steal bases. Players who just steal bases swipe numbers. Blue Jays outfielder Shawn Green stole 35 bases in 1998; his teammate Jose Canseco swiped 29. But they really aren't base stealers. I'm not sure Jose wants to hear that. Canseco was awfully proud of those 29 stolen bases, coming as they did during a season in which he turned 34. But I think he was so focused on running up his stolen-base totals, he hurt his team. Catchers threw out Jose 17 times, which means he had a .630 success rate, far too low to have any real value for his club. At this stage of his career, Jose should save his legs for trotting around the bases rather than sliding into them. When a player continues to run in the face of so much failure, it looks as though he's more interested in gratifying his ego than winning ballgames. And it gives managers such as Buck Showalter additional ammunition when they downgrade the stolen base.

Your 24-karat base thief is someone who can swipe a bag with the score tied in the ninth while everyone in the park is aware of his intent. Base stealers run with the game on the line. Put Rickey Henderson on first in the final inning of a tight game—I don't care if it's opening day or a World Series finale—and he will find a way to get to second. Players who just collect numbers rarely run

beyond the seventh inning. Their hearts may overflow with lar-
ceny during those situations, but their feet remain honest. For
them the stolen base is a statistic; for the bona fide base thief it's a
weapon.

Under my definition, players like Henderson, Tim Raines,
Maury Wills, Lou Brock, Davey Lopes, Tommy Harper, Rodney
Scott, and Ron LeFlore have all been card-carrying members of
the base burglars' fraternity. And, yes, I counted myself among
their number. Sparky Anderson has often told people that he
never had to waste an out to move me into scoring position during
the late innings of a close ballgame. If we were tied or down by a
run, I would steal second to set the table for the hitters behind
me. I took great pride in the fact that players who can deliver in
those situations unsettle teams.

Kenny Lofton, Tom Goodwin, and Brian Hunter are three of
the few modern players who are felonious in the clutch. I also like
what I've seen of Toronto's Shannon Stewart and Tampa Bay's
Randy Winn. Rickey Henderson, whose 66 steals led the American League in 1998, is obviously still a force. Those players can
swipe victories as well as bases.

Unfortunately, their numbers are dwindling. Houston second
baseman and lead-off hitter Craig Biggio, who pilfered 50 bags in
1998, is one of my three or four favorite players in baseball. He's
among the league leaders in stolen bases every year. During the
1998 National League playoffs between the Astros and Padres,
Craig was on first in a 0–0 ballgame with Kevin Brown pitching.
You won't get many scoring opportunities against Brown. A true
base thief should feel obligated to take off for second with the
game at such a crucial juncture. Yet Biggio remained riveted to the

bag. Houston eventually lost and was on its way to playoff elimination. Had Biggio stolen second as a prelude to scoring, it might have turned around the game and the series. Your prime-time base stealers can do that.

The irony of the running game's decline is that players today are faster than ever. Not that you need a lot of speed to steal bases. Maury Wills, the first player to swipe over 100 bases in a season during this century, wasn't even the fastest guy among his Dodger teammates. Willie Davis, Junior Gilliam, and Lou Johnson all could have bested him in a 100-yard dash. Baseball is a game of 30-yard sprints between the bases, however. Over that distance of ground, quickness was the difference between Maury and all comers. Wills accelerated to top speed in only three steps; it takes most players ten to twelve strides before they are running full throttle.

Maury also knew you couldn't rely on speed alone to be a high-performance base stealer. He studied pitchers and catchers with a Talmudic scholar's discipline. Like all great base stealers, Maury didn't see a pitcher on the mound; he saw a traffic signal and could instinctively recognize whether the light was flashing green or red. I can't tell you how often I hear players today say they have to take their time reading those signals. Wrong! If you want to make a living as a thief, you must immediately pick up your next victim's "tell." Linger at first a split second too long, and you're just another notch on some catcher's arm.

If there is one thing recent baseball history has proven, it's that base-stealing is a skill that can be acquired. During a two-year span (1975–76), Johnny Bench stole 24 bases in 26 attempts, many of them in big situations. That's a fabulous percentage, especially since John was only a step or two faster than Luciano Pavarotti (actually, Bench was much swifter than the tenor, but I like to jab him whenever I can). He swiped those bags with his brains and his eyes rather than his feet. Yankee rightfielder Paul O'Neill, another relatively slow runner, stole 15 out of 16 in 1998 by meticulously reading the pitcher while picking his spots. There are few major-leaguers who can't steal in the double digits every season if they simply learn how.

So why aren't more players swiping bags?

For one thing, most big-leaguers refuse to expend the same amount of concentration on base-stealing that they do on hitting. Base-stealing is one of baseball's delicate arts; you have to invest time to master it. Detroit Tiger centerfielder Brian Hunter became a base-stealing champion (he led the American League with 74 in 1997) by working exclusively on his base-stealing mechanics four or five times every week.

You don't see many players today demonstrating the same commitment. Why is that? Because management doesn't provide them with the financial incentive to do so. Clubs pay the big bucks for sluggers, and the players know this, which is why so many of them spend every spare moment working on their hitting while ignoring other, less overtly lucrative aspects of the game.

To be a great base stealer, you must focus as much from the bench as you do when you're on base. You have to continually study the pitchers, catchers, and infielders. Note their tendencies with runners on. Most players who could steal bases if they applied themselves would rather think about their most recent turns at the plate. Some even venture inside the clubhouse to study tapes of their last at-bat. So they miss the opportunity to do the base stealer's homework.

I learned how to steal bases during a season in which I played only a handful of games. In 1968, I suffered a knee injury that kept me out of the lineup for most of the season. Instead of staying home, I sat in the stands every night studying the pitchers and catchers while watching how the defenses set up. I kept asking myself, "What is the pitcher giving away? Does he move his foot or his shoulder first when he's going to throw the ball home? Is the catcher doing anything unusual before he throws down to first?" Things like that.

The following season, all that studying paid off. I stole forty-nine bases, a career high to that point. Gene Mauch, who was managing the Montreal Expos at the time, said he never saw any player who could read a pitchout as well as I could. It really wasn't any big deal. Any player can decipher a pitchout as long as he knows what to look for. Nine times out of ten, the pitcher or catcher's body language reveals whether a play is on. For example, if a pitcher looks for a sign, he expects to see 1 for a fastball, 2 for a curve, 3 for a slider, or 4 for something off-speed.

When the catcher flashes something unusual, such as a closed fist for a pitchout, it can give a pitcher pause. He might hesitate ever so slightly. If you're focused on him, you can't miss this clear red light. Stay rooted, because the pitchout is probably on. (Reading the pitchout correctly not only helps you on the basepaths, it aids the hitter as well. Any time a catcher calls a pitchout, and the runner doesn't go, it's a ball.)

Some pitchers will accelerate their motions during the pitchout; they want to get the ball to the plate as quickly as possible. Or a catcher might betray his intent by looking down at the base runner before giving a sign. Players can pick up this data simply by being more observant.

They can also learn a good deal by seeking out tutors. Today's young players need mentors. Most of them are brought up through the minor leagues too rapidly to absorb fundamentals. So, for many of them, on-the-job training is a must.

When I first joined the Astros, you could get advice from all over the league. Maury Wills was a Los Angeles Dodgers superstar. When it came to swiping bags, he was The Man. He was also my guru. It was Wills who advised me to steal third base more often because it was actually easier than stealing second. You could take a big lead off second without drawing many throws. Pitchers generally find it more difficult to pick runners off second than first. You can depart from second base before the pitcher releases the ball; you have to wait for the pitcher to start his motion before you can take off from first. And while the catcher has a shorter throw to third, the big lead you can take from second compensates for that.

Many baseball people will tell you that stealing third with two out is a bad percentage play because you can score just as easily from second in that situation. They are wrong. Maury taught me that standing at third rather than second offers you nine more opportunities to score with two out. For those of you who want to thrill and amaze your friends with your baseball acumen, here they are:

1. a balk
2. a wild pitch
3. a passed ball
4. a one-base infield error
5. an infield hit

6. a fielder's choice (where the hitter and any other base runners are safe)
7. catcher's interference
8. base-running interference
9. a steal of home (now there's a lost art!)

Watching Wills dance along the basepaths, I noticed how his feet worked in unison with his brain. He would set up at first with his right foot a little open toward second base; most runners keep their front feet perpendicular to the bag. Maury would turn his foot toward the bag, then spin as he took off. That was the secret behind his instant acceleration. Other base runners usually took their leads in back of the bag, behind the baseline. Maury took his lead in front of the baseline; this created the illusion that his lead was much shorter than it actually was.

Wills wasn't my only instructor without portfolio. Rod Carew of the Minnesota Twins gave me tips on bunting. I'd seen him play enough times on television to know he had something I wanted. I spoke with Willie Mays about base-running and reading the outfielders because no one ever went from first to third better than he. Whenever Willie decided to take an extra base, he rarely got thrown out. It didn't matter to Maury, Rod, or Willie that we were on opposite sides; they were making baseball better by sharing their insights.

We don't see as much of that today. I recently asked Tony Gwynn how many players talked to him about hitting. This eight-time National League batting champion replied, "Practically none, and I don't know why that is. I would love to talk to other players about hitting, whether they are on my team or not."

Maybe young players today are too intimidated to approach a Tony Gwynn. They shouldn't be. Players should take advantage of every opportunity they find to enhance their skills.

Fear is another factor depressing the running game. During the 1998 season, Craig Biggio offered this quote to *USA Today Baseball Weekly:* "It's gotten to a point where if the pitcher doesn't want you to steal, you can't steal." In the recent past, talk like that would have gotten a player permanently chucked from the base stealers' union.

Unfortunately, many managers are—to borrow a term from the Oprah Winfrey nineties—enabling their players' paranoia. In that same article, Astros manager Larry Dierker supported Biggio's timidity when he said, "Pitchers are making a conscious effort to stop the stolen base. A lot of teams figure it's not worth taking a chance when you have so many guys who can hit it out."

Gee, Larry, are pitchers actually trying to prevent stolen bases? When did that happen? Since baseball began, hurlers have lain awake at night trying to devise methods, legal or otherwise, to apprehend base thieves. However, players like Davey Lopes, Rickey Henderson, Kenny Lofton, and I have always felt as if there wasn't a pitcher alive who could stop us when we wanted to swipe a bag. Hitters must take the attitude that they can adjust to anything a pitcher does. They have to carry that same confidence on the basepaths. (And to underscore how cockeyed my friend Larry's sentiments are, just imagine if a manager said, "My hitters don't want to come to the plate because the pitchers are determined to get them out." The front office would be fitting him for a straitjacket.)

Fear of injury is a legitimate player concern. Stealing bases is a dangerous business. The catcher's throw can hit you in the head. Infielders might spike you. You can catch your own spikes on a bag and tear a ligament or, worse, break an ankle. But outfielders have suffered serious injuries while diving for fly balls. What should they do, never dive for a ball again? Baseball is a sport of calculated risks. Players can't allow trepidation to take them out of their games.

Many ballplayers I've spoken with cite the slide-step as a primary reason for the curtailed base-stealing. When a pitcher slide-steps, he eliminates his leg kick while using his lower body to drive his arm. This reduces the time it takes the pitcher to deliver the ball to home plate. Shaving a split second from his delivery allows the catcher a better opportunity to eliminate base-stealing wanna-be's. The funky motion also throws off the runner's timing.

When Jim Kaat pitched for the Philadelphia Phillies, he eliminated his leg kick in favor of a "no-windup windup." It wasn't quite a slide-step; he'd just rear back with his upper body to deliver a pitch while his legs drove off the mound. I always had difficulty getting a good lead off first when "Kitty" was the opposing hurler. Man, he was tough. If you stole a base while he was pitching, you usually stole it on his catcher. So I know a slide-step can be a base-stealing deterrent. *But you can't let it stop you from running.* Whenever a base stealer induces a pitcher to slide-step, he's grabbing an advantage for his side by taking the pitcher away from his natural motion, upsetting his rhythm.

You see, a slide-step doesn't enhance a pitcher's effectiveness. If it did, pitchers would use them all the time. So even if the runner never leaves first, he can help his team. And he cannot do this unless he poses a viable base-stealing threat. Roger Clemens won't slide-step with Frank Thomas looming on first, but he will when the speedy Ray Durham is on base. That gives the White Sox an advantage. They might be unable to exploit it on the scoreboard, but any edge you can grab on a Rocket Roger has tremendous value. And your team can't get that edge if it rarely runs. Today, even the top thieves aren't taking off as often as they used to. Throughout the 1980s, you usually couldn't lead either league in stolen bases unless you swiped at least 70 bags. The Cardinals' Vince Coleman stole over 100 bases in three consecutive seasons (1985–87). In 1998, Rickey Henderson, who was all of 39, led the majors with only 66 steals. The National League used to be the speedster circuit. It hasn't had a stolen-base leader swipe more than 60 bags since 1992.

Okay, I think we can agree that there is a problem here. Now let's look at some solutions. How can baseball revive the running game? First, front offices must scan their organizations and identify those players who have the quick reactions or speed required to steal bases. Remember, these are two distinct components. Quick players can react to pitchers immediately and swipe bases even if they aren't particularly fast. Players with blazing speed can outrun the combination of throws from the pitcher to the catcher to the bag.

Once teams identify which of their players possess base-stealing aptitude, they must hire the teaching masters who can maximize that potential. One of the reasons base-stealing has declined is that there are few coaches, in the majors or minors, who can pass on the art. I can think of only four who are currently working in the big leagues. Davey Lopes of the Padres, Tommy Harper of the Expos, Mookie Wilson of the Mets, and Al Bumbry of the Indians were all accomplished base thieves. Those men have studied every aspect of base-stealing; they know how to impart their wisdom to others. Baseball needs more of them. Each team should have at least one coach or roving instructor with the background to inject some flash into their offense.

With the roadrunners in their lineup ready to rock and roll, it will be the manager's responsibility to unfetter them. This means skippers such as my friend Mr. Dierker will have to alter their present mind-sets. If they lack any incentive for making the change, they need only turn their eyes toward that juggernaut in the Bronx.

Joe Torre's 1998 Yankees were a band on the run, a club in perpetual motion. They played what used to be known as National League baseball in American League parks. Torre's road warriors stole bases, pulled the hit-and-run, bunted, and squeezed runners home. The Yankees tormented pitchers and defenses alike by exerting constant pressure on both. Six major-league clubs outhomered them, but they led everyone in scoring. By the end of the season, Torre wasn't issuing any statements about how difficult it was for his team to steal bases. He was too busy picking up his team's World Series trophy,

I suspect there's a lesson in that, don't you?

We saw an excellent example of how the Yankees' running game could unravel a pitcher when they played Cleveland in the opening game of the 1998 American League Championship Series. Jaret Wright started for the Indians. In his brief major-league career, he had become something of a Yankee-killer. Wright had beaten New York twice in the first round of the 1997 AL play-offs. He was also one of the few pitchers to win as many as two games against the Bombers during the 1998 regular season.

New York came right at him in the bottom of the first inning. Yankee second baseman Chuck Knoblauch—who, by the post-season, was looking a lot more like the pesky player he had been with Minnesota—led off with a base hit to right. With Derek Jeter at the plate, Knoblauch took a long lead off first. There was no question he had designs on stealing second base. Wright has a terrible pick-off move and is unusually slow delivering the ball to the plate. To neutralize Knoblauch, he tried shortening his stride. This took just enough off his fastball for Jeter to smack it into right center for a base hit. Paul O'Neill then singled in Knoblauch for the first run of the game. Bernie Williams followed with another single to score Jeter for a 2–0 lead.

With runners on first and second, Tino Martinez hit into a force play that pushed O'Neill to third base. That set up the play of the game. As Tim Raines struck out, Martinez—who had stolen just two bases all season—swiped second. Cleveland catcher Sandy Alomar Jr. didn't even try to throw him out.

When Wright threw a wild pitch to Shane Spencer, O'Neill scored while Martinez rumbled into third. Spencer walked. By now it was obvious that Wright had been psyched right out of the strike zone. A single by Jorge Posada plated the Yankees' fourth run and drove Wright from the game.

Scott Brosius's flaring base hit off Cleveland reliever Chad Ogea scored Spencer with the fifth and final tally of the inning. The game had barely started, yet the Indians were as good as done. Six well-placed singles, a walk, a stolen base, a wild pitch. Not a long ball in the bunch. A lot of little baseball produced five big runs. It was Martinez's stolen base that set up the last three. His successful gamble put two runners in scoring position, kept the Yankees out of the double play, and brought Jaret Wright to the cusp of the abyss. In that one inning, Cleveland discovered that you don't always need a lineup heavy with Dirty Harrys toting .44 Magnums to whack out a club. Speed can also get the job done.

Speed kills.

4

Winning the Arms Race

I s this irony enough for you? I spent my entire playing career try-ing to make life miserable for pitchers. Now I'm taking on the role of their protector. And do they ever need protecting. Over the past few seasons, earned-run averages have been rising faster than blue-chip tech stocks. After seeing their best pitches hammered into the stratosphere by today's super sluggers, hurlers are refusing to challenge hitters as they have in the past. Instead, they are trying to paint the corners, which translates into more walks, longer games, and a sloppier brand of baseball. I know fans love offense, but they also want to see faster-paced, more efficiently played games. That's exactly what we will get if teams adopt the following measures to restore the competitive balance between pitchers and hitters:

Just for Starters: Let's Resurrect the Four-Man Rotation

From 1900 until the mid-1960s, most major-league teams used four-man rotations. Then, perhaps because the New York Mets had so much highly publicized success with it, clubs began shifting to five-man rotations. By 1980, Earl Weaver's Baltimore Orioles were the only team relying almost exclusively on four starters. The practice all but ended after Weaver first left Baltimore at the end of the 1982 season (he would return for a brief managing stint three years later).

Given the scarcity of good pitchers today, I'd like to see baseball return to the four-man rotation. Most teams don't have the resources to fill five spots with quality starters (for some of them, even four is a stretch). Twenty percent of today's games are being started by pitchers who twenty years ago would have been middle relievers if they were fortunate enough to be on a major-league roster at all. Too many clubs are rushing young pitchers into the majors to work as number-five starters. This practice hurts the team, who have to trust 30 or so starts to an arm that might not be ready for prime time, as well as the pitcher, who would be better off developing his mental and physical skills in a less pressured environment.

Pitching on three days' rest rather than four sharpens most pitchers' control. Logic tells us that when a pitcher works more regularly, he's more likely to throw strikes and build arm strength. Since few managers ever employ four-man staffs for even short spurts during the season, it's difficult to prove this. But what little empirical evidence has been gathered over the last twenty years indicates that the four-man rotation is an idea worthy of reconsideration.

For example, in his groundbreaking work *The Diamond Appraised,* statistician par excellence Craig Wright tells how Kansas City Royals manager John Wathan used a four-man rotation from the opening day of the 1988 season to May 10. During that time, Bret Saberhagen, Mark Gubicza, Charlie Leibrandt, and Floyd Bannister started each one of Kansas City's first thirty-two games. The Royals quartet posted a 3.13 ERA while pitching on "short rest." Their ERAs climbed to 3.78 after Ted Power was added to the rotation. According to Wright, the Royals starters not only pitched better with the four-man setup, but also pitched longer: an average of seven innings per start, as opposed to six and two-thirds innings pitched in their other games.

After joining the rotation, Power performed abominably. His ERA was 5.94 in 12 starts. When it became obvious he wasn't going to turn his season around, Kansas City traded him to Detroit. Instead of going back to the four-man rotation that had functioned so superbly, however, Wathan inexplicably stayed with his five-man setup. A former catcher, Wathan may have been leery about pushing the arms of young Saberhagen and Gubicza, both of whom proved to be fragile later in their careers. Wathan instead used a potpourri of starters, none of them particularly effective, in the fifth spot. His reluctance to further buck what had become a baseball fashion made his 32-game experiment more intriguing than instructive.

Fortunately, we do have other examples of the four-man rotation's efficacy. Throughout the 1970s, the Baltimore Orioles had the best pitching staff in baseball. As noted at the top of this chapter, their manager, Earl Weaver, was a firm believer in putting his best four pitchers on the mound as often as possible. His starters frequently pitched on three days' rest; Weaver would use a long reliever as a swing man to start the occasional second game of a doubleheader or to give a starter an extra day off whenever the manager felt he needed it. It's no coincidence that Earl's staffs were usually among the league leaders in ERA and fewest walks allowed. Weaver's pitchers could throw strikes while unconscious, and they were especially effective at throwing breaking-ball strikes while behind in the count. It's safe to say that their work schedules had something to do with that.

I know that many managers today are timid about going to four-man rotations because they fear excessive wear and tear will damage their pitchers' valuable arms. Pitchers and their agents will probably raise the same objections. To them, I would point out that in his sixteen years as a major league manager (1968–82, 1985–86), Weaver helped produce 22 20-game winners and six Cy Young Award recipients. Only two of his pitchers—Jim Palmer and Dennis Martinez—suffered sore arms while working in his four-man setup. Both recovered to continue their stellar careers.

You want more examples of how durable pitchers can be despite working on only three days' rest? Just take a trip to Cooperstown. Bob Gibson, Jim Bunning, Don Sutton, Ferguson Jenkins, and nearly every other starting pitcher whose plaque hangs in the Hall of Fame pitched four-man rotations. All of them maintained their effectiveness late into their careers. Warren Spahn took his regular turn as part of a four-man setup for most of his twenty-one-year career. It took so much out of his gifted left arm, he was able to win only 23 games when he was 42 years old. Steve Carlton, one of the last hurlers to work regularly on three days' rest, was a Cy Young Award winner at 38. Gaylord Perry, another workhorse of the old school, led the National League in wins at 40, after a ten-year period in which he *averaged nearly 37 starts a season.*

Baseball conditions haven't changed so much in the last 25 years that pitchers can't thrive in a four-man setup as they did in the past. I believe it's all a matter of mind-set. Yes, there are fewer days off because of the tighter modern schedule, so managers would have to work in an occasional swing starter when he thinks his quartet is being overtaxed. But that's no different from what Earl Weaver and others did, back when we played those double-headers nearly every Sunday. Granted, there are some pitchers who, owing to age or infirmity, probably wouldn't flourish in a four-man rotation. But you could use them in a modified rotation that featured three pitchers taking their regular turn while alternating two swing men in the fourth spot. Under that system, you would at least get maximum use out of your three best starters.

I see three advantages to reviving the four-man rotation. First, pitching quality would improve immediately throughout the majors just because teams would be giving their four best pitchers an additional five or six starts each (you would assign 8 to 12 to those swing men) while they eliminated 32 starts by their worst starters. Second, teams like the New York Yankees, who have a solid fifth starter in Hideki Irabu, can upgrade their relief corps by sending the number-five man to the bullpen. If he's not suited for relief (which Irabu probably isn't), they can trade him for something they need, thus improving themselves and the starting rotation of some other team.

And finally, if, as Earl Weaver's staffs proved, pitching in a four-man rotation enhances a pitcher's control, we'll see quicker, more crisply played games, a real bonus at a time when we hear so many complaints that baseball games are too long. Knowing that they are going to see more strikes, hitters will be more aggressive when they come to the plate. Fewer walks means hurlers will be working more efficiently, throwing fewer pitches to each hitter. They will be able to work deeper into games. When a pitcher throws strikes, his defense improves because his fielders stay alert. Take it from a retired second baseman, nothing puts a fielder back on his heels like a pitcher walking the ballpark.

One Man's Vote for a Higher Mound

It's funny how life works. I suffered a knee injury during the first month of the 1968 season that limited me to only 20 at-bats for the whole year. Given my druthers, I would have played every inning of every game that season. But because I was hurt, I was spared the agony of participating in a season that was every hitter's worst nightmare. The major-league batting average that summer was .237, a record-setting low. Carl Yastrzemski led the American League while batting only .301. Oakland's Danny Cater finished second to Yaz at .290. Only five National Leaguers topped .300. Just three major-leaguers—Willie McCovey, Hawk Harrelson, and Frank Howard—drove in 100 or more runs.

Throughout the fifties and early sixties, premier pitchers usually had ERA's between 3.00 and 3.50. In 1968, the combined ERA for both leagues was 2.98, which meant average pitchers surrendered less than three runs every nine innings. The Washington Senators had the worst pitching staff in baseball, yet its 3.64 ERA would have led the American League in 1998. Between the two leagues, 48 pitchers who threw enough innings to qualify for the ERA championship recorded marks below 3.00.

In his 34 starts, Bob Gibson of the Cardinals pitched 28 complete games while notching a remarkable 13 shutouts. His ERA was a National League record-setting 1.12. Cardinals manager Red Shoendienst lifted Gibson for a pinch-hitter six times during that season. Schoendienst never once removed him from a game while he was working on the mound. You know what that means? Not a single team could knock Gibson out of the box. In the American League, Detroit's Denny McLain became the first pitcher since Dizzy Dean to win 30 games in a season. The number of runs scored by both teams per game, 6.83, was the lowest average since 1908.

All that run suppression had a calamitous effect on baseball's box office. Major-league attendance dropped by over a million. Several franchises—most notably the Senators, Indians, White Sox, and Pirates—were under such severe financial duress that many thought they would go under. It was around this time that people started complaining that baseball had become boring, that it was now little more than a languid game of catch between the man on the mound and his teammate behind the plate, with only intermittent bursts of action. Who would pay to watch that? Desperate to resuscitate baseball's rapidly expiring offense, rule makers shrank the strike zone and lowered the mound.

The strike zone modification was slight but meaningful; instead of extending from the top of the shoulders to the bottoms of the knees, as it had from 1963 to 1968—a period that saw run production decline with each season—it returned to its pre-'63 dimensions from the batter's armpits to the tops of his knees. That might not seem like much of a difference, but it deprived power pitchers of that chest-high strike that batters found nearly unhittable. Since this was a time when most umpires diligently enforced the rule book strike zone, the smaller dimensions had an immediate effect. Walks per team rose by over 20 percent in both leagues.

Lowering the mound from 15 inches to 10 was an even more momentous alteration. Without that higher hill to use as leverage, most pitchers lost some velocity. Home runs increased by 30 percent, runs scored by 20 percent. Pitchers weren't as dominant as they had been, but they weren't completely disadvantaged, either. Your better hurlers still had ERAs around 3.00, and the real mound studs like Gibson, Steve Carlton, Juan Marichal, and Tom Seaver were under 2.50. Attendance revived as the confrontation between hitter and batter regained a semblance of its traditional symmetry.

But over the last 20 years, things have tilted too far in favor of the hitter. Batters are bigger and stronger, and they're swatting a baseball so lively that Dave Parker, the recently departed St. Louis Cardinals hitting coach and a former National League MVP, likens it to hitting Titleist golf balls. Pitchers can put the ball precisely where they want, yet still surrender a long ball even if the hitter doesn't make solid contact. This has scared hurlers out of the strike zone, another reason why you see so many of them nibbling at the plate when they should be coming right at hitters.

Raising the mound another three inches will restore some order. Conditions are so favorable to modern batters, there's no way this modification will revive the run-scoring malaise that afflicted baseball during the 1960s. In the last section, we pointed out the advantages gained when pitchers throw strikes. Elevating the mound is another piece to this. With a few more degrees restored to their heaters, pitchers will get some swagger back.

They'll start challenging the hitters again. Instead of interminable walk fests punctuated by occasional home runs, games will be faster-paced, more balanced contests that will still feature enough offense to satisfy the hungriest of long-ball fans.

A New Closing Time

Here's something I've never understood. It's the eighth inning and your starter has been struggling, though he's still holding a two-run lead. The opposing team opens its frame with a single and a double, both scorched. Now they have the tying runs in scoring position and their best hitters coming to the plate. You have to get your exhausted starter off the mound. So whom do you bring in with the game on the line? The second-best pitcher available, naturally.

Huh?

Nonsensical as it may seem, that is exactly what most managers do when confronted with the scenario I just described. There seems to be a universal agreement among major-league skippers that they shouldn't use their closer, usually the best arm in a pen, until the ninth inning. So you rarely see Trevor Hoffman, Mariano Rivera, or Jeff Shaw pitch the eighth. And when they do punch in for work that early, it's not unusual to see them get lit up à la Hoffman in the third game of the 1998 World Series. Hey, you can't blame Trevor for his pitching line that evening—two innings pitched, two hits, one walk, two runs, one loss. Instead of concentrating on the Yankee hitters, he probably spent most of his time on the mound wondering what the hell he was doing out there. Closers have developed a one-inning mind-set and find it difficult to adjust their body clocks to any unexpected wake-up calls.

This is a relatively new phenomenon in baseball. Saving your closer for the ninth started with Herman Franks when he managed the Chicago Cubs and Bruce Sutter in 1979. Yankees manager Dick Howser and his relief ace Goose Gossage perfected the practice in 1980. Howser reasoned that if he saved Goose for one-inning stints whenever possible, he'd be able to use him more often. Gossage's cameo appearances also gave hitters less time to gauge his blinding fastball.

Howser's plan worked because he had a deep bullpen that usually held leads until Gossage took his star turn. In a pinch, the manager would extend Goose for more than one inning, but for the most part he reserved his closer's heroics for the ninth. Gossage averaged only one and one-third innings per appearance that season while tying (with Kansas City's Dan Quisenberry) for the major-league lead in saves, with 33. New York won 103 games and took the AL East title.

The Yankees' success inspired emulation throughout both leagues. By the late eighties, most managers tried to save their closers for the ninth inning. Oakland's Tony LaRussa took the strategy one step further by building his bullpens from the inside out; he packed his relief staffs with specialists who could hand the lead to Dennis Eckersley in the ninth. Eckersley's role became so sancrosanct that he was averaging less than an inning per appearance by 1994.

This was a complete departure from the way managers had used their closers before Howser and the Goose. Pitchers like Rollie Fingers, Clay Carroll, Lindy McDaniel, Sparky Lyle, and others would often pitch two or even three innings to earn their saves. Gossage himself averaged nearly two innings per appearance when he closed for the Pittsburgh Pirates in 1977. All that work put such a strain on his arm that he was only able to strike out 151 batters in 133 innings while recording a minuscule 1.62 ERA. The following season, as a New York Yankee, he averaged more than two innings per appearance while leading the American League in saves.

When you examine the careers of these durable relievers, you find no evidence that their workloads shortened their pitching lives. McDaniel pitched in the majors for 21 seasons. When he was 38, he averaged nearly three innings per relief stint and had one of his finest seasons: 12–6, 10 saves, with a 2.86 ERA. Fingers, Carroll, Gossage, and Lyle all pitched in the bigs for 15 years or longer. They're not an isolated group. Your baseball encyclopedia is filled with the names of bullpen workhorses who enjoyed long major-league careers.

Since pitchers evolve rather than devolve, I don't see any reason why today's closers can't pitch longer outings. Sure, I understand their managers want to save their arms so they can not only save today's win but tomorrow's as well. But that's contrary to sound baseball thinking. Unless your name is Nostradamus, you can never be certain that your team will even *have* a lead to protect in tomorrow's game; you have to do whatever you can to grab the victory that's in front of you. If a manager picks his spots carefully and develops a second closer to spell his main man, there's no reason why bullpen aces can't once again pitch 100 innings or more without fear of injury or loss of effectiveness. Getting those closers into the game before the ninth will assign a greater percentage of a team's innings to one of its top guns, which is the whole point of this exercise. As it is now, the modern manager is limiting one of the two or three best arms on his staff to fifty or so innings. That's crazy. Since there aren't enough quality arms to go around, we need to get the better pitchers on the mound as often as possible.

Making Every Pitch Count

A general lack of arm strength may be the most alarming crisis in pitching today. It's not that modern pitchers can't throw hard; there are more young flamethrowers in baseball than ever before. It's just that many of them lose velocity just as the game reaches its critical point. A "five-and-fly" mentality has taken hold. Too many starters are content to throw five or six innings before turning things over to their bullpens. As a consequence, they don't know how to get tough outs during crunch time.

There are still mound warriors who can make hitters uncomfortable in the late innings. Roger Clemens, Randy Johnson, Chuck Finley, and Curt Schilling, to name just a few, can even turn up the heat in the batter's box from the seventh inning on. But they are a dying breed.

Pitch counts and flawed training theories are two big reasons why starters are no longer as durable as they once were. I think anyone who dismisses pitch counts out of hand is foolish. They do have their place in baseball. For example, managers and coaches should use them to closely monitor pitchers who are coming back from injury. When Kerry Wood returns to the Cubs from his recent elbow ailment, I'd expect Chicago to keep him on a conservative pitch count for an entire season or more. You might also put an older player who has experienced periodic arm problems on a tight pitch ceiling. Pitchers like the Yankees' 36-year-old David Cone or Boston's 35-year-old Bret Saberhagen, both of whom have recently felt the surgeon's blade, are going to have longer shelf lives if you limit the strain on their now somewhat fragile limbs.

Teams should also apply gradually escalating pitch counts to pitchers under the age of 25 or 26, a time when they are still developing their arms. From Robin Roberts to Dwight Gooden, baseball history is dotted with stories of pitchers who lost their best stuff before they turned 30 because they threw too many pitches in their late teens and early twenties. I want to make it clear that it's not the number of starts that hurt their arms; Dwight Gooden, for instance, has thrown in a five-man rotation for nearly as long as he's been in the majors. Yet, by his twenty-ninth birthday, he was trying to adapt to life without his once-dominating fastball.

Gooden's career provides us with a lesson on why pitch counts should be used with still-maturing arms. Dwight was, without question, the greatest teenaged pitcher ever to toe a major-league rubber. When he joined the New York Mets as a 19-year-old in 1984, he had an explosive fastball that seemed to accelerate as it got closer to the plate, and a curve ball so knee-buckling that batters didn't even refer to it as "Uncle Charlie," the name they reserved for the very best breaking pitches. Instead they called it "Lord Charles." Gooden led the NL in strikeouts that season with 275, a major-league record for rookies. Because he pitched so well, he worked deep into nearly every game. Because he struck out so many, he often had outings in which he threw 120 or more pitches.

That trend continued in 1985, when Gooden redefined the word *awesome*. At 24–4 with a league-leading 1.53 ERA and 256

K's, Dwight was the best pitcher in the game by a wide margin. But he was once again throwing an inordinate number of games with pitch counts over 120. The abuse began to take its toll in 1986, when Gooden was only 21. Though he had an excellent year (17–6, 2.84), his velocity was down. He struck out 200 batters in 250 innings—an impressive total, but certainly less eye-popping than the numbers he had accumulated in his first two seasons, when he punched out more than a hitter per inning. Dwight was also having a harder time finishing off batters. They weren't taking as many called third strikes, and they were battling him into deeper counts.

Gooden pitched the following five years (1987–91) with roughly the same effectiveness he had demonstrated during the 1986 season. He kept winning in the high teens, but he was never again a 20-game winner. There were many times when Gooden appeared as unhittable as ever, but he was no longer consistently dominating, despite the fact that he was in what should have been his pitching prime. In '92 and '93, he lost more often than he won, though he pitched better than his record. His velocity, however, had fallen precipitously. By 1994 he was having trouble getting anyone out; his ERA ballooned to 6.31 as he surrendered more hits than innings pitched for the first time in his career. Before that season ended, Gooden had to submit to a surgeon's scalpel, an old arm at only 29. Doc has come back from surgery to pitch credibly. He even pitched a no-hitter against the Seattle Mariners in 1996. But he has never again put up the kind of numbers that made him look like a sure-shot Hall of Famer before he was 25.

Gooden's oft-reported drug problems no doubt exacerbated his decline, but it didn't cause his arm impingement. It was all those pressure-packed pitches he threw before his arm was ready that did the damage. I saw the same thing happen to former teammates Larry Dierker, Don Gullett, Gary Nolan, Jim Merritt, and Jim McGlothen. All had been young phenoms with great stuff who were overworked in game after game during their formative years. Not a single one of them experienced a winning season after the age of 30. I believe that if they had been subject to pitch counts early in their careers, their primes would have been extended.

Though I support the concept of keeping young hurlers on pitch counts, teams should never hold them to arbitrary ceilings. Instead, coaches should customize the counts according to each pitcher's natural arm strength, mechanics, conditioning, and size. Then they should gradually raise the counts from season to season as pitchers establish new thresholds of endurance.

After they've reached their mid-twenties, when past experience tells us most pitchers' arms have acquired full maturity, I don't see the point in pitch counts unless a hurler has clearly demonstrated that he will almost always run out of gas once he reaches a certain number. Owing to the current ultra-dependence on pitch counts, many pitchers are coming out of games while they still have good, albeit not necessarily their best, stuff; they're not learning how to work out of jams, a toughening experience that produces better pitchers. I can't tell you how many times I've seen pitchers cruise in the early innings, only to start looking over their shoulders to the bullpen the moment they get into trouble after the fifth. How can that possibly be good for them or baseball?

Without putting in a call to Rocky Balboa, let's help these guys rediscover the eye of the tiger. Managers, coaches, and catchers should pay more attention to a pitcher's stuff, instead of counting pitches. When they see his velocity decline for four or five consecutive pitches late in a game, they should get him off the mound, because that's when he's going to get hurt.

Coaches should also ask their pitchers to throw more often. Warren Spahn and Bob Gibson have both told me that the primary reason modern pitchers lack endurance and control is that they don't throw enough between starts. The most durable staff in baseball during the nineties has been the Atlanta Braves, the one team where Cys do matter. Their award-winning starting rotation usually pitches more innings more effectively than any rotation in the majors, and its pitchers rarely break down; only John Smoltz has suffered any arm miseries over the last ten years. (We should note that Smoltz threw an inordinate number of high-pitch games before he was 25. He also features a vicious slider that is as rough on his elbow as it is on hitters.) Braves pitching coach Leo Mazzone has his charges light-toss every single day. That regimen builds and maintains arm strength. He also watches his pitchers carefully and gets them off the mound the moment they start to labor. Every team in baseball should adopt or at least adapt the Mazzone protocol.

Pitchers in general should also start throwing more fastballs. Too many hurlers have fallen in love with trick pitches like the split-fingered fastball. Despite its name, the split-finger is really an off-speed pitch that resembles a fastball as it approaches the plate, then suddenly drops out of the strike zone. You can make batters look foolish with it.

However, like most breaking pitches, it takes a lot out of your arm (which is why power pitchers usually last longer than breaking-ball artists, reference Nolan Ryan). And the less you use your fastball, the quicker you'll lose it. Once that happens, pitchers are in trouble because it's the good heater that permits them to go inside on hitters. As Sandy Koufax once said, "Show me a pitcher who can't pitch inside, and I'll show you a loser." I'm not advocating that hurlers completely abandon the split-fingered pitch or their other breaking stuff, but they'll be much more formidable if they go back to using their fastballs as primary weapons. They should assemble the rest of their arsenal around it. I hope they do it soon, because if they don't develop the weaponry to better attack batters inside, we might have to put pitchers on the endangered species list.

5

Managing to the Max

Managing. It sure isn't what it used to be. Leading a major-league club today certainly requires different skills than it did ten or twenty years ago. Talk about a change in job descriptions. Skippers in my day were a lot like Darth Vader. Only scarier. When a manager shouted "Jump!," not a soul in the clubhouse stopped to ask "How high?" We just took to the air. Dropping into a manager's doghouse was like falling into one of those black holes in outer space; once you took up residence, you might never be heard from again.

Managers back then could motivate or punish players by humiliating them. Though your better skippers would rarely roast anyone in public, they could sautée you to a crisp in the confines of their office or during a closed team meeting. If you were guilty of stupidity, a manager would merely berate you, unless, of course, the condition was chronic. Then you stood a good chance of being benched.

Fail to hustle, though, and he might take sterner measures to make an impression. In 1969, I remember New York Mets manager Gil Hodges sending out a sub in the midst of an inning to relieve Cleon Jones, his star leftfielder. Cleon had been, shall we say, a bit tardy chasing down a fly ball. Hodges personally escorted Jones from the field in front of a nearly packed Shea Stadium. Yankees manager Billy Martin did the same thing to Reggie Jackson during a nationally televised game against Boston in 1977. When something like that happened to a player, he felt about as tall as Tom Thumb; he knew that when he got to the clubhouse he was in for a tongue-lashing and a stiff fine. And there wasn't very much he could do about it. Even if he felt his manager was wrong, he'd more than likely endure his punishment in silence.

There's a New Sheriff in Town

You know what gave a manager all this power? His pencil. Filling out the lineup card gave every skipper tremendous leverage over his team. Unless you were a superstar, he controlled your playing time and, by extension, your compensation. You had to remain in a manager's good graces back then. If you didn't he could sit you down, demote you to the minors, or ship you to another team. Do as he required and the manager became your ally during salary negotiations. Come up short and you were on your own. Or worse, the manager would present the front office with a laundry list of reasons why you didn't deserve a raise.

Free agency gradually ended all that. It took a while to sink in, but as players realized they controlled their own destinies, managers lost their omnipotence. Today, if a skipper is foolish enough to cry "Jump!," most players ask "Why?" Sparky Anderson—my manager with the Cincinnati Reds—best summed up baseball's new world order when he told me, "It not true anymore that the 25 players have to get along with one manager. Now it's the manager's job to get along with the players. You have to adjust to 25 different personalities, or you don't belong in the clubhouse."

Established players know they are going to get their at-bats. Everyone in baseball understands the game's golden rule: He who has the gold, rules. If your salary is hefty enough, your manager pretty much must pencil you into the lineup most of the time or he'll catch grief from the front office, the media, and the fans.

How has that changed the game? Let me give you an example. In 1972 the Baltimore Orioles were the consensus pre-season choice to win their fourth consecutive AL championship. However, the team got off to a sub-.500 start when most of its veteran hitters—including All-Stars like slugging first baseman Boog Powell and Hall of Fame third baseman Brooks Robinson—fell into a protracted, collective slump. The only way O's manager Earl Weaver could jump-start his offense was by inserting three talented rookies into the lineup—shortstop Bobby Grich, outfielder Don Baylor, and catcher Johnny Oates. As soon as they started hitting, Baltimore started winning; the Orioles just barely missed capturing another pennant.

That was then; it sure isn't now. You couldn't apply Weaver's remedy today without first purging your team's roster through trades and other transactions. For example, Joe Torre is a decisive manager who's not afraid to confront hard choices. But, trust me, if Bernie Williams—the Yankees' new $12 Million Man—is hitting

.240 at the All-Star break, do any of you think that Rickey Ledee, Chad Curtis, or anyone else will be usurping his position? Don't bet the house on it. Bernie might be worried about fan reaction, media criticism, and his swing, but he won't be worried about job security. As long as he has a pulse and Mr. Steinbrenner's checks don't bounce, Bernie will be the Yankee centerfielder.

When modern managers publicly criticize their players, they invite trouble. Their targets can throw barbs right back without fearing retribution. During the 1997 season, New York Mets manager Bobby Valentine questioned his catcher Todd Hundley's off-the-field habits. Valentine wondered out loud in front of several reporters if Todd was "getting enough sleep." The journalists inferred from Bobby's remarks that Hundley was spending too many late nights in too many pubs. When the journalists confronted Hundley with his manager's comments, the catcher responded by suggesting, in so many words, where Bobby could stuff his innuendo. Over the next few days, a war of words was waged between Hundley and Valentine. It brought a friction to the New York clubhouse that would not have existed at a time when players were afraid to confront their managers openly.

Don't get the idea, though, that I think Hundley should have kept his mouth shut. He had no choice but to defend himself. Valentine was completely in the wrong here. If a manager has a problem with a player, he should settle it with him behind closed doors. Nothing positive could have come out of attacking Hundley in the press. Bobby should have known that. But then, he's not exactly a "people person." Valentine is cocky to the point of being arrogant and often acts as if he's reinventing baseball. His attitude has turned off a lot of people throughout the game. As one respected baseball man told me just before the start of the 1999 season, "Let's face it. Nobody likes Bobby and anyone who says he does is lying."

Today's managers can't even use their players' pocketbooks to motivate them anymore. Players don't need a skipper's help with salary negotiations. That's what they have agents for. Should a player feel he is spending too much time on the bench, he has numerous ways to force a trade to some team that will put him in the lineup more frequently. Managers may still fine players for various infractions. However, the maximum penalty they can impose is chump change for even a team's lowest-paid rookie. And a player can always get the fine reduced or eradicated (if it exceeds $499.99) by filing a grievance through the Players' Association.

Let's See Your Résumé

As you can see, player-manager relationships have evolved radically in a short time. Managers can no longer simply command their players' fear; they have to earn their respect. So I think teams give themselves a decided edge when they hire managers who have excelled as players. That's not to say that you can't manage unless you once hit .300 or won 20 games. Jim Leyland has proven you can be an All-Star manager without ever having been an All-Star player. But a record of accomplishment as a big-league hitter or pitcher will get the immediate attention and respect of today's teams.

When I was in the majors, managers such as Sparky Anderson, who batted .218 in his lone big-league season, or Earl

Weaver, who couldn't hit his way out of the minors, established credibility with their clubs by demonstrating what they knew. Players today don't care about that. Before trusting you with their careers, they want to know what you've done.

Here's an example of what I mean. During the 1998 season, I saw Texas Rangers coach Rudy Jaramillio attempt to correct a flaw in a young player's swing. The player, who didn't want Rudy tinkering with him, listened to Jaramillio for a bit before asking, "And when did you hit .300 in the big leagues?" Rudy had been a career minor-leaguer, and the player knew it. He was really asking his coach, "How can you teach me to do something that you couldn't do yourself?" (An impertinent question, since Mr. Jaramillio has proven to be one of the best hitting instructors in the business.)

That player had an attitude problem, but he's not alone. Frank Robinson recalls, "When I managed in Baltimore [1988–91], the front office wanted me to bring in a minor-league manager as hitting coach. I asked, 'What are his credentials?' He's never played in the major leagues. You make someone like him the hitting coach, and my players are going to ask, 'How can he tell us what to feel and what to do when he's never experienced what we go through on this level?' Sure enough, when word got out that he might be appointed, that is exactly what my players asked. And I had a lot of veterans on my club."

Before they'll listen to you, many big-leaguers—particularly the younger ones—want to know what you hit, how many games you won, and how many pennant winners you've played on. I don't think that's right, but its something that organizations must deal with. That's why teams looking for managers should first consider marquee names—former All-Stars and MVPs like Dusty Baker, Joe Torre, Phil Garner, Lou Piniella, and Felipe Alou. What I'm proposing is a distinct break from the past, when many managers were marginal former players like Ralph Houk, Bill Rigney, Gene Mauch, and Dallas Green. For decades, the common misperception in baseball was that stars rarely made good managers because success had come too easily for them; they supposedly would not have the patience to tolerate a less gifted athlete's shortcomings.

Now we see that a successful playing career can be a tremendous asset for a manager, particularly during his rookie season. In 1997, Larry Dierker, a former teammate of mine, came out of the broadcast booth to manage the Houston Astros. Had he never been anything but an announcer whose playing career had been undistinguished, it would have been difficult for him to establish credibility with veterans like Jeff Bagwell, Craig Biggio, and Derek Bell.

However, everyone on the team knew that Larry was a former All-Star pitcher and 20-game winner with the Astros. They automatically assumed he had something to teach them. Larry was able to command his players' respect the moment he put on the manager's uniform. And, of course, his pitchers paid attention to him as though they were investors listening to the president of Smith-Barney.

Managers have to set a tone. Because the season is so long, they cannot blow any one play, game, or event out of proportion. After all, the best teams are going to lose 60 to 70 games; the best hitters will fail 70 percent of the time; and your top pitchers will drop a third or more of their starts. Adversity is part of baseball; if a manager can't cope with it, his team will suffer. Terry Collins, the skipper of the Anaheim Angels, learned that lesson when he was with Houston. The Astros were a talented team when Collins was there (1994–96). They finished second three times, but failed to make the playoffs because the manager exerted too much pressure on them. He was so uptight, his players thought every pitch was life-and-death. It wasn't anything Terry said; it was his demeanor. Collins was edgy in the dugout during the games, always looking like someone who was just waiting for disaster to strike. And the moment anything actually went wrong, you could smell the panic on him. Players pick up on that. To alleviate the tension the manager is bringing to the clubhouse, they put added pressure on themselves to perform well, which invariably chokes off their natural abilities so that they can't play their best. It's no coincidence that the Astros became a post-season participant once Houston replaced Collins with Larry Dierker. I don't know if Larry knows more about baseball than Collins, but he does have a laid-back attitude that immediately puts his players at ease. Dierker kept the pressure off his team by reminding them that while the goal of winning is serious, the game is still essentially supposed to be fun. (By the way, I've been watching Collins since he joined the Angels, and he's a much more laid-back skipper. When I complimented him on the change, he said former Angel infielder-outfielder Tony Phillips had talked to him about relaxing more and that it had really made an impression.)

If you don't have that glittering players' résumé, a strong record as a minor-league manager or major-league coach is a must. The Tampa Bay Devil Rays picked Larry Rothschild as their manager after he served as the world champion Florida Marlins' pitching coach. Larry never played in the majors, but that World Series ring he wears inspires confidence. That can go a long way in baseball. When players believe that you know how to win, they'll rarely hesitate to follow your lead.

Despite Rothschild's strong credentials, I'm not a big advocate of hiring former pitching coaches as managers. I can't think of too many who have been successful. Take Ray Miller. He was probably one of the greatest pitching coaches of the last 25 years. In 18 seasons with the Baltimore Orioles and Pittsburgh Pirates, his clubs finished first or second ten times. Ray helped produce seven 20-game winners and three Cy Young Award recipients (Mike Flanagan, Steve Stone, and Doug Drabek). But when the Orioles named him manager in 1998, they were exercising baseball's version of the Peter Principle. Miller, like most pitching coaches not named Roger Craig, doesn't know how to handle the egos of everyday players. Starters work only every fifth day, and relievers never know when they are going to get into a game. Your regulars know they are under the gun every day, so they tend to get frustrated quicker. You have to be ready for that. Your rotation determines how much rest a starter gets, and you can easily monitor a reliever's workload. But you have to develop a feel for when to give one of your regulars a day off. Managers also have to know when to trust their judgment. When I was with the Giants in 1982, we were playing a game against the Astros in the midst of a pennant race. Our manager, Frank Robinson, excluded me from the original lineup against Houston starter Bob Knepper. When I asked why I wasn't playing, Frank responded, "Because you're only one for five against this guy." I said, "You're right, but if I play today, I'll be three for nine." Frank had been a Hall of Fame hitter, and he knew what I was saying. Knepper had gotten me out, but I had hit him hard. This game it would be my turn to have the base hits drop in. Frank penciled my name into the batting order, and, by the end of the game, I was 3-for-9. Frank trusted me because he had been through that sort of situation many times himself. A pitching coach just can't relate to that.

The "I" Word

Few, however, will follow if they don't trust where you're taking them. As manager of the Yankees, Athletics, Tigers, and other teams, Billy Martin was infamous for talking out of both sides of his mouth. When the Yankees traded for shortstop Bucky Dent in 1977, Martin greeted Dent by taking credit for the deal. Then Billy told the incumbent shortstop, Fred Stanley, that the trade had been George Steinbrenner's idea; Martin even claimed that he had argued against the transaction.

Martin could get away with that kind of duplicity because players back then more or less had to accept whatever a manager said. Athletes today, though, can challenge a skipper if they suspect he's being less than honest, and they won't hesitate to confirm something he tells them with another source. Once players discover their manager fudges the truth, his effectiveness ends. A skipper often must ask his players to make sacrifices for the good of the team. For example, he might have to persuade a valued bench player to accept a limited role for one season by promising him a full-time position for the following year. No player will buy that if he suspects the manager is being anything but straight with him.

Because integrity matters so much, I think the Toronto Blue Jays were correct in firing manager Tim Johnson last March 17. Johnson had placed himself in an untenable position during the 1998 off-season. For years the former Marine had been telling people, including his players, that he was a Vietnam War veteran who had spilled blood on the battlefield. Johnson used his "war experiences" to motivate his players. Stories circulated of how he once told pitcher Pat Hentgen that the right-hander didn't really understand adversity, that "pressure was Vietnam." The manager also allegedly claimed he'd once had to kill a 12-year-old Vietnamese girl who was working for the Viet Cong. In another story, he supposedly claimed he had strapped live hand grenades to Vietnamese children. As a newspaper article later disclosed, Johnson did serve in the U.S. Marines during 'Nam, but he never got close to any fighting. When the truth about his military service got out, Johnson was forced to make an embarrassing public apology. He admitted that he had spent most of his service time in the reserves, teaching mortar training to Vietnam-bound troops. (Even that story has since been questioned, since it was atypical for the Marines to give someone in the reserves a training assignment.)

Even though Johnson apologized, the issue wouldn't go away. Journalists continually questioned him about his fabrications, and openly wondered what effect they would have on his team. I felt for him. Tim's a good guy, and I like the way he managed a ballgame. But the reporters were right to raise the issue. Toronto's front office had just embarked on a youth movement. Young players need leadership. Whom do they follow when the manager is a liar? No way you can make that work. For the good of the Blue

Jays, Johnson should have resigned. Or Toronto should have dismissed him immediately. I have no idea why they waited so long.

Joe Torre understands the importance of integrity as well as any manager in the majors. As David Cone told us, "The players always know where they stand with Joe." Which is huge when you have 15 or 16 talented non-pitchers on your roster and only nine of them can play at the same time.

For example, on paper, left field was the only open position as Torre's New York Yankees arrived for spring training in 1998. Four men were vying for that spot. All four were, not incidentally, among the lowest-paid members of the team: Chad Curtis, the best fielder and a team spark plug; Rickey Ledee, the Yankees' best minor-league prospect; Tim Raines, probably the best pure hitter of the bunch; and Darryl Strawberry, the club's biggest home-run threat.

On some American League teams, the manager could use the DH slot to work at least three of these four players into the offensive mix. Torre, though, didn't have that luxury. Chili Davis was set to handle the designated hitter's chores on the Yankees. Mr. Davis, a devastating clutch hitter with power from both sides of the plate, makes $4.5 million a year; Torre wasn't sitting him down any time soon.

By opening day, Joe had to explain to three of his four left-field candidates why they weren't starting. If those ballplayers couldn't trust that Torre would find them some playing time, the Yankees would have had three disgruntled athletes on their roster. Their grousing might have threatened the Yankees' clubhouse chemistry, the esprit de corps that was such a vital part of the team's astounding success in 1998.

As it turned out, Yankee fans didn't have to lose any sleep

over that possibility. An overabundance of talent is a problem every big-league manager prays for. Joe has proven repeatedly that he knows how to transform log jams like the one he had in left field into an advantage. A little good luck disguised as bad also helped. The Yankees discovered that Ledee needed more seasoning, and sent him back to the minors. An ankle injury to Chili Davis kept him on the bench for a good part of the 1998 season. Torre used the open DH spot to rotate his leftfielders—including Shane Spencer, a minor-league slugging sensation who joined the club in September—into the lineup. Had Chili been healthy, Joe would have found another way to get the job done. And because his players trusted him, they would have given him the time and the latitude to solve the left-field puzzle.

One way a manager can command a team's loyalty is to stick his neck out in support of a player, even when it means risking his job. I thought Jimy Williams of Boston blew it when he failed to back up Mo Vaughn during the first baseman's final seasons with the Red Sox. Boston general manager, Dan Duquette, and his front-office minions spent a lot of time painting Vaughn, one of the best guys in baseball, as an ingrate and a mercenary while they were trying to cajole him into accepting a contract far below his market value. This was part of an ongoing battle between Duquette and his top player. When Mo was arrested on a DWI charge, he protested his innocence. Did his ball club come to his defense? Are you kidding? Duquette and the Red Sox acted as if Vaughn were Sacco *and* Vanzetti. They had him guilty before any of the evidence was in and subtly used the incident to raise questions about the first baseman's unimpeachable character. Then they went mute when a jury exonerated Mo of all charges.

Throughout the Vaughn–Red Sox wars, I never heard Williams utter a single word in support of his superstar. That is unforgivable. Mo had taken care of Jimy on the field; Vaughn drove the club to the playoffs in 1998. Without him, the Red Sox would have been fortunate to finish above .500. Williams should have reciprocated by taking care of Mo off the field. Instead, he let Duquette drive away the player who had been the heart and soul of the Red Sox for most of the nineties. Williams's silence hurt Mo, and, in my opinion, it has hurt his club. Boston entered the 1999 season desperately needing offense. Bernie Williams, Albert Belle, and Rafael Palmeiro all turned down strong offers from Boston to sign elsewhere. I think they took one look at how Mo was treated and they knew this wasn't the clubhouse for them.

This, by the way, is the same Jimy Williams who, in 1997, gave pitcher Steve Avery an end-of-the-season start that automatically kicked in the option year of his contract. The Red Sox front office wasn't pleased with that move. It cost them more than $2.5 million. But this was one time when Jimy was looking out for the club. "Players have to know that we honor our agreements or they won't come here," he told the press. Good thinking, Jimy. Except that Avery had an ERA over 5 at the time and had pitched atrociously for most of the year. He didn't deserve another start. Yet Jimy risked his position for Avery, while abandoning his best player, Vaughn. Talk about needing a priority check.

The Nine-Inning Manager

Besides being honest, today's major-league managers have to be quick on the draw. Throughout my playing career, skippers often didn't make many critical decisions until late in a ballgame. Starters usually took you into the sixth or seventh inning, so you didn't have to choose many pinch-hitters, pinch-runners, relievers, or defensive subs until the game's final third. If you made a bad decision or two in an early inning, a strong starter could bail you out by shutting down the opposition.

Because expansion has thinned out so many starting rotations, managers have to be at the top of their game from the first hitter on. Make a single misstep with your starter—remove him a batter too early or too late—or choose the wrong arm out of your bullpen, and the opposition can bury you.

The emphasis that clubs place on their bullpens has also changed the way managers go about their business. Up until the 1980s, most bullpens were built around two pitchers—a closer and a setup man. If you were lucky, you also had a reliable left-handed relief specialist who would pitch almost exclusively to left-handed batters. The other relievers were often failed starters who basically mopped up in lost causes.

Tony LaRussa, while managing Oakland, took a different approach by filling his bullpen with gifted arms, each with a specific purpose. On LaRussa's 1989 world champion A's, right-hander Gene Nelson usually came in whenever the opposition stomped an Oakland starter early in the game. His job was to hold the score while the A's mounted a comeback (which, more often than not, they did). Southpaw Matt Young was LaRussa's man when the skipper needed to get a left-handed hitter out during the first six innings.

Flamethrowing right-hander Todd Burns was the setup man for the seventh and eighth. Ricky Honeycutt was his left-handed counterpart. Both could be used to get a pivotal out or two during the late innings. And both were also used to save games whenever Dennis Eckersley, Oakland's Closer Maximus, required a respite.

In 1990, Cincinnati manager Lou Piniella perfected the all-purpose bullpen when he teamed right-handers Rob Dibble and Tim Birtsas with left-handers Norm Charlton and Randy Myers to unleash a scorched-earth policy throughout the National League. Known as the Nasty Boys, this fearsome bullpen used wall-to-wall heat to wilt its opponents while leading the Reds to a World Series title. Since that time, every major-league team has tried to follow the LaRussa-Piniella bullpen model.

Just look back at the 1998 Yankees. They had five relievers— Mariano Rivera, Jeff Nelson, Mike Stanton, Ramiro Mendoza, and Graeme Lloyd—to stop offenses cold. When they were on, and they were infrequently off, they transformed the traditional nine-inning game into a six-inning contest. If you didn't beat the Yankees before the seventh, odds were you weren't going to beat them at all.

Admittedly, most teams' bullpens aren't as well stacked as New York's was last season. However, nearly every club has at least three relievers—a closer, a setup man, and a left-handed specialist—who can get decisive outs during the late innings of a ballgame. All of which means managers must make things happen early.

Managing the Media

And sometimes making things happen early means making them happen before the game starts. Every modern manager should take a course in media relations. Handling the press is more important today than it's ever been. It's practically become an art form. Frank Robinson concurs: "When I first started managing (with Cleveland in 1974), the press would pop into your office all at once at a certain time, ask a few questions, and you were done until after the game. Nowadays, the press is at the ballpark at noon for a night game. You have to deal with them from the moment you're on the job. And they come at you in waves, two here, two there. You're answering questions right up to the start of the game. This leaves you less time for your players, so you have to know how to use that time."

If a team is playing poorly, a manager's job can hinge on public perception. Franchises will stick longer with a competent manager who is also a fan favorite. Conversely, when enough angry callers rant about some skipper's "boneheaded" strategies to the talking heads on sports radio, the front office starts tuning in. And pretty soon the manager is moving out.

Players, on the other hand, have more leeway in choosing how they interact with the press. If Barry Bonds doesn't want to talk to a reporter, he doesn't have to. The Giants aren't going to trade the National League's best player because he gets a few bad write-ups. (Despite what you may have heard, Barry doesn't dislike all of the press. He just has no respect for any writer he deems clueless about the finer points of his game. And, yes, he thinks there are a lot of those guys running around. Last season, when I noted that few reporters were picking the Giants to contend, he chuckled and said, "Joe, if I had to place bets based on what most of the media thinks, I'd be straight homeless.")

Unlike his leftfielder, San Francisco manager Dusty Baker must absorb a little heat. That's part of what the Giants pay him for. And that hot seat in his office has never been more scorching. As Peter Pascarelli, who covered the Phillies for the *Philadelphia Inquirer,* recently told me, "When I joined the *Inquirer,* being a baseball beat writer covering a team was the most coveted job on any paper. It no longer is. Many of today's beat writers see it merely as a stepping-stone to a column or becoming a featured writer in another part of the paper. So they look for the big story, the exposé that is going make their names as reporters. Which is why they are more probing and combative. I'm all for a probing press; we don't want to go back to the time when reporters were practically on the payrolls of ball clubs and wrote nothing but soft news. But some of today's writers—like the guy who rummaged Mark McGwire's locker and discovered he was taking androstenedione—definitely went out of bounds." (Peter's got that right. A player's locker is his private domain. When a reporter goes through a player's locker without his permission, it's like a policeman searching your house without a warrant.)

Managers must learn to discern which writers they can trust as their conduits to the public. Many beat writers are extremely knowledgeable about the game and its nuances. They respect the sport and they'll give managers a fair hearing in the press. Those are the journalists you work with to get your message out.

When managers discover that a writer doesn't really know the game, they shouldn't dismiss him out of hand. Instead, they should go the extra step to ensure that the writer understands everything they say, especially when they are explaining a complex strategy or some potentially controversial issue. A media-wise manager is one who knows how to educate the press without patronizing it.

Managing at Crunch Time

Like players, managers must be able to respond to pressure, to step up their games when a season is on the line. Some managers who perform boldly during the regular season become less daring when the calendar reads October. San Diego's Bruce Bochy is a fine skipper. It's hard to find fault with a guy who took his club from last to first in 1998. But you'd have to question many of the decisions he made against the Yankees during the World Series. For example, in Game One, he watched four relievers throw away a win because he didn't want to use his ace Trevor Hoffman for more than one inning and was leery of bringing him on before the ninth. He was sticking with the formula that had been so successful for him during the season. But this was the World Series, and his team was outgunned at nearly every position. The Yankees were clearly the more talented club, so he should have done something unorthodox to beat them.

With his team leading 5–2 in the seventh and the Yankees threatening, Bochy should have brought in his closer to end the New York rally. Sure, it's a gamble, but one worth taking in the Series when you have an opportunity to steal a game in the other team's home park. Hoffman never even warmed up, while Donne Wall, Mark Langston, Brian Boehringer, and Randy Myers surrendered six runs and the game (including one that was charged to starter Kevin Brown) to New York. In that situation, if you're going to get beat, get beat with your best.

Bochy compounded his mistake again by neglecting to use Hoffman the following evening. The Yankees battered San Diego to take a 7–0 lead by the third inning. New York's onslaught was a brutal thing to see, like watching a car wreck in slow motion. Even the Yankee outs were hard hit. With his team down by 6 in the eighth inning, Bochy should have brought Hoffman in. That first pitch or at-bat in a World Series is unlike any other appearance a player will make in his career. There is so much pressure, so much adrenaline running that it takes you a while to get your feet on the ground. Bochy missed a chance to acquaint his closer with the Fall Classic's heady environment in a no-pressure situation while getting him some much-needed work. Hoffman hadn't pitched in several days, and by the time he did get into Game Three of the Series, he was too strong. With San Diego leading 5–2 in the eighth, the right-hander came in overthrowing his best pitch, the change-up. He threw two off-speed pitches out of the strike zone to Scott Brosius. After Brosius fouled off a fastball for strike one, Hoffman tried to even the count with another heater, which, of course, the third baseman promptly hit over the centerfield fence for a three-run homer and a lead the Yankees never relinquished. If Bochy had gotten Hoffman the work he needed, his ace might have been at his best when he needed him most.

Bruce also mishandled his third baseman Ken Caminiti during that Series. Caminiti, who is one of the grittiest players in the game, was troubled by bad legs throughout the 1998 season. He could still hit, but he could barely move in the field. Bochy could have used him as the DH in the first two games of the Series. This would have kept Ken's batting eye sharp while affording him some much needed rest. Instead, he played him at third and by the end of the Series, Ken was virtually helpless at the plate and in the field.

Handle with Care

Some managers do things that I just don't understand. Take Jim Riggleman, who led the Chicago Cubs to the National League wild card in 1998. The most valuable commodity on his club, next to Sammy Sosa, was 20-year-old fireballer Kerry Wood. But a complete tear of the ulnar ligament in Wood's elbow, an injury he sustained during the 1998 season, has jeopardized the pitcher's future. After the Cubs announced that Kerry would be lost to the team for the entire 1999 season, Riggleman said, "I think this was inevitable. It wasn't just last year. His problems go back to his teenage years in high school. Certainly, in the minor leagues he had some ups and downs with his arm. When he got to the big leagues, it was lingering. That's a sign that there's a problem."

Well, you know what is also a sign that there's a problem? A manager and organization who know their young pitcher's elbow may be fragile, yet allow him to throw 115 or more pitches in a game on 13 separate occasions. Which is precisely what Riggleman did in 1998 when Wood averaged 109.2 pitches per start. According to Stats Inc., that's the sixth highest average recorded by pitchers 23 or younger in the last ten years. Four of the five pitchers ahead of Kerry on that list—Ramon Martinez, Wilson Alvarez, Alex Fernandez, and John Smoltz—have all spent time on the disabled list in the last three years. The leader in this category, Livan Hernandez, hasn't gone down yet, but you can already see he's starting to struggle. And that's not a recent pattern. History has taught us that managers should carefully monitor their young pitchers until their arms fully mature. Wood was only twenty, and Riggleman acknowledges that he thought "the elbow was damaging itself every time he [Wood] threw the ball." Yet he allowed Kerry to put an inordinate strain on his priceless arm in start after start. What could he have been thinking of?

Keeping Things in Order

Given today's deep, dominant bullpens, building a lineup may be a manager's biggest challenge. As I mentioned earlier, until recently, most teams were blessed if they had just one good lefty reliever on their rosters. Today it's a rare club that doesn't have two capable left-handers in its pen. (Lefties who can throw strikes are valuable commodities; unlike right-handers, they don't even need good stuff to be successful. The reason? A southpaw's ball naturally runs away from right-handed hitters. Any pitch that moves away from the batter is tough to handle. So soft-tossing lefties can still get hitters out long after their best stuff has deserted them.)

With so many capable arms lurking in major-league bullpens, managers can't stack their lineups with too many batters who hit from the same side. Start four or five consecutive left-handed hitters, and the opposing manager won't hesitate to bring in a southpaw to whittle their bats or force them out of the game in some early, crucial situation. Alternating right-handed and left-handed hitters also makes it difficult for the opposing starter to work himself into a groove. Pitchers are prone to make more mistakes when they have to modify their pitching patterns from batter to batter.

The most efficient lineups blend speed and power, allowing managers to scratch out a run if a Greg Maddux or a Randy Johnson neutralizes their sluggers. Each spot in the batting order carries a different responsibility. To demonstrate how those duties vary, let's look at what I consider to be an ideal major-league lineup:

Your lead-off hitter has to work the pitcher deep into the count, especially during his first at-bat. When starting pitchers routinely went seven innings, a batter could count on getting four or five plate appearances against him. Today's starters generally don't stay in the game past the sixth. So the lead-off man has to give his teammates ample opportunity to gauge how the pitcher's whole array of stuff is moving for that game. He must be a patient batter who can take a lot of pitches.

A lead-off man's batting average doesn't have to be particularly high, provided he maintains an on-base percentage of .370 or better. Getting on base by whatever means necessary so his teammates can drive him in is the lead-off man's primary function. Pete Rose, Eddie Yost, and Mike Hargrove were all good lead-off hitters, even though they weren't fast.

However, I prefer bona fide base stealers at the top of my lineup. They can use their speed to get into scoring position and race home from second on a single. Cleveland's Kenny Lofton, Detroit's Brian Hunter, and Pittsburgh's Tony Womack are all good lead-off hitters. But the greatest lead-off hitter I've ever seen is Rickey Henderson of the New York Mets. This right-hand hitting leftfielder walks over 100 times a year, steals bases at will, and, as a bonus, can put an opponent in a quick hole with a lead-off home run.

I'd want my second-place batter to possess many of the same skills as a lead-off man. He should be capable of stealing a base if the first hitter doesn't get on. He must also have unerring bat control. Your number-two hitter must make consistent contact so that he can move runners around via the bunt or hit-and-run. You don't want him striking out into a double play if a runner is caught stealing on a two-strike count.

There is a paucity of genuine second-place hitters in the major leagues today. Some, like Atlanta's Walt Weiss, have great bat control and know how to reach base, but they aren't fast. Cleveland's Omar Vizquel is fast, but he doesn't get on enough.

Houston's Derek Bell is a fine hitter, but he strikes out too often to bat second, as he frequently did last season. (Bell is really a number-three hitter.)

At least one batter has all the attributes I'm looking for in that second spot: Cleveland's switch-hitting Roberto Alomar. Batting left-handed, Alomar can block the catcher's view of the man at first, allowing the runner a better chance of stealing second. With the first baseman holding the runner, Alomar can also pull the ball with authority through the hole on the right side of the infield. As a right-handed hitter, Robbie can slash a pitch the other way through that same opening.

Whether he bats righty or lefty, a team's best hitter should bat third. This is a player who can both score runs and drive them in, a high-average hitter who will take a walk. He doesn't need base-stealing speed (although that's a welcome plus), but he must be able to go from first to third on a single, or score from first on a double. You want diverse power from your number-three hitter, someone who hits doubles and triples as well as home runs. San Francisco's Barry Bonds or Atlanta's Chipper Jones can fill this role. But the obvious choice is the best player in baseball, Seattle Mariners centerfielder Ken Griffey Jr.

Whoever bats fourth doesn't need a high batting average, or much speed. Mental toughness and power are the tickets here. A clean-up hitter's eyes should light up whenever he comes to the plate with runners in scoring position. Met catcher Mike Piazza, Cub rightfielder Sammy Sosa, and Orioles leftfielder Albert Belle all possess the clean-up hitter's mentality. But nobody is fiercer in the clutch than the Texas Rangers' right-handed RBI machine, our rightfielder Juan Gonzalez.

A number-five hitter often bats with two outs, so he must be able to power the ball to plate runs; a clean-up man will have more opportunities to drive in runners with singles and sacrifice flies. I could bat Mark McGwire, Cleveland's Manny Ramirez, or Colorado's Dante Bichette fifth, but I'm looking for a left-handed bat to complement Gonzalez. Someone like Anaheim's first baseman, Mo Vaughn.

Theoretically, whoever bats sixth gets the lineup rolling again. Seattle shortstop Alex Rodriguez, a right-handed hitter, has the speed to score runs and the power to bring them home. Seventh-place hitters usually don't hit for high averages. They should compensate for that with walks and home runs. Los Angeles catcher Todd Hundley, a switch-hitter who's at his best from the left side, is my choice (provided he's recovered from the arm ailments that have hampered his play).

A number-eight batter should be able to get on base much like a secondary lead-off man so the pitcher can move him over with a bunt or an out. He doesn't have to be fast, but he should be one of the smarter base runners on the team. Opponents don't expect much run production from this spot; any eighth-place hitter who can drive in runs with timely hits is an asset to be cherished. Throughout 1998, right-handed-hitting Scott Brosius of the New York Yankees was the most productive bottom-of-the-order hitter in baseball. He is our third baseman.

As a National League traditionalist, I didn't name a DH to this lineup. But if we had to play by American League rules, the Yankees' Chili Davis would be my designated hitter. Chili is a switch-hitter with power and a knack for driving in runs. He doesn't have speed, but he knows his way along the basepaths. You could plug him into this batting order anywhere from fifth slot down.

Five You Can Follow

Most managers don't have the luxury of plugging in an All-Star-quality player at every position as we just did. They have to win with whatever talent the front office gives them. There are many good managers currently filling out batting orders in the major leagues. Atlanta's Bobby Cox, Los Angeles's Davey Johnson, Cleveland's Mike Hargrove, Seattle's Lou Piniella, and Texas's Johnny Oates are all proven winners. Younger skippers, like the Chicago White Sox's Jerry Manuel and San Diego's Bruce Bochy, have quickly earned reputations as sound tacticians and motivators. Given time (and some good teams), they could be among the managing elite.

I should mention that there are also a lot of inept managers. As many as half of the skippers currently leading major-league clubs are clueless; they make more mistakes in a single game than Bill Clinton has made in a career. I've often heard it said around baseball that you don't have to be a genius to manage a team. The guys I have in mind seem to be going out of their way to prove that point. They abuse their pitching staffs, continually fumble their lineup selections, are always caught on the short end in pitcher-hitter matchups, and aren't above ripping their players in the press when things go wrong. I'm not naming names; you guys know who you are.

I'm often mystified why teams hire certain guys. When my old club, the Reds, tabbed Jack McKeon as skipper, he had a career record that was barely over .500. There's no question that Jack is a solid baseball man; he was a topflight general manager renowned for his creativity and daring. "Trader Jack" is what they called him, and he was never afraid to pull the trigger on a trade that could help his ball club. He's a nice guy who works hard, but, at 69, his time has passed. I can't understand how the Reds expect him to relate to all of his young players such as Dimitri Young, Pokey Reese, Sean Casey, and top minor-league pitching prospect Robbie Bell. I have to admit he had the Reds playing better than anybody expected in the first half of the 1999 season. I still wonder, though, if he is the man to take this young team to the next level.

Then there are organizations that hire skippers who are clearly out of their element. Two years ago, the Dodgers gave Bill Russell what is perhaps the most prestigious manager's job in baseball. Russell had played for the Dodgers for 18 seasons (1969–86). During that time he had demonstrated no leadership qualities whatever. Ron Cey, Davey Lopes, Jimmy Wynn, Steve Yeager, Reggie Smith, Mike Scioscia, Steve Garvey—they were the leaders on all the championship clubs Russell played on. Yet the Dodgers put him in command. When the team didn't win, everyone blamed Mike Piazza and Raul Mondesi for failing to provide leadership. But they weren't getting any direction from the manager, so what were they supposed to do? Eventually, the Dodgers realized they had erred and removed Russell. But you have to ask why they ever hired him in the first place.

Five You Can Learn From

Five current managers stand out as the best in their trade. They are all role models for the modern baseball manager. If everyone managed like these skippers, the quality of major-league play would be elevated.

Felipe Alou, Montreal Expos: Alou's teams have played below .500 for the last two seasons. Doesn't matter. Felipe is baseball's best manager because he gets maximum performance from whatever players he has on hand. Alou keeps his teams well schooled in fundamentals. Even though they lose more often than they win, the Expos are nearly always competitive. You rarely see Montreal blown out of any ballgames.

That's quite an accomplishment when you consider the quality of Alou's personnel. Montreal has one of the lowest player budgets in baseball. Each season it has to shed another star or two out of economic necessity. Larry Walker, Moises Alou, John Wetteland, Delino DeShields, Pedro Martinez—you could win a World Series with the players who have passed through the Expos clubhouse since Felipe came on board. To replace them, the organization has been forced to rush many of its top minor-league prospects to the majors before they were ready.

As a result, Felipe must conduct on-the-job training for a new crop of rookies nearly every year. Most major-league managers resent having to teach their players the basics; they complain to me about it all the time. Working with young players, however, is Alou's long suit. He embraces the challenge as one of the most rewarding aspects of his job. Felipe has repeatedly told me, "Joe, I love to teach." His entire coaching staff takes its lead from him.

Alou knows how to dole out tough love. It's one of the reasons the 64-year-old manager is able to command the respect of his young charges. He can sense when a player needs a pat on the back or a kick in the rear. Players like Wilfredo Cordero and Delino DeShields have reputations for being difficult, but you never heard a bad word about either of them when they were playing for Alou.

Rushing green talent through the minor leagues is a growing trend in baseball. Expansion is only one of the reasons for this. Teams shelling out big-buck bonuses to their top draft picks want to realize a return on that investment as soon as possible. In the future, you can expect to see more players reaching the majors with less than a year of professional seasoning. Like it or not, managers and coaches are going to have to spend many hours teaching the game. They could learn some valuable lessons themselves just by watching the way Felipe Alou prepares his troops to play baseball.

And do they ever know how to play this game! Outside of Vladimir Guerrero and Rondell White, Felipe has few long-ball threats in his lineup. So he makes sure his players do all the little things that produce runs: steal timely bases, bunt, hit and run. His teams rarely pass up an opportunity to take an extra base. When the Expos' offense is cooking, they will first-and-third you all day long.

Aside from what he does on the field, I also appreciate how Alou supports his players. When everyone in baseball was screaming that Pedro Martinez (the talented right-handed pitcher who now works for the Boston Red Sox) was a headhunter, Felipe rushed to his defense. He went out of his way to explain through the media that Martinez was simply fighting control problems while attempting to pitch inside. Alou's PR campaign worked; you rarely hear anyone refer to Martinez as a headhunter these days.

We're not just talking about sticks and stones here. Umps will scrutinize a headhunter more closely than other pitchers, and they will quickly eject him if they suspect he's trying to hit someone. That plants a negative seed in the pitcher's head. He's not going to come inside as often, and batters, knowing that, will take advantage by sitting on his outside stuff.

Opposing players are also more likely to retaliate against a pitcher with a headhunting rep, even when it is obvious that he isn't trying to hit anyone. When Pedro was with Montreal, he hit Reggie Sanders, then of the Cincinnati Reds, with an inside fastball. Reggie, all six feet two inches and 220 muscular pounds of him, charged the mound, prepared to separate Pedro from his throwing arm. I can understand a hitter trying to protect himself. However, Pedro was pitching a perfect game at the time. There was no way he would jeopardize his shot at baseball immortality by hitting Sanders. Reggie wasn't reacting to the pitch; he was responding to Martinez's rep. That's when Alou took to setting everybody straight in earnest.

Pitching for Montreal, Pedro won the National League Cy Young Award in 1997. After he was traded to Boston, the Red Sox made him the highest-paid player in baseball. Martinez owes much of his extraordinary success to Alou. Had all those hard-eyed umpires and angry hitters ever intimidated Pedro to the point that he stopped pitching inside, I doubt he would have been nearly as effective. It's just another example of how Felipe is always fighting to grab every advantage for his players.

Jim Leyland (Colorado Rockies): Jim knows as much about baseball strategy as any manager on the planet. His teams play good defense and never stop coming at you. Leyland makes sure everyone on his roster understands his role against the context of the team. You'll never see his players come to the park unprepared. They respect Leyland's knowledge, and respond to his keen sense of loyalty. I noticed this when Jim managed the Marlins in the 1997 World Series against Cleveland. His lead-off hitter, Devon White, was struggling at the plate. I suggested that Devon might relax if Jim gave him a game off. White looked as though he was pressing with every at-bat. Leyland said, "Joe, I'm not going to do that. This guy helped us get here, and I know he'll break out of this." Devon led the team to a win that very night.

Before the seventh game of that same World Series, several journalists wondered how Leyland could pick left-hander Al Leiter to start the most important game of the year. Leiter had not pitched well in the post-season. Leyland responded, "If Al has his control and stuff, I have no doubt that he can get the job done today."

Starting pitchers need that kind of support even more than hitters do. If you're a starter who gets knocked around, you have four or five days to beat yourself up before your next start. A batter who goes 0-for-5 knows he can straighten things up the very next day. Leyland's words gave Leiter some added confidence; he pitched a strong, gutsy game that the Marlins eventually won in extra innings. Both the White and Leiter episodes vividly demonstrate how players will reward a manager who sticks by them during adversity.

Leyland uses anticipation to broaden what has become the modern skipper's thin margin for error. For instance, in a game against the Arizona Diamondbacks last summer, Marlins starter Brian Meadows took a 4–1 lead into the sixth. Meadows had not allowed more than two base runners in any one inning.

Arizona opened the bottom of the sixth with singles by centerfielder Devon White and second baseman Andy Fox. That's when Meadows toughened. The right-hander stranded both runners by retiring the next two hitters on two flyballs and a strikeout. Meadows had pitched economically throughout the ballgame. He had thrown only 74 pitches, a modest total for six innings of work. Most managers would have sent him out to start the seventh. But Leyland summoned his bullpen. He had seen something undetected by almost everyone else in Bank One Ballpark.

Meadows's fastball hadn't lost any velocity, but it was straightening; both fly-outs were hard-hit balls to center field by Jay Bell and Matt Williams. Leyland didn't need a pitch count to know that the Diamondbacks were honing in on the Meadows fastball. He got his young pitcher out of the game before Arizona could damage his ERA or his psyche. Meadows came away with his confidence intact and with a W on his record. That, my friends, is managing.

Dusty Baker (San Francisco Giants): When I was with the Reds, I asked Sparky Anderson whom he considered the best manager in baseball. He replied, "Earl Weaver because he's won with so many different kinds of clubs." That's what Dusty Baker has done throughout his career with San Francisco. Baker usually goes into battle with a patchwork lineup. Leftfielder Barry Bonds, who prefers to bat fifth, has to hit third because no one else on the team is suited for that spot. Second baseman Jeff Kent, who would be a number-five hitter on most teams, bats cleanup. First baseman J. T. Snow would be better off batting sixth or seventh, but he frequently hits fifth for San Francisco. The top of Baker's lineup isn't any more orthodox. The Giants haven't had a legitimate lead-off hitter in nearly a decade.

One might assume, then, that it's the pitching staff that provides the Giants with their glue. Guess again. San Francisco's starting rotation may be the most anonymous in baseball; as the team entered spring training in 1999, it didn't have one starter with as many as 100 career wins. So for me this team's recent success all comes down to the manager. Somehow Baker finds a way to make this hodgepodge work. He has proven that he can mold 25 disparate talents and personalities into a cohesive unit that outperforms its individual stats.

Dusty—out of design as much as necessity—never stays with a pat hand. Bonds, still the National League's finest player, and Kent, who has matured into one of baseball's best clutch hitters, are the only constants in his lineup. He constructs the rest of the batting order around them. Dusty has demonstrated a fine knack for picking a hot hand. He knows exactly when to plug a bench player into the lineup, let him run for two weeks, then replace him with someone else who contributes for another ten or so games. He doesn't consult a seer to work his magic. "I talk to my players all the time," says Dusty. "I know their habits, their feelings, even their diets. For instance, I have one player who's a vegetarian, and I have a good idea when he's going to run out of gas. Before that happens, I rest him. There's nothing mysterious to it."

Dusty also knows how to keep the players who do sit upbeat. That's not an easy thing to do. While there are utility men who are content just to be on a major-league roster, you don't want them on your team. The best role players are starved for playing time.

They come into the lineup with something to prove; that attitude can energize your team for weeks.

When Charlie Hayes was with the New York Yankees from 1996 to 1997, he was rarely smiling even though he was playing for a world championship club. As a right-handed hitting third baseman, Charlie platooned with the left-handed hitting Wade Boggs. Boggs did the bulk of the playing. Hayes despised the arrangement and wasn't shy about sharing his displeasure with anyone.

Charlie thought he would find a better situation in San Francisco. However, he is not even a platoon player with the Giants. Bill Mueller is the everyday third baseman. Mueller is a young switch-hitter who bats with equal authority from both sides of the plate. If he's healthy, Mueller is going to start 140 games, which doesn't leave many at-bats for Charlie. Yet Hayes has told me that playing for Dusty is a joy. He knows the manager is going to give him the opportunity to help the club win ballgames. Hayes trusts that Baker will never let him languish on the bench. Charlie will spell Mueller at third, play some first when a tough left-hander forces Snow from the lineup, pinch-hit, and give the Giants a lot of late-inning defense. Baker has taught him to think T-E-A-M all the time. (Integrity, which I mentioned earlier, plays a role here. If Hayes didn't believe Dusty's promises of playing time, he wouldn't be quite so content.)

Dusty was a great hitter when he played with the Braves and Dodgers; he's taught his team how to make adjustments at the plate depending on the pitcher and the situation. This is an invaluable skill in a time when batters might see as many as five different pitchers in any given game. It's difficult to defeat any big-league club that takes a lead into the seventh inning. Baker's teams score late and often while producing many comeback victories, because their hitters continually adapt.

All managers should pay attention to the way Dusty coordinates his pitching staff. As he told me recently, "We start the season earlier than ever now. So there just aren't enough games in spring training for my starting pitchers to build up to full arm strength." With that in mind, Dusty will go to his bullpen early and often during April and May. Come June, as his starters' arms stretch out, he gives the bullpen more rest. This delicate handling usually means his entire staff is clicking on all cylinders as the pennant race enters its stretch drive.

During 1998, Dusty's starters weren't giving him the innings they had in the past; he had to go to the bullpen sooner than he would have liked throughout the entire season. You know what? He still found a way to win. That's another reason I think Dusty is a role model for other managers; like his lineup, he adapts all the time.

Joe Torre (New York Yankees): You know something that annoys me? Torre has won two world championships in the last three years, yet he still may be the most underrated manager in baseball. I hear people say he wins because he has such a good team. But it was Torre who transformed it into a good team by teaching it to play National League–style baseball in American League parks.

Buck Showalter, the Yankee manager before Torre, played station-to-station ball. His Yankees took one base at a time while waiting for someone to crank up a long ball. Torre arrived and immediately unleashed New York's hidden running attack. Suddenly the Bronx Bombers were a team of sprinters bunting, stealing bases, executing the hit-and-run. And they still got their share of home runs. The other teams in the American League weren't prepared for this brand of edgy, wide-open baseball.

Though he's stamped his personality on his team, Torre's managerial style is not intrusive. Any manager who attempts to exert too much control over the game is invariably going to limit his club's success. Gene Mauch, who managed the Phillies, Expos, Twins, and Angels, was unquestionably one of the most brilliant baseball minds I've ever encountered. But he tried to control the pace of every game like a college basketball coach. It's one of the primary reasons Gene never won a pennant despite having managed his share of formidable teams.

When a manager tries to direct nearly every move a player makes, that player starts to look over his shoulder too often. Baseball is a game of confidence, instinct, and improvisation; you undermine all three when you make your players tentative. Since today's players are so independent, a good manager will put them in situations where they can excel, then let them play their natural game.

Torre does exactly that. He not only knows what buttons to push on his veteran team, but when to push them. When the Yankee offense is percolating, Joe lays back, content to let his hitters do their thing. But if it appears that runs are going to be scarce, he's all hands-on.

Just look at how he managed the first game of the American League Division Series against Texas last year. Ranger right-hander Todd Stottlemyre started against Yankee left-hander David

Wells that day, and you could see right away that both pitchers had their best stuff. Torre knew one or two runs would probably decide the ballgame.

In the second inning, New York had one run in with leftfielder Chad Curtis on third and third baseman Scott Brosius on first. Texas's catcher was Ivan Rodriguez, a fellow who throws heat-seeking missiles from behind home plate. Even the best base stealers stay close to first when Rodriguez is on watch. And Brosius is one of the slowest men on the Yankee roster (although he's also the team's cagiest base runner). No one in the ballpark expected him to test Rodriguez's arm. So what did Torre do? He flashed Brosius the steal sign.

As Rodriguez tried to cut down Brosius with a throw to second, Curtis took off from third. Brosius forced a rundown that lasted long enough for his teammate to sneak home with the Yankees' second run. That was the ballgame. Neither team scored again. Torre's aggressiveness and the Yankees' superb execution stole a run and a victory.

As a former All-Star catcher, Torre appreciates the value of strong defense. When he first joined New York, Mike Stanley, a clutch-hitting slugger with lower-than-average defensive skills, was behind the plate. After the front office decided to let Stanley go (he was a free agent), Torre and bench coach Don Zimmer lobbied management to trade for Joe Girardi of the Colorado Rockies. Girardi was one of the best defensive catchers in all of baseball.

Irate fans complained loudly on the New York sports talk radio shows when the Yankees let go of the popular Stanley. But Torre knew what he was doing. New York became a better team the moment Girardi stepped behind the plate. He immediately solidified the Yankee pitching staff with his astute game-calling. And though he couldn't come close to matching Stanley's power, Girardi has proven to be a solid professional hitter who seems to be in the middle of almost every Yankee late-inning rally.

Something Derek Jeter told me about last season's Yankee team indirectly underscored what may be Torre's greatest value as a manager. When I asked the Yankee shortstop how good his club was, he said, "We can be as good as we want to be, as long as we don't become complacent. We're not the kind of team that shows up trying to win two games out of three, or three out of four. We think we can win every game we play. And we don't rely on any one star to carry the load."

It is nearly impossible for any team to maintain that intensity throughout spring training, a 162-game schedule, and the post-season. But 1998's world champion New York Yankees rarely let up for even an inning, because Joe Torre's relentless style of play kept them engaged.

Tony LaRussa (St. Louis Cardinals): The original nine-inning manager. Most skippers come to the park prepared; Tony is ultra-prepared. He and his coaches study all the charts, scouting reports, and other data they can obtain to grab an edge over the opposition.

Managers throughout both leagues have access to the same information, but LaRussa knows how to use it better than most. Tony is so thorough he scouts his own tendencies throughout the season in order to detect whether he is falling into a strategical pattern. "If I always hit-and-run on 1–0," he explains, "the opposing manager is going to start pitching out on 1–0."

As I wrote earlier, LaRussa was the manager who took major-league bullpens to the next level. He'll use four setup men to get key outs on the way to his closer. Tony will bring in a southpaw to get out a left-handed slugger with the game on the line, even though he knows his pitcher will face only the one batter; his relievers usually lead the league in one-batter appearances. LaRussa employs so many pitchers because he battles throughout all nine innings to get the pitcher-hitter matchups that will best serve his team.

Like Joe Torre, LaRussa is aggressive. Even when he has a lineup packed with power, he mixes in the running game to manufacture runs. He's also an innovator who doesn't always do things by the book. For example, LaRussa was managing a floundering Oakland pitching staff in 1993 when he unveiled a novel strategy: working his pitchers for 50-pitch stints every other day to keep them sharp. He experimented with the plan only for a brief stretch, and it wasn't particularly successful. But that's not the point. Oakland had the worst pitching staff in baseball that season; LaRussa demonstrated a willingness to try something that had never been attempted before to improve its performance. Most managers would never even consider such an out-of-the-box strategy, much less have the guts to put it into practice.

I am less sanguine, though, about his latest tactical wrinkle. During the 1998 season, with his first baseman Mark McGwire bearing down on Roger Maris's home-run record, LaRussa batted his pitchers eighth instead of ninth. He explained he was doing this to get McGwire more at-bats.

The math is against Tony on this one. Over the course of a full season, each spot in the batting order will come to the plate 18 to 20 more times than the following spot. So how does getting more plate appearances for your pitcher, the worst hitter in your lineup, translate to more swings for McGwire? If anything, the lineup switch should reduce Big Mac's hitting opportunities. Which is exactly what it did in 1998. When the pitcher batted eighth, the Cardinals scored fewer runs than when he batted ninth. And McGwire came up with fewer runners on base or in scoring position. Despite this, LaRussa stated his intentions to revive his unorthodox batting order in 1999. Then, when the season started, he dropped the idea. Guess he got a good look at those numbers.

. . .

All five of the managers on my list share at least one attribute: they let their teams play. Four of the five played in the major leagues. (Leyland being the exception. Before managing in the majors, Jim made his reputation as a member of Tony LaRussa's coaching staff.) Baker, Torre, and Alou are former All-Stars and Joe was the National League MVP in 1971. They talk straight while defining each player's role on the team. None of these skippers ever take too much credit for the club's success. That's important. Any manager who believes that he is the reason a team wins is going to lose all rapport with today's athletes. As Sparky Anderson has told me, "Players are like dogs; they can smell you. If you're a fake or a swelled head, they'll sniff it out and turn on you in a minute. So any manager who discovers he's fallen in love with the guy who looks back at him from the bathroom mirror has two choices: get a divorce or get out of the clubhouse."

6

Ten Who Will Keep
the Turnstiles Spinning

For years, major-league baseball has been reluctant to bally-hoo its greatest asset—the players. Owners reasoned that if you made someone the focal point of your team, you would have to pay him more money. With salaries so high, that's a moot point today. Baseball should follow the lead of the NBA by casting a spotlight on its stars. Here are ten players who can deliver the siz-zle—to use the parlance of Madison Avenue—to any marketing campaign, ten luminaries who bring center stage with them wher-ever they stride:

Mark McGwire (St. Louis Cardinals): Quickness is the key for some sluggers. Hitters like Nomar Garciaparra and Bernie Williams (hitting from the right side) use their tremendous bat speed to generate home runs. Others are so strong—Anaheim first baseman Mo Vaughn comes to mind here—that they simply over-power the ball. Mark McGwire, like Ken Griffey Jr., is that rarest of hitters; he's both quick and strong. He propels a picture-perfect, compact swing without a hint of wasted motion. Just after impact, he removes his top hand (the right one for right-handed hitters) from the bat for greater extension. During the 1998 season, our ESPN BatTrack measured his bat speed at 99 mph. No one else in the major leagues was as fast.

Which is why no one mistreats a horsehide like Big Mac. I've played with and against many Hall of Famers, but I can't recall anyone like Mark. He is a figure out of folklore, a Paul Bunyan with bigger biceps and a better batting eye. Most of his home runs are majestic; they seem to travel as high as they do far. I remember Mickey Mantle, Willie Stargell, Frank Howard, and Richie Allen hitting McGwirean moon shots, but not nearly as often as Mark does. Sinewy power hitters such as Frank Thomas and Jim Thome are so bulked they make their bats look too small when they tote them to the plate. Mark is the only hitter I know of who can make *ballparks* look too tiny. When you come to the stadium, there is always a chance you might see him do something unprecedented. It wouldn't surprise anyone if he became the first player to hit a 600-foot home run. (It has been said that Babe Ruth, while still a pitcher-outfielder with the Boston Red Sox, hit a 600-foot homer in an exhibition game against the New York Giants on April 4, 1919. However, there is nothing beyond anecdotal evidence to support this claim.)

What made Big Mac's record-breaking performance so remarkable is that from midseason on, he only got two or three good pitches to hit per game. Can't blame the pitchers for that. You have to be a masochist to enjoy facing him. McGwire's home runs not only rattle stadium seats, they rattle around in a hurler's psyche. As Junior Griffey told me, "When I hit a home run 425 feet, the pitcher only gets so upset. But when McGwire hits one 500 feet or so, the pitcher is embarrassed."

Challenge McGwire inside too often, and there's a good chance six of your friends are going to be carrying you around by the handles. You have to vary your pitches, speeds, and arm angles, or you won't get him out consistently. Atlanta's pitchers threw everything but the kitchen sink at McGwire and were able to contain him for most of the season. On August 30, however, Braves right-hander Dennis Martinez threw Big Mac two consecutive fastballs. Mark took one for a strike, then launched Martinez's second offering a mere 501 feet for home-run number 55. In that same game, he smacked a laser-beam single so hard it nearly cleaved Atlanta shortstop Ozzie Guillen in two.

Throughout the National League, McGwire draws crowds of 25,000 or more to his batting practice sessions. I've never heard of anyone doing that, not even Babe Ruth or Ted Williams. He will continue to be big box office for years to come, not only because America loves all things large, but because the public senses he's a decent guy. He's donated over $1 million to establish the Mark McGwire Foundation for sexually abused children

Ken Griffey Jr. (Seattle Mariners): Batting title contender, Gold Glove perennial, and home-run champion Junior Griffey will always be a fan magnet because he is baseball's complete package. What impresses me most about him is his love for the game. In that respect, he reminds me so much of Willie Mays; you can always tell he's having fun out there.

Junior enjoys making great plays—and he makes a ton of them—as much as getting a base hit. That's rare these days. His concentration sets him apart from the rest of baseball's center-fielders. Bernie Williams, Brian McRae, and Andruw Jones might all be swifter than Griffey, but they lack his focus and commitment to catch every ball hit in his direction. Junior believes he can glove any fly ball that stays in the ballpark. You can't be a great fielder without that conceit.

Kenny has all the range any centerfielder could want. When he plays, center field isn't just that area bordered by left and right; it's wherever he chooses to roam. He can flash in to cut off a line-drive single. Then, in the very next play, he might devour yards of real estate to snatch yet another base hit out of the box score. I'd pay money just to watch him cavort on defense. With nine Gold Gloves already resting on his mantel, he is on a pace to break Willie Mays's record of 12 Gold Gloves for center-field play.

When Junior comes to bat, pay attention to his hands. They're the best in the game. Once he reads a pitch, his hands react quicker than most other hitters. That's what makes him so explosive at home plate. Also, notice the sound the ball makes when it jumps off his bat. Junior hits the ball hard almost every time up. Unlike McGwire, who usually hits towering fly balls, Griffey tends to hit line-drive homers. He is one of the few left-handed hitters whose power doesn't suffer against left-handers.

Before the 1998 season opened, I kidded Junior that Barry Bonds was a 40–40 man (40 home runs and 40 stolen bases in a season), while he was only a 10–50 player. He said that he and (Seattle manager) Lou Piniella had decided that it was time for Ken to run more. Junior set 20 stolen bases as a goal; he swiped exactly 20 bases while getting caught only five times. Which should tell you that he can do pretty much anything he sets his mind to.

He's terrific with the fans, a fixture in Seattle. Ken acts a spokesperson for the Boys and Girls Club of America. He throws an annual Christmas party for 400 Seattle kids and their families, and last year he flew 45 Seattle students who had improved their grades down to his Orlando home for a trip to Disney World. I joined him for dinner in Seattle not too long ago. The moment he walked in, every kid in the place started beaming. Junior signed autographs all night and never lost his smile. He has a childlike exuberance that attracts young fans. Baseball marketeers often act as if they are on a mission to find their sport's Michael Jordan. They can stop looking. He already plays in Seattle.

Sammy Sosa (Chicago Cubs): When he first entered the major leagues, Sammy was an erratic fielder and an undisciplined hitter. No one projected him as a player who could bash 50 homers, much less 66. But he has surpassed everyone's expectations because of his tremendous work ethic.

Last season, for example, Sosa made a major adjustment in his batting style. In past seasons he stood as close as he could near the top of home plate, making it difficult for him to protect the inside corner. Pitchers regularly got him out by popping him inside. Cubs hitting coach Billy Williams moved Sammy back and off the plate. This gave him more time to recognize pitches. It also meant he was better positioned to handle anything thrown inside. Now, instead of worrying about the pitcher jamming him, Sammy could just see the ball and react to it. He immediately started depositing into the upper deck pitches that used to tie him up.

Throughout the 1998 season, Sammy comported himself as a consummate team player who thought more about his team's pennant chase than his home-run race. He became an excellent situational hitter. Most sluggers look to pull everything. But with a man on second and his club down by a run, Sammy would smack the outside pitch the other way to right field for a run-scoring single. Unlike McGwire and Griffey, Sosa isn't particularly quick at the plate. He has a longer swing than Griffey or McGwire, so he must overpower the ball to be effective.

Sammy has also invested enough sweat equity in his defense to become a competent outfielder with a strong, accurate throwing arm. He was always fast, but he's learned how to read pitchers to become a productive base stealer. That's something I've admired about him ever since he was a rookie: No matter how much he achieves, Sosa never stops elevating his game.

That's Sammy the player. Here's all you need to know about Sammy the person: After the Cubs' second playoff game against Atlanta in last year's National League playoffs, he and some of his teammates worked late into the night loading trucks with supplies for Dominican hurricane victims. Once those playoffs ended, Sammy chartered a plane to fly him to the Dominican Republic with even more supplies. Many athletes will write checks for different causes, but Sammy also contributes his time. That's special. He has financed an office complex to create hundreds of jobs in his hometown, San Pedro de Marcoris. Last season, his Sammy Claus Program distributed 7,000 Christmas gifts to the underprivileged in the United States and the Dominican Republic. And of course we've all seen the Sosa smile; it could brighten even Billie Holiday's stormiest Monday. No wonder fans adore him. When Chicago signed him to a contract that averaged $10 million annually, nearly everyone—including me—thought the Cubs were overpaying. Now baseball's Good Humor Man is one of the game's biggest bargains.

Unlike most of the great sluggers who played before them, McGwire, Griffey, and Sosa all use relatively light bats, either 31 or 32 ounces (I used a 32-ounce bat myself). I think this is a harbinger rather than an aberration. Bat speed is the new priority for today's power hitters; smaller bats give you that.

Orlando Hernandez (New York Yankees): Fans should be packing the stadium whenever this right-hander pitches. Hernandez is a veritable rock-and-roll laser light show on the mound. No pitcher in baseball throws more pitches from more different angles. His ultra-high leg kick, hesitation motion, and downright nasty stuff can keep hitters off-balance no matter how often they face him.

The thing I like most about him is his composure. When I watched the Yankees take batting practice before game four of the American League Championship Series against Cleveland, I could tell they were tight. The fans and the media had expected New York to bulldoze their post-season competition right up through the World Series. Now they were down in the playoffs, two games to one, to a tough team that had upset them in the ALCS only the year before. You could sense the doubts they were all experiencing as they grimly prepared for that evening's contest.

All of them, that is, except Hernandez, whom Torre had tabbed to start that critical fourth game. During a team brunch, Hernandez had joked with his teammates while serving them platters of food. The night of the big game, he was the loosest guy in both clubhouses. It was as if he didn't know he was starting.

When a reporter asked him how it felt to pitch in such a big game, he said, "Oh, this is nothing, I've pitched in big games before." Then he reminded us of how he had hurled his teams to championships before huge, exuberant crowds in the Cuban National Series.

Prior to his ALCS start, El Duque hadn't pitched in nearly two weeks. It showed in the first inning. You could tell he was struggling with his command. He allowed a couple of base runners, but Cleveland first baseman Jim Thome ended the inning with a deep fly ball to right that nearly left the field for a three-run homer. After that threat came to naught, Hernandez was untouchable. He pitched seven shutout innings in a 4–0 New York victory. That win lifted the anvil off the Yankees' backs. The next day, you could see the swagger was back in their strides. Hernandez had reminded them that they were the Yankees, the best team in baseball.

Besides a great attitude, Hernandez has great stuff, and, boy, does he know how to use it! When he first came to the Bronx, he was successful even though he seemed timid about coming inside on left-handed hitters. Once that got buzzed around the league, lefties jolted him a few times. Orlando quickly adjusted, though, and that's the sign of a good pitcher. Now he comes inside hard on lefties. When they try to speed up their bats, he mixes in a change-up right out of Pitching 101.

Hernandez has the same charisma that Luis Tiant displayed when he pitched for the Boston Red Sox during the 1970s. You just can't keep your eyes off him. I usually scan the entire field when I'm broadcasting a game. When El Duque takes the mound, though, my focus never leaves him. His gravity-defying gyrations, 99 different arm angles, and great command of the strike zone make him one of baseball's more entertaining figures. Even the way he takes his signs from the catcher exudes panache.

As for his pitching repertoire, El Duque has a deceptively good fastball that tops out around 92, but has all kinds of movement within the strike zone. His change-up is a fabulous pitch; once he gets you looking for it, he can overpower you with hard stuff (as Cleveland discovered). Hernandez throws his curveball sidearm and three-quarters at varying speeds, so it's like having five or six different pitches.

This is a special athlete. Any time you can bring your left knee up to your nose, you are some kind of flexible. The Yankees team physician told us there wasn't a single Yankee—not Bernie Williams, Paul O'Neill, Derek Jeter, Chad Curtis, or Tino Martinez—who was better conditioned than Hernandez. He fields his position like a Gold Glove winner. When I first met him in the Yankee clubhouse, Hernandez greeted me warmly, though I doubt he knew who I was. Funny and outgoing, El Duque is going to be a fan favorite for a long time. It wouldn't surprise me if he eventually becomes a twenty-game winner.

Derek Jeter (New York Yankees): You want to know what kind of determination Jeter has? He was ten years old when he decided he was going to play shortstop for the New York Yankees. Derek is a throwback in this age of the pull hitter. He hits straightaway, and starts most at-bats trying to shoot the ball to right center. He will pull off-speed stuff, or pitch inside. Derek has average bat speed; he strikes out a lot because he must commit to pitches early. But his approach is sound, since he rarely tries to do too much with the ball. Jeter takes what the pitcher gives him.

As a fielder, Derek positively seethes with talent. He has a powerful arm—the best among major-league shortstops—that allows him to do things I could never imagine. During the playoffs against Texas, he got to a slow roller by Ivan Rodriguez, and threw him out on the run. It was an audacious play. Any other shortstop would have needed an extra step to plant his back foot before throwing. Saving that step secured the out.

Derek possesses excellent lateral movement, broad range in and out, and increasingly sure hands. He improves every aspect of his game each season. As Yankee pitching ace David Cone recently told me, "He's very much a student of the game. Derek watches the pitch selection and adjusts his positioning depending on what pitch is going to be thrown. He's learned the nuances of how to cheat (lean) one way or another depending on the pitch, the hitter, and the situation."

He has also learned the importance of putting his team first. The little things Jeter does—bunt, hit-and-run, move runners along with productive outs—demonstrates that he counts wins ahead of individual stats. Every player should have his attitude. Last year, after I congratulated him on his near-MVP season, he said, "Thanks, but I still have a long way to go." Here's a player who has been Rookie of the Year, an All-Star, and a member of two World Series winners, yet he's still not satisfied. He has that competitive hunger common to all winners.

Derek also has that indefinable something extra that would have marked him as a star in any era. Nike has plastered his picture on the side of a building in New York City. A caption within the illustration asks in bold letters, "CAN YOU JETER?" When a mega-company uses your last name as a verb in its advertising campaigns, you know you've arrived as a star. Of course, the Yankees' female teenaged fans didn't need a Nike sign to tell them that. They think he's the hottest thing since Leonardo DiCaprio. Jeter is fan-accessible and knows that his obligation to the team extends beyond the ballfield. I expect him to be the next Yankee captain.

Alex Rodriguez (Seattle Mariners): I've never understood his batting approach. He looks like he should be quick at the plate, but more often he powers the ball for hits. Despite that, he doesn't pull most of his home runs. Alex hits the ball the other way as often as some slap hitters, only he hits everything hard. Does he hit fastballs better than breaking balls? Who knows? I've seen pitchers retire him with both, but I've also seen him homer off the same pitches. There's no discernible pattern to him.

But there must be a pattern in his mind; this guy can flat-out hack. Alex is the most gifted of baseball's elite shortstops. He may be the prototypical middle infielder of the future: big and powerful at the plate (he's bigger, in fact, than teammate Ken Griffey Jr.), quick and rangy in the field.

Alex is not as good as Jeter defensively, even though A-Rod has the advantage of playing on artificial turf. Derek is more flexible and shows better hands. Alex makes more errors, but he can play his position. Any talk about moving him to third base is premature. With his speed and long strides, he covers as much ground as any shortstop. Alex also positions himself well. A smart player.

If Rodriguez has an offensive ceiling, no one has noticed it. During his first full major-league season (1996), Alex, a mere 21 years old), hit .358 to become the third-youngest batting champion of all time. Only Hall of Famers Ty Cobb and Al Kaline were younger when they won batting crowns. He became a 40–40 player last season, the first infielder to post that double.

People ask me if he will surpass Griffey as a hitter. Hard to say. Griffey has the advantage of being a left-handed hitter, a decided plus when the majority of pitchers are right-handed. Alex, however, is certainly on a par with Junior at comparable stages of their career. Both Junior and A-Rod will be free agents after the 2000 season. If Seattle can afford to keep these two together, they could lead baseball into the next millennium as the most explosive hitting combination since the Yankees had Gehrig and Ruth.

Albert Belle (Baltimore Orioles): Albert has one of the game's most powerful swings, and he can focus on each pitch as few hitters can. Once he hones in on a ball, he makes a commitment. That is the difference between an average hitter and an elite one. This may surprise you, but 90 percent of today's major-league hitters fail to commit. When they see a pitch, they think, "This is a fastball (or a curve). I'm going to try to hit it." When Albert recognizes his pitch, he thinks, "I'm going to knock the hide off of it."

Do you know the difference that kind of confidence can make? With a 2–0 count on him, any major-league hitter knows a fastball is coming, so he should be ready to drive it. Yet you'll see too many batters swing late on that pitch. When a pitcher goes 2–0 on Albert, you know he's going to cream the next offering if it's anywhere near his hitting zone. And if he doesn't get the pitcher this time, he'll get him the next, because Albert is also mentally tough. A hurler may get him out consistently with sliders away, but Belle will keep fighting until he eventually does something with that pitch. That's why he puts up Hall of Fame–quality numbers season after season.

Belle's powerful swing is a product of his stance as well as his strong upper body. Notice the way he keeps his front shoulder in most of the time. He turns it just a tad back toward the catcher as the pitcher prepares to deliver the ball. That gets him into a great hitting position. He reminds me of my former teammate George Foster, who hit 52 home runs during 1977, when he won the MVP Award, only Albert is bigger and stronger. His public persona might not attract many fans to the ballpark, but his accomplishments at the plate will. Albert will be playing his home games in Camden Yards in 1999, a park so small you have to believe the architect was someone who was raised to hate pitchers. Hitting in that bandbox, Albert could drive 60 or more home runs.

Owing to his somewhat menacing reputation, Albert often absorbs more than his share of unwarranted criticism from the press as well as the fans. For instance, in 1996, while a member of the Cleveland Indians, Albert took Milwaukee Brewer second baseman Fernando Vina out of a double play with a body block that knocked Vina into the middle of the next century. The media crawled all over Belle for that; you would have thought he was a combination of Hitler and Jack the Ripper. Even American League president Gene Budig treated Belle as if he were a criminal. There was only one thing wrong with all this outrage: Belle was totally in the right.

As a member in good standing of the second baseman's fraternity, I'm here to tell you that it was Vina's responsibility to get out of the way on that play. Belle had been hit by pitches twice in that game. Every major-league second baseman knows that a hit batsman standing at first is probably going to target the first fielder who gets in his way for some retribution. Whenever a pitcher on the Reds would hit Bob Watson, a former teammate and buddy of mine, I knew I had to be nimble on any force plays at second or the Bull was going to cream me. It's part of baseball.

Belle was in the runner's lane, his territory, when he advanced on Vina. His hit on Fernando was certainly violent, but it was also clean. The second baseman should have stepped to his left or right and tagged Albert from out of harm's way. Forget the revenge angle; Albert was just doing his job trying to break up the double play. What he did was no different from a base runner colliding with a catcher who's blocking the plate. It would have been wrong for Belle to just slide gently into Vina's tag. He would have been letting down his teammates and manager.

One year after the Belle-Vina crackup, Robin Ventura of the White Sox, one of the nicest guys in the game, upended Cleveland second baseman Bip Roberts on a similar play. No one said a word about it. You can draw your own conclusions.

We covered that game on ESPN, and I criticized Roberts, as I had Vina, for not eluding Ventura's charge. Someone must have told Bip about my comments, because during the next inning he held up a sign to one of the cameras. It read: "Joe, You're Right!" Roberts understood that he had no one to blame but himself for the collision.

I first met Albert when I watched him play for Louisiana State in the College World Series. My former Astros roommate, Jimmy Wynn, was his idol, so we hit it off right away. In private,

Albert is a terrific guy, gracious, respectful, and highly intelligent. Believe it or not, he's a people person. He regularly donates large sums to such organizations as the Boy Scouts, the Make-A-Wish Foundation, the American Heart Association, as well as numerous church groups and reading programs. More important, Albert gives of himself. Having been a 3.0 student at Louisiana State, he spends hours talking to young people about the importance of education and religion.

When spring training opened in 1999, it looked as though we might see a different Albert off the field, someone more media-accessible and fan-friendly. He saw the adulation heaped on Sosa and McGwire, and I thought he might want some of that. Unfortunately, his intensity got the better of him. After going 0-for-4 in an early spring training game against the Mets, Albert launched into a clubhouse tirade that the press commented on the following day. The next time the media saw him, he vowed never to speak to them again. Sportswriters play a large role in shaping a player's public image. When fans read only about the surly Belle, they never get to know the complete man—which is too bad, because they would love Albert if he just gave them the opportunity.

Juan Gonzalez (Texas Rangers): Former Texas first baseman Will Clark told me that the Ballpark at Arlington is a challenging stadium for sluggers; you really have to drive the ball to hit it out. That doesn't seem to handicap Juan Gonzalez, baseball's best cleanup hitter. As the old-time scouts like to say, Juan can hit the ball over the wall in any park, including Yellowstone.

He's more than just a slugger, however. Juan's extensive plate coverage makes him one of the game's most versatile hitters. He goes to the ball with his powerful upper body; most hitter just can't do that. When he's in the batter's box, Juan's feet stride in the same spot almost every time, but his body takes him wherever the pitch is. That makes it difficult to get Juan out on either side of the plate. For example, in the third inning of a May game against the Indians last season, Cleveland right-hander Jaret Wright threw Juan an inside, 0–2 fastball. Juan pounded it to right field for a line-drive single. Two innings later, Wright threw Gonzalez a 99-mph fastball on the inside corner. A nasty pitch, especially for a right-handed hitter. Gonzalez ripped it into left field for an RBI double. How do you pitch to someone like that? Carefully, very carefully.

Like most genuine clean-up hitters, Juan is at his most dangerous with men on base; he's averaged more than an RBI per game for the last four years. He relishes hitting under pressure. The major-league RBI record for a single season is Hack Wilson's 190 (1930). Should his teammates keep getting on base in front of him, I think Gonzalez can threaten that mark.

Vladimir Guerrero (Montreal Expos): Giants manager Dusty Baker told me that Guerrero "throws like Roberto Clemente, hits like Willie Mays, and runs like Bo Jackson." You think a player with all those tools isn't going to become a big drawing card? If Montreal is going to survive as a major-league franchise, this is the guy the front office must build around.

In 1998, Guerrero hit .324 with 38 home runs and 109 RBI. The scary part (for pitchers) about those numbers is that Vladimir is still learning his craft. He pounds pitches in the strike zone, but I've found he's not quite as patient early in the count as he should be. His feel at the plate will improve with experience. The one part of Vladimir's game that doesn't need much tinkering is his defense; it has been a plus from the time he joined the professional ranks. When Guerrero was in the Eastern League, his peers voted him the circuit's outstanding defensive outfielder, a rare honor for a rightfielder. He and Pittsburgh rightfielder Jose Guillen have the most powerful, accurate outfield throwing arms in baseball.

Vladimir stole only 11 bases last season, while catcher nailed him nine times. That's an atrocious percentage, particularly for someone with his speed. I'm betting he will improve those figures as soon as he absorbs base-stealing fundamentals such as how to read a pitcher. He has the perfect teacher in Expos coach Tommy Harper, a Rhodes Scholar in base thievery. A graceful big man, Vladimir has the talent to become baseball's next 40–40 player.

Kerry Wood (Chicago Cubs): He's the new gunslinger in town. Nolan Ryan, Steve Carlton, Sandy Koufax, Roger Clemens: throughout baseball history, power pitchers have put a lot of fannies in the ballpark seats. Wood's fastball is the genuine article, a 95-to-98-mph rocket that forces hitters to consider alternative careers. Trying to swat the Wood curveball is as easy as hitting a drunken Frisbee; it careens to the plate with a swift, downward breaking motion that has a little bit of extra bite at the finish. Kerry's big, hard-breaking slider cracks the speedometer at 95 mph, which means it has more giddyup than most pitchers' best fastballs. You can't read it because it's on top of you so quickly and veers at the last moment.

But what makes the 21-year-old Wood so special among power pitchers is his control. He strikes out three hitters for every man he walks, a phenomenal ratio for someone whose ball moves so much. Early in his career, Nolan Ryan, the major leagues' all-time strikeout king, walked nearly as many hitters as he struck out. (Ryan's control did improve, but he never acquired the accuracy Wood demonstrated in his rookie year.) In the minors, Wood averaged 11 K's per nine innings pitched. When the batters weren't whiffing, they weren't doing much of anything else against him; in Wood's 55 minor-league starts, hitters mustered only a .179 batting average against him. He hasn't looked any less imposing since joining the Cubs in 1998.

Which all goes to say that Kerry has the stuff to throw a no-hitter or, given his terrific control, a perfect game any time he takes the field. When he struck out 20 Astros to tie the major-league record, even his teammates were awed. "I've never seen anything like that," said 13-year veteran left-hander Terry Mulholland, "not even in Little League. Not only did he strike all those guys out, but he did it with only 120-something pitches. And he didn't walk anyone. Houston was a terrific offensive club last year, and he went through them like they were Swiss cheese."

Besides his scintillating fastball and impeccable control, Kerry also has the one trait you can't teach a pitcher—mound presence. In that regard, Wood reminds me a little bit of Bob Gibson, the St. Louis Cardinal Hall of Famer. When Gibson pitched, his whole demeanor said, "You can't hit me." Wood carries that same imperiousness onto the field, which is suprising since he's such a soft-spoken, modest kid. It's something you don't see much anymore. Roger Clemens, Kevin Brown, Randy Johnson, and John Smoltz (especially in big games) have it, but each has spent ten or more years on the major-league stage. If he can survive his arm woes (and that's a big if, because a torn ligament in Wood's elbow, an injury he apparently suffered near the end of the '98 season, ruined the 1999 season for him), Kerry can be an annual Cy Young Award candidate. Let's hope he makes it. As Atlanta Braves manager Bobby Cox said when he learned of Wood's arm problem, "You want to see players like that back on the field, even though you hate to see them on the other side. They bring people out to the park. That's good for baseball."

Don't Kill the Umpires!
(Just Teach Them the Strike Zone)

U mpires, in general, do an extremely professional job. They may not get it right all the time, but who does? Ninety-nine percent of them are consistent and fair to both sides, which is all you can ask for." At least, that's what a prominent baseball executive initially told us when we asked him to grade major-league umpiring. However, when we let him go off the record, he wasn't quite so sanguine. "The umpiring stinks," he declared, "and the veteran umpires are worst of all. Many of them look like they are just going through the motions, as if they are coasting toward retirement. A lot of them don't hustle, and have strike zones that change with the weather. They are a joke, but you can't quote me on that. Those guys hold grudges forever. If they ever find out I said this, they'll kill my team."

While his reaction may be a trifle extreme, I agree that the umpiring standards in both leagues have deteriorated steadily over the last decade. If you want evidence of this, just take a gander at something this frustrated executive referred to—the elastic strike zone.

For years, it seemed to me that most umpires called the same strike zone with only slight variations. I prided myself on having a good eye; it's one of the reasons I'm ranked fourth in career walks behind Babe Ruth, Ted Williams, and Rickey Henderson. I don't recall questioning many umpires' calls. Back then, no matter who the umpire was, you knew a pitch above the knees on the corner of home plate was a strike, a pitch below the knees off the corner a ball.

Today, you'll see umpires such as Durwood Merrill, Eric Gregg, or Frank Pulli calling strikes on balls that aren't in the same zip code as home plate. When you criticize a Merrill or a Gregg, they defend themselves with the tired mantra, "This is my strike zone," as if it were something so malleable they could bend and shape it according to whim.

Oh, does that make me fume! Maybe someone should tell these guys that baseball has an official rule book. If you look though it, you will find that the strike zone "is that area over home plate, the upper limit of which is a horizontal line at the midpoint between the top of the shoulders and the top of the uniform pants, and the lower level is a line at the hollow beneath the knee cap. The strike zone shall be determined from the batter's stance as the batter is prepared to swing at the pitched ball." In other words, if a pitch is over the plate and arrives between a batter's knees and the letters on his chest while he's in his natural stance, it's a strike. Read that rule again and see if you can find any wiggle room there.

There isn't any. Yet for some reason, most umpires behave as if the rule were open to interpretation. Durwood Merrill was talking for many of them when he recently said, "Every one of us (umpires) will see the ball a little differently. We're not all alike.

Our personalities are different and our approaches to the game, mannerisms, and our zones are going to be different. We are human." Doesn't Merrill make it sound as if someone were asking him to perform a task that he can shade with individual emotion, nuance, and perspective? Come on, no one is asking him to play Beethoven's Fifth here. Calling balls and strikes isn't an art; it should be an exact science. Hitters and pitchers have a hard enough time adjusting to each other; they don't need a third, inconsistent element to make their jobs tougher. Players have to cope with weather changes, diverse park conditions, and whatever strategic surprises the opposing team chooses to spring on them. Umpires should be the one constant amid all these variables.

Let me tell you how bad things have gotten. You often hear how pitchers and batters keep books on each other. Tony Gwynn, the San Diego Padres batting champion, maintains an extensive video collection that documents nearly every swing he has ever taken in a major-league game. Well, players like Roger Clemens now keep books on the umpires. Clemens can identify which umpires call strikes on high or low pitches, which ones have wide strike zones, and which ones will squeeze a pitcher. Roger shouldn't have to be doing all of that. When you're facing the Mo Vaughns and Frank Thomases of the world, your focus should be only on them, not on the man calling the game from behind the plate.

In the confrontation between the hitter and the pitcher, the umpire must be a neutral party, in order to preserve the game's delicate balance. Yet you have some arbiters like Frank Pulli, a 27-year veteran of the National League, who are known as a pitchers' umpires. Pitchers love Pulli's wide strike zone; if you just get the ball near the plate, there is a good chance Frank will call it a strike. What I find most astounding is that Pulli does this by design. He has stated publicly that his liberal zone helps move the game along, because it motivates hitters to come up hacking. Well, that's all very nice, Frank, but it's not your job. You are on the field to enforce the rules. Let everyone put his own slant on the rule book and we'd have chaos. Don't you wonder how Pulli would like it if a player told him, "My basepath is 89 and a half feet instead of the regulation 90. If I come within six inches of the base before the ball arrives, I'm safe." You think Frank would buy that argument? Merrill is another umpire who prides himself on being a pitcher's best friend. He has justified his runway-wide strike zone by saying, "If you bring the plate out one ball wide on each corner, that makes the plate 23 inches instead of 17. A good hitter can hit that. I don't apologize for having a wide strike zone. Pitchers love me to work their games."

Which is another way of saying, "I don't care what the rule book declares, I'm going to alter the dimensions of the playing field arbitrarily." Who gave him the right to do that? Since he's apparently so concerned about what pitchers think of him, why doesn't Merrill just shrink the size of the baseballs by a third while he's at it? He'd probably call that an absurd idea, but it's just as absurd as his setting up his own strike zone. If you're an umpire and pitchers love you, that should be a clue that you're doing something wrong. At least Merrill and Pulli are consistent; hitters know what they are up against when either of them is behind the plate. Many players will tell you that's not the case with Ken Kaiser, who's been umpiring in the American League for 22 seasons. His strike zone seems to change from batter to batter. And if you complain about his inconsistency, get ready for an explosion. Kaiser is known as an umpire with a low threshold for dissent.

When an umpire's idiosyncrasies become intrusive, he's detracting from the game on the field. And he can, in some instances, affect its outcome. Once an umpire does that, he has overstepped a boundary. For example, during the fifth game of the 1997 National League Championship Series between the Atlanta Braves and the Florida Marlins, Eric Gregg's strike zone was so wide it nearly became a national scandal. From the first inning on, Gregg was calling strikes on pitches that weren't just an inch or two outside. They were well off the plate.

Charles Johnson, the Marlins catcher that day and one of baseball's smartest players, immediately recognized what Gregg was calling; he coaxed his pitcher, Livan Hernandez, to work the umpire's hyper-expanded zone all day long. Pitching as though the plate were high and outside, Hernandez shut down the Braves, 2–0. The Marlins would clinch the National League pennant in the very next game.

Gregg's calls that afternoon didn't directly favor one side over the other. But his strike zone neutralized an advantage usually enjoyed by Hernandez's mound opponent, Greg Maddux. Few can match Maddux's command of the strike zone; Hernandez has never had control nearly as fine. But with Gregg behind the plate, it didn't matter. Pee Wee Herman could have thrown strikes through a zone that spacious. Had Gregg enforced a smaller strike zone, Livan might not have been as effective as he was that afternoon. Or he might have been even more unhittable. We'll never know, and that's a shame, since this was, after all, a league championship series.

Incidentally, I was in the broadcast booth for that game. Though I knew Gregg's strike zone was wide, I couldn't tell how generous it was from watching on our monitors. Pictures can be misleading. When the center-field camera is perfectly centered behind the mound, or the overhead cam is aligned with the middle of the plate, you usually get a genuine representation of where a pitch is. But shifting those cameras by a fraction can distort your perceptions; you can't always tell if you are looking at a true strike zone. We try to get that right for all of our ESPN games. The first thing I ask our producer before every broadcast is whether we have a true read on home plate. If we don't, I let the viewers know.

I must admit that while I was doing the game, I had little sympathy for Atlanta's predicament. No staff in baseball has taken greater advantage of the umpires' elongated strike zone. Just watch Javy Lopez and the other Atlanta catchers. They all set up with their gloves off the outside of the plate before calling for a pitch. If Maddux, Tommy Glavine, or John Smoltz merely hit the catcher's target, many umpires will call it a strike even if the pitch is off the plate. This has helped make the Braves' pitchers that much more dominant—and, believe me, they don't need any help.

It does appear, though, that the league is finally catching on to Atlanta. During the 1998 National League Division Series, Houston second baseman Craig Biggio, a former catcher, told me something the Astros were planning to do if they faced the Braves in the League Championship Series. He called my attention to the catcher's box behind home plate in the AstroDome. Catchers must stay within that box until a pitch is thrown. It's supposed to be outlined in chalk, but few ground crews bother to do that, since most catchers will obscure those lines within a few innings.

Since Atlanta's catchers rarely set up with their feet in the box, you'll never see it marked in Turner Stadium. But the Houston crew was going to make sure it was clearly delineated throughout every inning of any home games against Atlanta. Larry Dierker, the Houston manager, could then insist that the umpires keep Javy Lopez within the lines.

The Astros never got a chance to employ this tactic; San Diego won the right to play the Braves by beating Houston in that series. But the Padres must have gotten wind of Houston's plans, because they made sure *their* catching boxes were marked throughout the LCS against Atlanta. As a result, the Braves failed to get their usual ration of outside pitches called in their favor. This undoubtedly helped San Diego to an upset win, because it forced the Atlanta pitchers to alter patterns that had proven so successful for the better part of this decade.

Of course, the Braves' hurlers wouldn't have to adjust to any changes in the catcher's box if the umpires would just agree on what constitutes a ball or a strike. I'd like to think there is a quick remedy for this problem. In a perfect world, the leagues could reintroduce the umpires to the strike zone as depicted in the rule book, and insist that they call balls and strikes based on it. I'm not that naïve. Too many umpires seem intent on putting their own personal stamp on the game; their egos won't allow them to adopt a uniform zone. When Sandy Alderson of the commissioner's office sent out a directive last spring in an attempt to establish a more consistent strike zone, the umpires balked immediately. Alderson was partially to blame. His notice didn't instruct the umpires to enforce the rule-book zone; it instead redefined the zone as an area extending from the bottom of the knees to a point two inches above the top of a players' pants.

The umpires' union jumped on that immediately. "In a misguided edict attempting to raise the strike zone," said a statement issued by umpires' union chief Richie Phillips, "the commissioner's office in fact substantially lowered the zone and has done so in direct violation of the Major League Agreement, which requires a two-thirds vote of the rules committee in order to effect any rules changes." And Durwood Merrill chimed in, "There's a human element in it. What I might see as two inches up, [someone else] might not."

What a mess! Why Alderson didn't insist that the umpires call the official strike zone is anybody's guess. He certainly would have been working from a position of strength if he had. Instead, he succeeded in further muddying the issue by asking the umpires to replace their individual—one might be tempted to call them unique—zones with his own arbitrarily created version. So the chaos continues.

If the commissioner's office or the leagues can't enforce the rules governing balls and strikes through the current crop of umpires, they should consider a long-term approach. Both leagues should, at the very least, insist that any umpires currently working their way up through the minors enforce the regulation zone as a condition for promotion. Get them to do it at the start of their professional baseball careers, and perhaps they will form good lifelong habits.

Because their job is so demanding and difficult, we need umpires of the highest caliber. A home-plate umpire has to concentrate intently for 260 to 300 pitches per game. On the basepaths, umpires' calls must be as precise as microsurgery. That's because baseball is not, as some claim, a game of inches. More often than not, a mere tenth of an inch separates a ball from a strike, a line drive from a pop-up, an out from a safe call. So, even though they don't hit, pitch, or field, umpires make a crucial difference in every game they work.

During the first game of the 1998 World Series between the New York Yankees and the San Diego Padres, we saw an excellent example of how a single umpiring call can affect an at-bat, an inning, or even the final score. In the bottom of the seventh inning, Yankee first baseman Tino Martinez came to the plate against Padre reliever Mark Langston with two out and the score tied 5–5. After falling behind 2–0, Langston threw a fastball for strike one. Martinez fouled off the next pitch, another fastball in on his hands, for strike two.

With the count even, Langston served Martinez—who was evidently looking for something up in the zone where Langston likes to finish off left-handed hitters—a low fastball for strike three. Or so it seemed to nearly everyone in Yankee Stadium except home-plate umpire Rich Garcia. He called it ball three, granting a second life to Martinez, who looked as though he were ready to take that long stroll back to the dugout. Tino made the most of the opportunity. Realizing Langston had to come in with another fastball, Martinez looked for something hard and drilled it deep into the right-field upper deck for what proved to be a game-winning grand slam.

Every professional baseball player understands that no one play, call, or hit decides a game's outcome. To his credit, Langston refused to blame anyone but himself for the Martinez homer. After the game, he told us, "I thought the (2–2) pitch was in there (for strike three), but when you don't get that call, you still have to execute on the next pitch. I didn't."

Mark was absolutely right. He had his chance to retire Martinez and failed. He couldn't blame the umpire for that. But had Garcia called out Martinez on Langston's 2–2 pitch, San Diego would have gone into the eighth inning tied instead of four runs down. That would have set an entirely different tone for the remainder of the game. We'll never know if the Padres could have regained their momentum and the lead or, had San Diego had come back to win, how the Yankees would have responded to the pressure of losing that World Series opener. So while no one can claim that Garcia's call—which I think he missed—ultimately determined the outcome of the game or the series, its impact was enormous. That's why we must hold umpires to exacting standards.

One of the biggest mistakes any umpire can make is to anticipate the outcome of a play before it develops fully. When an umpire does that, he's often not sure what his eyes have just seen. We saw several examples of this during the 1998 American League Championship Series between the Yankees and Indians. Game Four of that match-up took place at Jacobs Field in Cleveland. In the top of the fourth inning, Tino Martinez batted against Cleveland right-hander Dwight Gooden, with Bernie Williams on third base. Martinez lofted a lazy ball to shallow left center. Indian centerfielder Kenny Lofton made the catch, then dropped the ball as he tried to grab it from his glove with his throwing hand.

According to the rule book, "In establishing the validity of the catch, the fielder shall hold the ball long enough to prove that he has complete control of the ball and that his release of the ball is voluntary and intentional." Lofton clearly had control of the ball, though he caught it one-handed. Kenny had obviously dropped it in his haste to throw out Bernie Williams at home. Yet umpire Jim McKean ruled no-catch as soon as the ball fell from Lofton's glove. Williams scored while Martinez was safe at first. McKean missed the call because he anticipated Lofton's making a trouble-free catch. When an umpire anticipates, his eyes and mind go out of sync, his internal computer short-circuits. He will often rule on what he thought he would see rather than on what actually transpired. McKean expected an easy, trouble-free catch; when he saw something else, he made the wrong call.

Though umpires can get themselves in trouble by anticipating an out or a safe call, they often must foresee where a play will develop so that they can position themselves to get the best possible view. At times, however, even making the right move can cost them. For an example of that, we flash back to another play involving Kenny Lofton, during the sixth and final game of that same series. It came during the top of the fifth inning, with New York's David Cone working the mound. Down 5–0, the Indians had Lofton on first and Enrique Wilson on third, with nobody out. Omar Vizquel, the Cleveland shortstop, touched Cone for a scorching liner that seemed destined for center field. It never got there. Instead, the ball struck second-base umpire Ted Hendry.

Under the rules, the embarrassed Hendry had no choice but to declare the ball dead. Since the liner had already passed David Cone in fair territory, Vizquel went to first on an infield single. But Wilson had to remain at third; Lofton could go no farther than second. Had Hendry not blocked Vizquel's line drive, Wilson would have scored while Lofton could have advanced easily to third.

To many, it appeared as if Hendry had committed a gaffe that, at least momentarily, cost the Indians a run. But he was doing his job correctly. Hendry would ordinarily have been able to avoid Vizquel's line drive. The reason he couldn't dodge the ball was that he had anticipated a stolen base by Lofton, who had broken from first with Vizquel's swing. Hendry was hustling toward second base to make his call on Kenny when the ball hit him. He had lost track of the play in front of him because he was trying to cover the play developing behind him.

Umpires have to make snap decisions like that all the time; no one can fault Hendry for the choice he made. In fact, there really was no wrong choice in that situation. (I think the baseball gods knew this and decided to bail out the umpire. David Justice followed Vizquel with a run-scoring walk. Jim Thome then rendered this whole situation moot with a grand-slam home run. But you could just imagine the uproar Indian fans would have raised had Cleveland failed to score.)

Hendry's umpiring was deserving of criticism in game two of that same series, however. He worked behind the plate for that contest, and his strike zone was so wide it would have made Eric Gregg blush. "He was calling terrible pitches on both sides," said Indian shortstop Omar Vizquel. The Yankees fanned 11 times, 4 on called third strikes. Cleveland struck out 9 times, an incredible 8 of them with their bats on their shoulders. Yankee manager Joe Torre concurred with Vizquel's assessment of Hendry's wall-to-wall strike zone when he said, "You couldn't reach some of those pitches with a bamboo pole."

Whether an umpire is behind the plate or working the basepaths, he must be decisive. A tardy call can unfairly reward or damage a team. For example, on April 5, 1998, Jon Miller and I broadcast a game between San Francisco and Arizona that featured one of the strangest plays of the year. With Arizona in front

3–1, Barry Bonds led off the Giants' fourth inning with a double off Diamondbacks right-hander Andy Benes. Jeff Kent advanced Bonds to third with a grounder to Jay Bell at short.

Giants first baseman J. T. Snow then rapped a Benes sinker back up the middle. From the booth, it appeared as if the ball had ricocheted off the mound to Bell, who threw Snow out at first, Bonds scoring on the play. Nothing extraordinary about that. After the out, the Diamondbacks threw the ball around the infield, as is the major-league custom when an infield out is made and the bases are empty.

Then the fun began. When the ball got to Matt Williams at third, manager Buck Showalter signaled for him to tag his base. As soon as he did, third-base umpire and crew chief Randy Marsh called Bonds out, nullifying his run while ending the inning. If you were scoring at home, that was a 1–6–3–4–5 double play, something you might never see again if you watched baseball for the next hundred years.

Why was Bonds out? Marsh had ruled (correctly, as our replay would soon reveal) that Snow's line drive had never hit the mound. In fact, it had never so much as grazed any part of the field. The ball, instead, had ricocheted off Benes's foot. Since the ball never touched the ground, Snow was out as soon as Bell made the catch (not that Jay realized that; he also thought the liner had struck the mound, which was why he threw the ball to first base).

Marsh called Bonds out for leaving third before tagging up after the catch of a ball that never touched the playing field. So instead of a 3–2 game with the bases empty and two men out, the score remained 3–1. The inning was over. It was a pivotal decision; Arizona went on to win that game 3–2.

Though Marsh ultimately made the correct call, his tardiness cost the Giants a run. Randy, who probably had the best view of the play, should have immediately ruled Snow out the moment Bell made the catch. If he had, Barry would never have left third base. Once Barry saw Bell set to throw, he took off. Which is precisely what he is supposed to do in lieu of an out call by the ump. But the fact that Barry was right didn't make him safe. Marsh had no choice but to declare him out, although it was his own act of omission that had sent Bonds scampering home.

By the way, I want to make it clear that I'm not knocking Randy Marsh. He is a prime-time umpire. Randy hustles all the time, has a consistent strike zone, and maintains a sunny disposition on the job. It takes a lot to get Marsh to blow his cool. If someone questions one of his calls, he'll take the time to explain his decision. He also has what I call Umpire's Alzheimer's. Argue with Randy today and, as long as you don't go too far out of line, he forgets about it by the following game.

There are more than a few umpires who should use Marsh as a role model. I hope this doesn't sound like another case of "things were better when I played the game," but I don't remember another time when umpires were ever so confrontational. Maybe that was because players in the past didn't dare argue with umpires as excessively as they do now. We looked at umpires the way lawyers might look at Supreme Court judges. If any arguing needed to be done, we usually left it to our managers.

I learned to respect umpires from the get-go. In my first major-league at-bat, Jocko Conlan, who eventually won a place in the Hall of Fame, was behind the plate. Jocko called a late-breaking pitch a strike; I thought it was outside. When I shared my opinion with him, he took off his mask and said, in a voice that would send shivers down a rock, "Young fellow, you can't stay in the game if you're going to argue with Jocko."

I got the message immediately, as had everyone else in the league. If you messed with an umpire back then, he could make your career one long hell of borderline pitches that always went against you. From that point on, I always treated the umpire with courtesy. Whenever I led off a game, I would say hello to the umpire and the catcher before we got down to business.

Umpires used to be more inclined to let you blow off steam, especially if they thought you had a legitimate gripe. During one game, the late Billy Williams called me out on a bad pitch with the bases loaded. I said, "Billy, that wasn't close to being a strike." He didn't react, which so infuriated me I started cursing. My outburst should have resulted in my ejection from the field, but Billy knew he had missed the call. Instead of thumbing me, he gently took me aside and said, "I heard you. Now don't ever do that again."

You could develop something of a relationship with umpires. During the height of the civil rights movement in the 1960s, Tom Gorman called a strike on a pitch that, to me, looked way outside. I said, "Tom, that pitch wasn't even on the black." ("The black" is what ballplayers call the narrow outer edges of home plate. Balls that are on it are strikes and difficult to hit. This pitch hadn't been close.) After I complained about his call, Tom said, "Well, that's the way it is now, Joe, the blacks are getting bigger all over the country." That cracked up both of us and eased the tension.

Most umpires back then were like Gorman. They were serious about their work, but they wouldn't bite your head off if you questioned a call. Many of today's umpires are about as personable as Saddam Hussein. In a 1998 survey conducted by *USA Today Baseball Weekly,* major-league players identified Joe Brinkman, Al Clark, Dale Ford, Ken Kaiser, Bob Davidson, and Joe West as officials who rarely tolerated players challenging their decisions. West seems to be his own worst enemy. He gives me the impression of being someone who works with a chip on his shoulder. In that *Baseball Weekly* survey, one player declared, "He's arrogant and rubs a lot of people the wrong way. You never know what his mood is from one day to the next." Which is a shame because, attitude aside, West is a solid umpire, especially when he's calling balls and strikes.

Joe Brinkman, an American League umpire for 26 years, has a personality that almost invites confrontation. You have to wonder why the league allows him to umpire in the pressurized atmosphere of post-season play. Yet there he was behind the plate for Game Two of the 1998 American League Division Series between the Indians and Red Sox.

Brinkman's strike zone was the size of a thimble that afternoon. Cleveland starter Dwight Gooden started complaining about it almost immediately. With a 2–0 count on Red Sox leadoff hitter Darren Lewis, Dwight threw what appeared to be a strike. Brinkman called it ball three.

Gooden yelled at Brinkman to call some strikes, and the umpire screamed right back. After they both vented, Dwight tried to play the conciliator. He held up his hands as if trying to restore some calm and said, "Okay, let's get back to the game." At about that same time, Indians skipper Mike Hargrove came out of the dugout to talk to his pitcher. Hargrove wanted to make sure that Dwight wouldn't say anything to provoke Brinkman further. The last thing the Indians needed was for Gooden to get tossed from the field. He had been one of his team's most reliable starters during the second half of the 1998 season.

After satisfying himself that Gooden was cool enough to continue, Hargrove lingered near the mound, prompting Brinkman to come out to break up the meeting. Which was exactly what Hargrove wanted. Mike made a few choice remarks to the umpire, who responded in kind. That tore it. The two spent the next several moments jawing at each other until Brinkman finally ejected Hargrove. The provocation? Hargrove had questioned the umpire's ball and strike calls. The rule covering this states that "managers or coaches leaving the bench of the coach's box to argue balls and strikes will not be permitted . . . if they start to the plate to protest a call . . . they will be ejected from the game." (When I later asked Mike why he had violated this tenet, which every manager knows will get him the automatic heave-ho, he replied, "Once Brinkman and I started arguing, I knew I was going to get tossed, so I figured as long as I was out there . . .")

When play resumed, Gooden walked Lewis as well as the next batter, John Valentin. I don't think Brinkman gave him a single close pitch. Dwight heated up to fan Mo Vaughn swinging. Then Nomar Garciaparra doubled high off the left-field wall as Lewis scored easily. But a great throw forced Valentin to slide as he approached home plate.

Brinkman ruled him safe, though it appeared Valentin was out. That was when Doc lost it. He challenged Brinkman to "get in the [expletive deleted] game!" Brinkman didn't need much more than that. He tossed Gooden after he had pitched only one-third of an inning. That, by the way, matched the shortest outing by a starter in the history of the playoffs.

All right, knowing who he was confronting, Gooden should have been more circumspect. But Brinkman was also wrong. Gooden had every right to question those earlier calls as well as the play at the plate. He was convinced his catcher had tagged Valentin a good half-foot in front of home plate (and he was not alone. I thought Valentin was clearly out). Baseball's rules do allow you the latitude to argue questionable decisions like that.

Though there is no way of proving it, Brinkman's safe call looked like a bit of payback. In the clubhouse after the game, Gooden said, "He [Brinkman] wasn't out of position, because we were both in the same position, but for some reason, he called him safe." Brinkman later claimed he had ejected Gooden for using foul language. That may be, but coaches tell me Brinkman is notorious for bad-mouthing players. When Doc chided him, Brinkman apparently told the pitcher to "throw the *&*&#*(@ ball over the plate."

If an umpire is going to be that provocative, he must allow a player a moment of madness, especially during the heat of a championship series. I felt Brinkman erred by making himself the dominant personality on the field that day. Whenever an umpire does that, he forsakes his responsibility to the game. Baseball fans buy their seats to watch some of the finest athletes in the world compete against each other. No one ever bought a ticket to watch an umpire call balls and strikes. Unless a player abuses or assaults him, a good umpire should go out of his way to ease a situation rather than exacerbate it.

Of course, umpires should never be patsies. If a player touches an umpire, spits on him, or is exceedingly profane, he deserves to be tossed, fined, or suspended. But the league offices should also crack down on umpires who follow angry players back toward the dugout as if inviting them to escalate matters. We see this all the time, and it's something relatively new in the game. Umpires are supposed to be above any fray on the field, the one person who maintains his equanimity while others rage. If he can't do that, he should find himself another profession. There are, fortunately, many top-notch umpires currently working in the major leagues. For example, Jerry Crawford probably doesn't comply with the official strike zone all the time, but he has the same zone from game to game, which is the next best thing. A terrific umpire on the basepaths, Crawford almost always gets himself in the best position to make a call.

Ed Montague is as focused as any umpire in the major leagues. He is on top of the game from first pitch to last. He also has a consistently wide strike zone that I'd like to see tightened. Players tell me Ed will allow them time to air a grievance, and is not above admitting when he blew a call. In that regard he reminds me of Harry Wendlestadt, one of baseball's legendary umpires. Whenever I challenged Harry on a pitch he missed, he would smile and say with a touch of irony, "Yes, Joe, I may have missed *one*. Now let's get on with the game." Players respect that kind of honesty and professionalism. They can, by the way, encourage those qualities by treating umpires with the same civility. If I challenged Harry on a call and one of my teammates told me the umpire got it right, I'd immediately let him know from the dugout that I had erred. Players don't do enough of that.

The American League's Dale Scott has radar for eyes, and always seems to angle himself properly to cover a play. During a 1998 game between Texas and Cleveland, which we broadcast on ESPN, he made a call that came right out of the textbook. Texas held a 4–0 lead with two men out and Kevin Elster on second in the bottom of the sixth inning. Rangers second baseman Luis Alicea smacked a Jaret Wright fastball into center field for a base hit. Kenny Lofton fielded the ball cleanly on the bounce and made a strong, accurate one-hop throw to his catcher Sandy Alomar Jr.

At first it appeared as if Elster slid into Alomar's tag for an inning-ending out. Scott, however, called him safe. Our initial replays were inconclusive, though they seemed to indicate that Alomar had touched Elster's heel before his foot struck home plate. Our overhead cam, however, caught the play perfectly. Scott had called it right; Elster's toe had touched home before Alomar nailed him. If Scott had watched the play from any other vantage point, he probably would have made the wrong call. That he didn't was a result of his hustle, know-how, and dedication.

I'd like to see more umpires as professional as Dale Scott, Rich Garcia, and Randy Marsh working in baseball. I certainly don't want to see any robots taking their jobs. Every season, it seems, someone suggests we replace umpires with electronic eyes. That would be a mistake. Machines are not infallible, and I don't see how any gizmo could adjust to each hitter's stance. Using replays to settle disputed calls as they have done in football would also be an error. Replays would slow the game down, and as we've seen countless times, camera angles can fool you. Maybe I'm just old-fashioned, but I never want the game to sacrifice the human element.

There are, however, steps we can take to upgrade umpiring in both leagues. We've already mentioned asking them to enforce the regulation strike zone. Hitters can actually help the umpires in this regard by learning the strike zone themselves. Why do you think batters like Wade Boggs, Frank Thomas, and Tony Gwynn have so many pitches called in their favor? Umpires realize that hitters like these know the zone, so they concentrate better. They can actually share a good hitter's focus. Conversely, if a batter comes to the plate swinging at just anything, the umpire will call more pitches outside the zone against them.

Besides getting umpires to agree on balls and strikes, baseball must also make them more accountable. As one general manager told us, "I think the last time we fired an ump was during the Roosevelt administration. Teddy, not Franklin. These guys are like tenured college professors; they practically have jobs for life. That gives them way too much power and comfort. Why should they maintain their skills when they know it's damn near impossible to remove them?" For the good of the game, the umpires' union and league presidents should devise a system that makes it easier to replace umpires for just cause.

National League president Len Coleman is doing his best to raise the umpiring standards in both leagues. In 1995 he helped create a five-man umpire review board. Its current members include former umpires Doug Harvey and Steve Palermo, former players Billy Sample and John Roseboro, and American League umpire coordinator Phil Jannsen. They tour both leagues, grading the umpires' performance in a variety of categories.

But those marks don't carry any weight when it comes time to hand out post-season assignments. That's because the umpires' union made sure its latest contract stipulated that no umpire can work the LCS or All-Star game in the same year. Umpires can work the Division Series and the World Series during the same season, but they can't appear in two consecutive World Series.

That system guarantees that 75 percent of the umpires will draw lucrative post-season assignments regardless of their ability. It also means there will be seasons when the very best umpires will be disqualified from working the World Series, the most important games of the year. That has to end. Baseball should adopt a merit system similar to the one pro basketball uses. There are 58 referees in the NBA. The league won't choose you to officiate during the playoffs unless you are among the top-ranked 32. To work the NBA finals, you have to be one of the top 11.

The other problem with the current evaluation process is that the results are never made public. Even the umpires don't get a chance to review their marks. Let's open the process. Who knows? Releasing those results to the media while reserving those plum post-season positions for the best-rated umpires might provide all the incentive that sub-par arbiters need to sharpen their games. After all, if someone hit you in your pride and your pocketbook, wouldn't it make a lasting impression?

Fighting for Fame:
Pete and Shoeless Joe

During the 1998 season, Ted Williams initiated a campaign championing Shoeless Joe Jackson's induction into the National Baseball Hall of Fame. For those of you who missed the movies *Field of Dreams* and *Eight Men Out,* Shoeless Joe was one of eight members of the 1919 Chicago White Sox who conspired with gamblers to fix that season's World Series against the Cincinnati Reds. Williams, always a soft touch for a good hitter, believes that despite any transgressions Jackson may have committed, he deserves a place in the Hall because of his almost unmatched prowess at the plate.

There's no doubt that Jackson was a formidable hitter. In ten years as a regular (1911–20), Shoeless Joe never batted below .300. His .356 lifetime batting average is the third-highest in major-league history (only the nonpareil Ty Cobb and Rogers Hornsby posted higher career marks). Even Babe Ruth emulated him. "I decided," the Babe once told a reporter, "to study the greatest hitter in baseball and copy his swing. Joe Jackson was good enough for me." Jackson wasn't a one-dimensional player, either. He was a heady, nimble base runner whose peers considered him one of the game's most accomplished outfielders.

I've seen the John Sayles film *Eight Men Out,* which painted the eight conspirators in sympathetic colors. As its central thesis, the movie claims that the players' chicanery was their only recourse against their tightfisted owner, Charles Comiskey. These White Sox—or Black Sox, as they came to be known—played well before the days of free agency or even minimum salaries; Comiskey literally owned his players' contracts for life. He could pay them whatever he wanted, and he did just that. Comiskey was one of those millionaires who threw money around like it was money. Though clearly the best team in baseball at the time, the White Sox had one of the lowest payrolls in both leagues. Jackson earned only $6,000 a year, less than half of what the other clubs were paying players of lesser stature. And Shoeless Joe was one of the biggest earners on the team.

So, yes, the eight Black Sox had a legitimate beef against their owner. But, to my mind, they chose the wrong means of settling it. Other baseball stars, such as the Philadelphia Athletics' third baseman Home Run Baker or the Cincinnati Reds' centerfielder Ed Roush, also engaged in vicious contract disputes with their clubs. When those players couldn't wangle the lucrative contracts they wanted out of management, they didn't call the nearest speakeasy to put in the fix with some local hood. Instead, they walked. Picked up their bats and gloves and played semi-pro ball for a season. What would have happened if the eight disgruntled Chicago players had threatened to strike a week before the World Series opened if Comiskey didn't sweeten their contracts? We'll never know, because they never explored that alternative. Instead, Jackson and his cohorts committed a felony.

Jackson always claimed that while he did indeed accept a $5,000 bribe, he played all-out to win against Cincinnati. Supporters like Williams point to his .375 Series batting average, the highest among regulars for both sides, as evidence of this. I think they're missing the point—JACKSON TOOK THE MONEY! He admitted as much to a grand jury. Even if he did play his best, he knew that his teammates were actively engaged in a conspiracy to tarnish baseball's crown jewel. That's crime enough to keep the Hall's doors barred to him.

But, in truth, even his defenders should take a close look at just how well he actually played. Jackson did much of his lustiest hitting with his team well behind the Reds. For example, in the final game of that Series, Jackson hit a solo home run in the third with Chicago down 5–0. He drove in two more runs in the eighth, but by that time, Cincinnati was coasting with a nine-run lead. Shoeless Joe did drive in the winning run during Game Six. But the conspirators were trying to win that contest because the gamblers had shortchanged them out of some of the bribe money.

During the Series, the Reds hit two triples over Jackson's head in left field. You could watch every inning of every game played during an entire major-league baseball season without seeing one triple hit to left, let alone two. And, as we've noted, Jackson was a superb leftfielder.

Despite his apologists' protests, Shoeless Joe's entire performance during the 1919 World Series was suspect. His fielding was questionable, and he padded his batting statistics with empty hits. Forget about Comiskey. Jackson and his co-conspirators betrayed their teammates—players like Hall of Fame second baseman Eddie Collins, pitcher Dickie Kerr, and catcher Ray Schalk, who played that Series on the up-and-up—the fans, and the game itself. When word of the fix became public, the ensuing scandal nearly wrecked baseball. Yet Ted, whom I love dearly, continues to lobby on Jackson's behalf.

Few players or journalists, however, are taking up Pete Rose's cause.

In 1989, Bart Giamatti, the late commissioner, placed Pete on the ineligible list for betting on baseball games and consorting with gamblers. Giamatti's action prohibited Rose from holding any position in the major leagues. Pete—who still maintains he never wagered on baseball—accepted Giamatti's sentence on the condition that he could petition the commissioner's office for reinstatement one year into the ban.

Had he not been suspended, baseball's all-time hit king would have been a first-ballot selection for the Hall of Fame. However, the institution's board of directors didn't want to risk the embarrassment of having baseball's latest bad boy enshrined in the sport's Valhalla. So it ruled that anyone on major-league baseball's suspended or ineligible list was also ineligible to appear among the Hall's annual list of nominees.

This was, in effect, the Pete Rose Rule. It was adopted just before I joined the Hall's board in 1991. The decision annoyed me. It seemed to me that the Hall should have entrusted any questions concerning Pete's eligibility with the electors who had served it so well for over 60 years. After all, the Hall had allowed the writers to consider Joe Jackson's candidacy during past elections.

It's not widely known that Jackson's name was placed in nomination for the Hall of Fame in 1936 and 1946; the electors found his offense so execrable that Shoeless Joe received only two votes on both occasions. That certainly demonstrated admirable discretion. Why, I wondered, wouldn't the Hall let the writers settle the question of Pete's eligibility, to trust them to discharge their duties as responsibly as they had in the past? I doubt that many of them would have voted for Pete, especially on the first ballot; write-in support for him has been weak and shrinks with each passing year. But that's not my point. It just didn't seem fair for the board to pass a rule specifically designed to keep one player from the ballot.

Don't misunderstand me. I do believe the Hall has the right, in fact the obligation, to set its own high standards for admission. Ours is supposed to be an elite institution; character should matter when we consider the qualifications of any candidate. It was the timing of this ruling—coming just before I could air my feelings on the subject—that rankled as much as anything. It was as if the board didn't want to hear from a potential Rose advocate.

Which was quite an assumption on their part. They had no way of knowing which side I would come down on. People often ask me if I think my former teammate should be in the Hall of Fame. Before I answer that, you have to know how difficult it is for me to be dispassionate on this question. Pete is family. If he needed my help tomorrow, I'd be at his side. When I first joined the Big Red Machine, he did everything he could to make me feel at home; he also helped make me a better ballplayer.

The charges against him are serious, however. Gambling is baseball's worst nightmare. The sport cannot tolerate any behavior that undermines its credibility. Pete claims he bet on the ponies and other sports, but never on ballgames. My heart wants to believe him when he says he did not violate the rules. But it's difficult for my head to accept his protestations of innocence.

You see, I'm certain that baseball possesses the proof to refute him. In 1989, I was interviewed for the job of National League president. During the process, someone asked me if I could impartially mete out a sentence to my friend if the evidence demonstrated he bet on baseball. I told them I loved Pete, but that no one was bigger than the game; I would treat him the way I would any delinquent player, manager, or coach. The interviewers then confided that they had the goods on Pete locked away in a safe. Two other executives who were later privy to the Rose file have since confirmed that for me.

Pete's own actions, or lack of them, also tell me he did something wrong. The Pete Rose I know is a consummate fighter. Had he been innocent, he never would have signed the document that banned him from the game he loves so passionately. Instead, Pete would have fought the commissioner the way he battled Nolan Ryan, Steve Carlton, Tom Seaver, and all the other pitchers who stood between him and another base hit.

This doesn't mean I think Pete is lying. I believe he's in denial on all this. He continues to tell people he was kicked out of baseball for betting on *Monday Night Football*. That's an insult to everyone's intelligence. Baseball would never banish one of its most popular figures and best ambassadors unless it couldn't support its allegations with hard evidence. What would be the point?

The information I've acquired along with my gut feelings tells me that Commissioner Giamatti and his investigators got it right.

Pete overstepped a well-drawn line; even the freshest rookie understands the consequences of betting on baseball. His behavior injured the game and was a disservice to its future as well as to its history. My friend has to pay a price for that.

But the question before us is how high should that price be?

I believe that Pete, having been estranged from baseball for a full decade, has already paid nearly in full. All that should be left is for him to publicly admit his mistakes while apologizing to all of baseball—the institution, its players, and its fans. If he did that, I would wholeheartedly endorse his reinstatement into the game as well as his induction into the Hall of Fame. I think a sincere act of contrition would win universal sympathy for his cause. After all, no one doubts Pete's statistical qualifications; his career numbers drip pure Cooperstown.

I've shared my feelings with Pete several times, but my words don't seem to make an impression. Pete recently applied to Commissioner Selig's office for a sentence commutation. So we know he wants to get back into baseball. Yet he does things that undermine his efforts at reinstatement. I recently heard that Pete has joined former football great Paul Hornung, who himself was briefly suspended by his sport for gambling back in the early sixties, on cable television to analyze football betting lines. (Of course, Pete may be sending a not-so-subtle message here: "Hey, Hornung gambled and football allowed him into its Hall of Fame.") He has publicly questioned Bart Giamatti's methods and motives, making it sound as if the late commissioner or his investigators were engaged in a vendetta against him. Bud Selig was close to Giamatti. He's bound to find any attacks on the Giamatti off-putting, especially since his friend isn't alive to defend himself. In a recent *Sport Magazine* interview, Pete declared that he has already made enough apologies; he still denies betting on baseball while maintaining he never had a "gambling problem." So it doesn't sound as if my friend will be chanting mea culpas anytime soon.

I'm often asked why Pete doesn't get it, why he is acting so self-destructively. People wonder why he can't at least *pretend* to be remorseful. The answer is as simple as it is complex. The thing that made Pete—whose physical skills were almost underwhelming—a great ballplayer was his transcendent confidence. That's what's killing him on this issue. Pete has always believed that, whatever the odds, he would always find a way to come out on top. He is convinced that he will eventually triumph; I'm telling him he can't win this thing on his terms. Pete can't see that because there's no quit in him. But perhaps it might help him if he knew how his peers viewed his predicament.

In 1995, the Hall of Fame inducted Pete's former teammate, Philadelphia Phillies third baseman Mike Schmidt. Mike made an impassioned acceptance speech in which he said he would be glad when baseball allowed Pete Rose to enter the Hall, "because he deserves to be here now."

During Hall of Fame induction weekend, we hold an alumni dinner in Cooperstown. Ed Stack, president of the Hall, both league presidents, the latest inductees, and most of the living Hall of Fame members attend. After we present the newest members with their Hall of Fame rings, several baseball immortals will rise to extend a few words of greeting. When Jim Palmer and I entered the Hall, Ted Williams ended his short speech by saying, "I want to welcome you, Joe, and you, Jim, into the greatest fraternity in the world!" Then immortals such as Stan Musial, Willie Stargell, and Warren Spahn led everyone in a round of warm applause.

You want to talk about goose-bump time?

After the greetings, we open the floor to discuss general baseball topics. We can talk about anything that is happening in the game or the Hall. On the night of Schmidt's induction, Robin Roberts, the former great Philadelphia Phillies right-hander, used this session to address the point raised by Mike that very afternoon. Robin wanted to know how the assembled Hall of Famers felt about Pete's ineligible status. He proposed that we discuss the issue to see if we could achieve some consensus that would form the basis for an official statement to the press. For the next hour, the ballroom became a war zone.

Opinions on Pete were as diverse as they were fervent. Since Pete and I were close, I said little while trying to keep an open mind to all sides. Everybody already knew how Schmidt felt. Reggie Jackson rose and said something like "I wanted to invite Pete to my own induction ceremony and I didn't. I feel gutless about it. He belongs here." Only Reggie's version was laced with several choice profanities. You could tell he believed strongly that Pete was getting shafted.

Then Jim Palmer stood to make a telling point. He asked the nine Hall of Famers at his table if they had ever bet on baseball. Each answered no. Palmer turned to the rest of the room, shrugged his shoulders, and said, "Then what are we talking about here?" Someone, I'm not sure who, followed by asking, "Why should we lower the standards of the Hall for someone who has shown such a blatant disregard for the game?"

By now, the mood in the room was decidedly anti-Rose. Players were shouting at each other. No one threw a punch, but you could feel a hint of physical confrontation in the air. I wasn't surprised by the vehemence of the exchanges. You have to understand that 99 percent of the players elected to the Hall break down in tears when they make their acceptance speeches. That induction ceremony is the culmination of our life's work. So deciding who you will share that parthenon with is no small matter for any of us.

I tried to play the conciliator before things got out of hand. Robin Roberts joined me on the middle ground by announcing, "I would be willing to listen to Pete if he would make a public apology." Many of the members agreed with that position; I thought we might be able to build our consensus around it. But then three of the greatest players in history—Warren Spahn, Eddie Mathews, and Bob Feller—stood up to oppose Pete's admission. Two of them vowed never to return to Cooperstown if Pete were allowed to enter the Hall. That got everyone's attention. After another half hour or so of heated discourse, the advocates on both sides could agree only to disagree. We left without issuing any public statements. Good thing for Pete, too. If anyone had called for a straight up-and-down vote, he would have lost in a landslide.

So c'mon, Pete, you need to do some fence-mending here. If you think you've made enough apologies, then one more won't hurt. Unlike Joe Jackson, you never threw a baseball game; you loved winning too much to do that. (Given the enormity of his crime, no one could justify admitting Jackson to the Hall while excluding Pete from the ballot; I mean, if Shoeless Joe goes in, Pete should be a shoo-in.) I think baseball would be a better game for your presence. You're the living embodiment of hustle, you can teach hitting to anyone, and you were once one of our game's best ambassadors (Pete could talk baseball for hours to a stump). Admit your mistakes, say you're sorry, and give the country, the writers, and the Hall a chance to embrace you once again. I'm not guaranteeing they'll do it, but I do think it's your last best shot.

9

Tweaking the Diamond

In the preceding chapters, I've tried to draw attention to some of the major issues facing baseball as it heads into the millennium. Now I'd like to kick back and do some fine-tuning. Here are some areas where a few small improvements can make a big impact on the game, the players, and the fans:

Let's Get Those All-Stars Snarling Again!

While baseball's popularity climbs, television ratings for its All-Star game remain flat. It's no mystery to me why fewer people are tuning in; the game has lost its intensity. This was driven home for me two years back when Shawn Estes, the Giants' left-handed ace, surrendered a game-winning home run to Cleveland catcher Sandy Alomar Jr. During the post-game interview, Estes said he didn't feel badly about the loss because Sandy is "such a nice guy."

Excuse me?

If a losing pitcher whimpered something like that with Frank Robinson or Bob Gibson as one of his teammates, someone would have had to order a hospital bed in advance. The name of our game is professional baseball. Its object isn't to bond with your opponent, enlarge your circle of influence, build character, or raise the world's consciousness. Its object is to win by any means fair. That's why they keep score. It rankles me that the All-Star Game has become just an exhibition. Its participants behave as if they are just there to have fun. And this lack of fervor is driving viewers away. If the players don't take the game seriously, why should the fans?

In past All-Star Games, the league president would make impassioned speeches, pleading with his stars to demonstrate their superiority over the other league. Chub Feeney used to come into the National League locker room to declare, "You guys aren't just representing your teams, you're representing the league. If you think this is a vacation, forget it! You are on the job, and your job is to win. The entire country is watching this game. Go out and prove to it that our brand of baseball is better than theirs." All right, it wasn't exactly the St. Crispin's speech Henry V gave before battle; no Dukes of York stepped forward, ready to slay the Dauphin. But it did rouse everyone for the contest. We need to get those competitive fires stoked again while raising the quality of play.

I think the game would be enhanced markedly if the managers of both sides didn't use substitutes quite so liberally. The eight starters on each team (I'm excluding the pitchers here) are supposed to be the best at their positions. Managers should keep them on the field until they've rolled up a comfortable lead. Reserves should be exactly that. If, however, a player on the bench is having a demonstrably better year than a starter chosen by the fans, the manager should get his bat into the lineup as soon as possible.

Outside of appealing to their pride, I'm not sure how to make the All-Star players more competitive. A few years back, some sportswriter suggested a way to motivate both teams. He proposed that whichever league won the All-Star Game should also earn the home-field advantage during the World Series. Since most of the All-Stars would still be in the hunt for a post-season spot, he believed they would play all-out to secure that extra home date for the Fall Classic. It's such a radical concept, I doubt it would ever receive serious consideration. But baseball may have to come up with an idea nearly that bold to instill this contest with drama and excitement. Unless it reverts to being a war rather than a showcase, I'm afraid the All-Star Game will continue to lose viewers.

The College Game: Loosen the Reins and Bring Back the Lumber

I've been covering the College World Series for the last ten years. Throughout recent tournaments, I've been struck by how many managers and coaches now exercise greater control over the on-field action. College baseball has become like college basketball, where coaches dictate the style and pace of the game.

It's not unusual to see a college coach call all the signals for his pitcher—the whole gamut from pitch selection to pitchouts. They are also implementing strange defenses that call for dramatic over-shifts against certain batters. When I spoke to some of the coaches about this trend toward overmanaging, they said it helps to keep their players alert and in the game. I think it hampers them. Players need to learn not only how to execute baseball fundamentals, but when. You can't play this game well if you are always looking to the dugout for instructions. College players have to sharpen their instincts so they can sniff out their opponents' strategies for themselves. Then they can react decisively and spontaneously.

Colleges should also lose all those aluminum bats. Give even an average hitter one of these ultralight bats with their big barrels (they're just like softball bats), and he can wreak havoc on college pitchers. This poses problems not only for the hurlers but for major-league scouts. Gauging a college hitter's ability is a difficult task because of those bats. You can't tell how quick a hitter will be once he has to swing the much heavier wooden bat.

For example, a few seasons back, the Boston Red Sox signed Jeff Ledbetter, the NCAA home-run champion out of Florida State, as a first-round draft pick. Everybody tabbed Ledbetter as a "can't miss" prospect. Unfortunately, as soon as he started swinging a wooden bat, the home runs stopped coming. He never made it past Double-A ball. Many scouts say they discount a player's average by as much as 150 points to compensate for the aluminum bat.

Those metal bats are so light that any hitter can get to virtually any inside pitch, even the high-octane fastball. Because of the thicker bat barrels, players don't even have to make good contact to hit line drives. An average wooden bat has a live power area of about 5 inches. There are nearly 25 inches of juice in an aluminum bat. I'm certain that's another reason that many major-league pitchers just up from the college ranks are reluctant to pitch inside. In college, if you pitch inside, you get burned. The hitter is either going to yank that ball a long way or hit a line drive back at the pitcher's head. With the way today's batters are bulking up, that's one scary thought. Could you imagine Mark McGwire wielding an aluminum bat and hitting a line drive back through the mound? All that would be left of the pitcher would be a pair of spikes with smoke coming out of them.

Most major-league hitters are vulnerable to the pitch inside; they generally picnic on guys who stay away. College pitchers now need two years in the minors just to shed the bad habits they picked up in school to learn the art of pitching hitters tight. Many otherwise good pitchers just can't make the adjustment. They leave a few pitches out over the plate, surrender some monster home runs, and trudge off the mound traumatized.

As we went to press, NCAA Division 1 Baseball had just adopted new specifications that require aluminum bats to be heavier, as well as thinner at the barrel. I applaud that decision, though coaches throughout the country tell me the ball still explodes off the new bats. A pitch in on the fists is still a line drive. College baseball conferences should soothe their pitchers' psyches by making the grand leap back to lumber. Should the expense of doing that prove prohibitive (replacing broken wooden bats can be costly), major-league baseball should consider subsidizing the transition. If the owners need an incentive to do that, all they have to do is examine ERAs throughout both leagues. It's obvious that we need to protect and nourish all the good pitchers they can find. They can also save themselves millions in wasted bonuses lavished on hitters who look like Mickey Mantle when they're swinging metal, but resemble Mickey Mouse when they have to carry some lumber to the plate.

Designate the DH to the Scrap Heap

When I was with Oakland in 1984, I was the designated hitter for two games; I went 1-for-4 both times. It was my only direct experience with the DH rule and—having already played over 2,500 games in the field—I enjoyed the novelty of it.

Still, I would like to see the DH interred alongside Tutankhamen. Before the DH, baseball had always demanded a price. If you could hit but couldn't field, your team had to weigh whether it was willing to trade off your defensive liabilities for your contributions with the bat. I liked that exchange. It meant managers had to be more alert in the late innings, had to intuit precisely when they should replace a slow-footed, iron-fisted slugger with a swifter, more sure-handed defensive caddy.

Pitchers also had to be more well-rounded. If they couldn't consistently hit as well as someone like the New York Mets' Dennis Cook, whose career batting average is nearly .280, they at least had to be able to move runners around with a bunt, the hit-and-run, or productive outs. The DH encourages hitters and pitchers to be one-dimensional athletes. It says if all you can do is hit, you can play.

Baseball is more than just hitting. It's strategy, defense, and all the other fundamentals that lend the sport its unique, exquisite nuance. The DH diminishes strategy, particularly in the late innings. AL managers call for the bunt, steal, and hit-and-run less than their National League colleagues. And they rarely call on pinch-hitters. This narrows the game, transforming it into a home-run hitting derby that is ultimately as numbing in the long term as it is rousing in the short. You often hear fans lament that players can't bunt anymore. Well, the way to learn how to bunt is to bunt. Often. Big-score baseball frowns on this.

One reason we should jettison the designated-hitter rule is that it's no longer needed. When the American League introduced the DH in 1973 (for you trivia buffs, New York Yankee Ron Blomberg was the first to take his swings in that role), offense throughout the circuit was at a nadir. Attendance was declining, and fans generally thought the National League played a more exciting, superior style of baseball. Most of the AL's most celebrated stars—such as Frank Robinson, Harmon Killebrew, Tony Oliva, Al Kaline, and Frank Howard—were losing their defensive spryness to age and infirmity. And it wasn't apparent that anyone was coming along to replace them.

American League owners were desperate to do something to ginger up their game. The DH was adopted as an experiment, one that has continued for these past 25 years. It gave the AL a boost at the gate (attendance rose by nearly 20 percent during the DH's first season) while allowing its older stars as well as some National League expatriates like Tommy Davis, Billy Williams, and Orlando Cepeda to thrill fans at the plate without risking catastrophe in the field.

But now the DH is a sidebar without a purpose. With its small ballparks and muscular sluggers, the AL is the flash-and-crash league, the theater of instant offense where baseball's brightest young stars—prodigies such as Alex Rodriguez, Ken Griffey, and Juan Gonzalez—wreak havoc on nearly anyone who dares take the mound against them. They don't need the artificial appeal of the DH to lure fans into their parks.

I'll tell you how strongly I oppose the DH and everything it symbolizes. Paul Molitor, whose 21-season major-league career included productive stints with the Brewers, Blue Jays, and Twins, was my kind of player, an unselfish leader and utterly unflappable in the clutch. One day he will undoubtedly be a Hall of Famer. But Paul played over 1,000 games, more than half his career, as a DH. His 3,319 career hits are his primary claim to Cooperstown immortality. Could he have amassed that many without the designated-hitter rule? Would his career have ended sooner if he had been forced to take his regular turn in the field? I'm not sure, and that troubles me. Dave Kingman hit 465 career home runs, the most of any eligible player who is not in the Hall of Fame. The reason he doesn't have a plaque in Cooperstown is that most baseball writers considered him a one-dimensional player. How different is he from Molitor, who carried his glove onto the field in barely 200 games during the last eight years of his career? Harold Baines, who has been a DH longer than Molitor, is going to retire with some impressive numbers. Harold will certainly attract a fair number of votes when he becomes eligible for the Hall. I have the same trouble with his candidacy, which I regret because these are two fine men who elevated the art of hitting. And they didn't make the rules that extended their careers.

Mostly, I want to see the DH go away so we can restore some balance between the two leagues. When it comes to the Hall of Fame, players like Molitor have an advantage over players who spend most or all of their careers in the National League. American League hitters in general are going to seem more productive than National League hitters because the DH gives them an extra professional hitter in the lineup, and therefore more opportunities to drive in and score runs than they would have if a pitcher was in the batting order.

Playing the World Series under two separate rules, one for the American League park and another for the National League park, has been and remains a travesty. With a world championship on the line, AL teams shouldn't be forced to send their pitchers to the plate when they haven't batted against serious pitching all summer. And NL teams, who reached the Series using a traditional nine-man lineup, shouldn't have to play someone who may have been little more than a sub during the regular season in the most important games of the year.

Getting rid of the rule will not be easy. The Players' Association opposes scuttling the DH on the grounds that such a move would reduce jobs for its members. Some owners have offered to expand the roster to 26 players if the union agreed to let the DH die. That proposal has no chance of flying. Any twenty-sixth man is going to be among a roster's lowest-paid players. A team's DH usually commands one of the biggest paychecks on the team.

American League diehards among the owners are also loath to discard the DH, essentially saying, "If it ain't broke, don't fix it." You could restore balance between the leagues by asking the National League to adopt the DH, but that's not going to happen, either. National League hard-liners—yes, there are still enough of them around to make a difference—tell me they will never accept that "American League abomination." (Which is ironic, since it was a National League president, John Heydler, who first proposed the designated-hitter rule back in 1928.) I'm not sure these differences can be resolved anytime soon, but that doesn't stop me from hoping.

Sprucing Up the Hall

The National Baseball Hall of Fame in Cooperstown made a big comeback in 1998. Attendance rose dramatically after several years of troubling decline. One of my favorite places, it's so steeped in the game's tradition, I'd be wary of tinkering with it too much. As a member of the Hall of Fame and its board of directors, however, I think there are some areas where we can change the institution for the better.

Marketing is one of them. Many people still think of the Hall as a musty, old-fashioned repository of artifacts. In fact, the Hall—which has undergone several renovations in recent years—is as cutting-edge as the Rock and Roll Hall of Fame. It is loaded with interactive multimedia exhibits that couldn't be more twenty-first-century, yet it retains its reverence for baseball's history. If the Hall of Fame is a time capsule, it's one that transports visitors into the future as well as the past. We need to do a better job of marketing that.

National sponsorships would enormously boost any Hall of Fame marketing campaign. Unfortunately, advertisers and marketing executives think of Cooperstown as provincial and out-of-touch (or so many of them have told me). They need a new perspective. The Hall of Fame is the Valhalla of the National Pastime. There's hardly a baseball fan in the country who doesn't realize its significance. The Hall's logo represents integrity, excellence, and durability; name a Fortune 500 company that wouldn't want its products associated with those three virtues. Madison Avenue and corporate America should wake up to the Hall's vast, untapped marketing potential.

I'd also like to restructure the Veterans Committee, which currently reconsiders the candidacy of players who were not elected by the Baseball Writers Association during their 15 years of eligibility. Right now the committee is composed largely of former players; they aren't always dispassionate when they cast their ballots. Some feel a sentimental obligation to campaign for former teammates who were good but not great players. For example, Ted Williams has recently been lobbying for the induction of Dom DiMaggio, who played alongside Ted in the Boston Red Sox outfield. I understand Dom was a fine centerfielder, nearly the defensive equal of his brother Joe, but he failed to get 200 hits in any single season, and has a mere 1,680 hits for his career. Dom hit .300 or better only four times in ten years. He never received more than 43 votes when the writers considered his candidacy. I can't see why he should be reconsidered now. I doubt that DiMaggio would have a shot if he weren't backed by a living legend like the once and always Splendid Splinter.

Williams isn't the first person to promote the candidacy of a friend. Phil Rizzuto, the starting shortstop on eight Yankee pennant winners, was elected to the Hall only after his former teammate Yogi Berra and former broadcast partner Bill White joined the Vets. Rizzuto was a terrific player, and perhaps his plaque should hang in Cooperstown. But there is something inherently wrong with a system in which your selection can be based more on who you know than what you did.

Throughout its history, the Vets Committee has made some of the more controversial picks for the Hall. Fred Lindstrom, a third baseman for the New York Giants during the 1920s and 1930s was elected when he received the Vets' nod in 1976; he never got more than seven votes when the baseball writers considered his nomination. The committee ordained George Kelly, a first baseman and teammate of Lindstrom's, in 1973. In seven separate elections, he received only fourteen votes, and only one in 1962, his final year of BBWAA eligibility.

And the list goes on. Most of the players selected by the Veterans Committee received meager support from the baseball writers. One of its picks, Rick Ferrell, received exactly five votes in five different BBWAA elections. That's right, one vote per year. I'm told Rick was a good defensive catcher, but he never drove in or scored more than 77 runs in any season. And get this: After Ferrell's election, at least one Veterans Committee member admitted that he had confused the catcher with his brother Wes, a six-time 20-game winner! Selections like these lower the high standards the Hall must maintain. (On the other hand, the BBWAA has generally done a splendid job at the ballot box.)

The Committee on Baseball Veterans (its official name) was founded in 1953. Its purpose was to review the candidacy of those players who missed election to the Hall during the early years of its balloting. Because baseball was over half a century old when the Hall of Fame opened, there was a backlog of worthy candidates who couldn't attract the necessary 75 percent of the vote needed for induction, simply because the field was so crowded with great players. The Vets Committee was supposed to offer the overlooked a last chance for induction. It was also charged with electing managers, club executives, and umpires. In 1971 the committee expanded its brief to include the selection of great stars from the Negro Leagues, players like Satchel Paige, Buck O'Neill, and Cool Papa Bell, who would have made the Hall if baseball hadn't remained segregated until 1947. Twelve men sit on the panel, and they meet annually to consider nominees. Successful candidates must garner 75 percent of the votes cast by those attending the yearly meeting. (During the last balloting, only nine electors showed up to cast votes; illness kept three committee members home.)

There is no longer any compelling reason to maintain the Veterans Committee in its present form. That backlog of talent has, with only a few exceptions, been cleared. There are now 16 Negro League inductees, and, sad to say, I'm not sure we can justify the addition of many more. Negro League baseball records are so sketchy, it's virtually impossible to verify the qualifications of those candidates who aren't already enshrined in Cooperstown.

I would like to replace the Vets with an oversight committee, which instead of meeting annually, would convene every five years. When a committee meets every year, it feels an obligation to elect someone. Expand the membership to 25: 12 of the most senior baseball writers currently working, 9 former players (preferably all Hall of Famers), and 4 former managers or executives. The larger field will make it more difficult for any group of two or three electors to sway the balloting for their favorite candidates. Choose alternates to ensure that there will be always be 25 members present for each vote.

This blue-ribbon panel should consider only those players who just missed selection during their 15 years of eligibility. I'm thinking of candidates like Gil Hodges, the Brooklyn Dodger first baseman who was a top-five finisher in the writers' balloting for 12 consecutive years. Any player who placed in the top five on at least two occasions, or who received 70 percent or more of the ballots cast in any one election, should get at least one more shot at the Hall. And only one. If a player can't make it after 16 tries, can anyone really think he belongs in a shrine dedicated to baseball's all-time greats? (For players whose careers started after 1945: The committee currently considers those players who gathered at least 60 percent of the vote in any one election. That always seemed low to me. If your career began before '45, as Rick

Ferrell's did, it doesn't matter if your name was on not a single writer's ballot; the vets could still select you. Under the system I'm proposing, players like Ferrell wouldn't even be considered.)

The present Veterans Committee can elect only one former major-league player, one former Negro League player, and one manager, umpire, or executive each year. They can also review any candidacy ad infinitum. The oversight committee would consider only the qualifications of players who competed in the majors. Since this panel offers candidates just one final crack at induction, it can vote in as many players as it deems worthy every five years. To win election by this select group, however, a player would have to receive at least 80 percent of the vote.

I would turn over the selection of former managers, executives, and umpires to the Baseball Writers Association. I can't think of anyone more qualified to judge the performance of nonplayers than the writers who followed them so closely. Add two to five spots on the regular ballot for nonplayers so that great managers like Sparky Anderson and the late Billy Martin can be inducted simultaneously. According to the current guidelines, the Vets can select only one nonplayer each year. Why make anyone wait?

There have been numerous suggestions for improving the current BBWAA balloting for the Hall. In his book *Whatever Happened to the Hall of Fame?*, author Bill James suggests that fans, players, broadcasters, and baseball historians participate in the selection. That's a dreadful idea. History has shown that many fans would more than likely vote for their hometown favorites, regardless of their qualifications, as they do in the All-Star Game balloting. As we've already noted, the players on the Veterans

Committee were behind many of the most controversial Hall of Fame selections. Broadcasters form alliances with their teams and build relationships with players that are bound to muddy their judgment. And I don't know who would decide who qualifies as a "baseball historian." There have been hardly any disputes involving the BBWAA electees; so let's leave the balloting in their capable hands.

There are a number of other players whose selection would enhance the Hall of Fame. Some are still active nominees who, I believe, are not receiving enough support from the electors. The others are no longer eligible for consideration by the baseball writers; the Hall's Veterans Committee, whatever form it takes, would have to consider their qualifications. I don't have a vote with either group, but if I did, these names would appear on my ballot:

My former teammate on the Big Red Machine, **Tony Perez,** missed election to the Hall by only a handful of votes last time out, and will probably make it on the next ballot. He should already be in. "Doggie," as we called him, was the most consistent RBI man of his time. It wasn't merely the number of runs he drove in that make him Hall-worthy, however, but the size of them. For example, everybody remembers Red Sox catcher Carlton Fisk's game-winning home run from the 1975 World Series. On the Reds, we are more inclined to remember Tony Perez's two-run homer off Boston left-hander Bill Lee in the sixth inning of Game Seven. We were down 3–0 at the time, and it started us back to a win and a World Series championship.

If Perez was on your side, he was the guy you wanted up with the game hanging in the balance. Doggie was dangerous in any situation, but with a runner in scoring position, he was the best hitter in baseball. Perez always hit the ball hard in the clutch. He was able to do that because, unlike most sluggers, he understood what he had to do in specific situations. With the bases loaded, many hitters go up to the plate swinging for the fences. If you gave Tony something to pull, he'd jack it, all right. But if the pitcher threw him a difficult outside pitch, Perez would drive it to right for a base hit and two runs. Tony drove in 100 or more runs seven times, 90 or more runs on five other occasions. Had he played today with the juiced-up baseball, diluted pitching staffs, and smaller ballparks, he'd drive in 125 runs every year.

To my mind, the selection of **Orlando Cepeda** last March by the Hall of Fame's Veterans Committee only strengthens Perez's case. Tony has more career RBI and runs scored than Cepeda, though Orlando has the higher lifetime batting average and slugging percentages. Cepeda drove in 100 or more runs 5 times (including a league-leading 46 home runs and 142 RBI in 1961) to Tony's 7.

I think Tony was the superior defensive first baseman. Though not quite a Gold Glover, Perez was surprisingly quick and sure-handed. I knew if I just got my throws in the vicinity of first base, Doggie would haul them in. Cepeda was slowed by knee injuries and lacked range, though he had excellent hands. A seven-time All-Star, Perez's 1,652 RBI are the highest total of any eligible player not enshrined in Cooperstown. That's a record he should surrender come the year 2000.

As long as we are pushing first basemen, **Gil Hodges** should have been inducted into the Hall long ago. His career stats, which include 370 home runs, seven 100-RBI seasons, and eight All-

Star team selections, put him on a par with Cepeda and Perez. His peers tell me Hodges was the fastest of the three, a swift, bruising base runner who could go from first to third on a single. Winner of the first three Gold Gloves awarded at first base, Hodges is generally regarded as the best-fielding first baseman of his generation. He was also a first-rate major-league manager. Gil's deft platooning and nearly flawless handling of a young, talented pitching staff were instrumental in bringing the New York Mets their first World Series title in 1969.

I've heard it said that **Ron Santo's** chances of making the Hall were damaged irreparably when Leo Durocher, his former Chicago Cubs manager, disparaged this third baseman's clutch-hitting prowess. "Five runs up or five runs down," Leo declared, "and Santo would hit all the three-run homers I could ask for. But one run behind, he was going to kill me." I know Leo was bald, but he was probably having a bad-hair day when he made that remark. No one on any of the teams I played for ever wanted to see Santo batting against us in tight situations.

One school of thought defines a Hall of Famer as someone who was a dominant player at his position for an extended period. Santo was every bit of that. From 1963 to 1973, Santo made the All-Star team nine times. He led the National League in on-base percentage twice and in walks four times, and he drove in 90 or more runs for eight consecutive seasons. Santo also could do it with the leather. From 1964 to 1968, he won five consecutive Gold Glove awards. Ron holds the major-league record for most seasons leading his league in total chances (nine). He also shares the NL record for most times leading the league in double plays (six), put-outs (seven), and assists (seven). Forget about what

Durocher said; anyone who played against Santo will tell you he was the National League's best third baseman during the 1960s; no one else was even close.

Bill Mazeroski, who played his entire career with the Pittsburgh Pirates, was the most extraordinary defensive second baseman I've ever seen. And I'm not alone in that opinion. Charles Faber, author of *Baseball Ratings,* has devised a method for measuring the defensive contributions of fielders; he awards points for assists, chances fielded, fielding percentage, and range factor. By his calculation, Mazeroski was the greatest fielder of all time, regardless of position. *Total Baseball,* the official encyclopedia of the major leagues, measures defense with a formula slightly different from Faber's, yet it has drawn the same conclusion. Anyone who ever saw Maz transform a sure hit into a double play can understand why.

Mazeroski was the quintessence of athletic economy; he rarely needed to take an extra step while eluding incoming base runners. On the double play, his peers called him "No Touch"; Maz would relay the throw from his shortstop to first base so quickly it seemed as if he never paused to touch it. Base runners discovered that trying to upend Maz on the double play was like trying to play tag with a ghost. His eight Gold Gloves represent the National League record for his position. He also holds the major-league marks for most years leading his league in double plays (eight) and assists (nine). Maz partipated in 1,706 career double plays, more than any other major-league second baseman *or* shortstop.

I always felt the best part of his game was his positioning; Mazeroski knew instinctively where to play every hitter, including those he had never seen before. His offensive stats don't leap from the record book, especially when compared to some of today's slugging second baseman. But Maz played at a time when middle infielders were generally singles hitters with little pop. In the context of his day, Bill had good power (138 career home runs). He was an excellent bunter and a timely hitter who seemed to drive in his runs when the Pirates needed them most. Talk to anyone who played for the 1960 New York Yankees to verify that. Mazeroski's World Series–ending home run against those Bronx Bombers remains one of the most storied blasts in baseball history.

I know what you're thinking, but my inclusion here of **Davey Concepcion,** another Big Red Machine teammate, *doesn't* reflect any bias on my part. Unless it's a bias toward talent. When people ask "Why Davey?" I point to Luis Aparicio, already a worthy member of the Hall, and Ozzie Smith, who, according to most of the baseball writers I've spoken with, will probably earn Cooperstown honors as soon as he is eligible. Both Luis and Ozzie deserve to be in the Hall for their superlative glove work and their longevity. Ozzie was a starting major-league shortstop for 20 years; Luis toiled at the position for 18.

Davey spent 19 years in the majors. Defensively, he was nearly the equal of Smith—considered by many to be the Rolls-Royce among shortstops—and probably a hair better than Aparicio. Smith was more athletic than Davey; Ozzie made the most death-defying, tumbling catches seem mundane. Concepcion couldn't leap as high as Smith, but he flashed just as much lateral range. He could match Ozzie going up the middle, and was better going into the hole. Davey frequently would beat me to plays on my side of second base, though I wasn't slow. He also possessed a more powerful arm than Smith.

No shortstop was more creative. I remember the day Davey

glided deep behind third base to snare a ground ball with a runner sprinting all out for first. Had he attempted a traditional throw, the runner would have been safe. So, Davey instead threw a one-hopper that bounded off the artifical turf and into Tony Perez's glove for the out. He used the bounce from the turf to accelerate his toss. I'd never seen anyone do that before. Until that moment, neither had Davey. He just made it up on the spot, and it became his signature play. Davey was that kind of player—gutsy, quick, innovative. I played alongside him for eight years without detecting a single defensive weakness.

Davey's glove alone should win him a spot in the Hall. However, he was also a terrific clutch performer, a more dangerous hitter than either Aparicio or Smith. Batting eighth in our lineup, he often drove in 60 or more runs, most of them big ones. For example, in the second game of the 1975 World Series against the Red Sox, Davey came to the plate in the ninth inning, with the Reds down by a run and two men out. He singled home Johnny Bench for the tying run, stole second, then scored the winning run when Ken Griffey Sr. doubled. No one in our locker room was surprised when Davey delivered under all that pressure. He did that sort of thing for us all the time.

Another shortstop, **Maury Wills,** revolutionized baseball by reviving the stolen base during the early 1960s. Wills led the National League in thefts for six consecutive years (1960–65). His 104 steals in 1962 broke the 47-year-old single-season major-league record formerly held by Ty Cobb (Maury's mark has since been surpassed by both Lou Brock and Rickey Henderson). He is one of only four shortstops to ever win the National League Most Valuable Player Award.

Wills was a first-rate hitter in a period when the average shortstop contributed little offense. His .281 career batting average is higher than that of 9 of the 17 shortstops currently enshrined in Cooperstown. The Los Angeles Dodgers dominated the National League during the early sixties. They won three pennants and two world championships from 1963 to 1966. Wills ignited the offense for each of those clubs. Hall of Fame pitcher Sandy Koufax recently told me that whenever he needed a run, Wills invariably found a way to get it for him. Koufax, pitcher Don Drsydale, and Wills made those Dodger teams special. Two of those players are already in the Hall; Maury deserves a spot alongside them.

From 1975 to 1988, **Jim Rice** averaged 100 ribbies a year. Read that again and savor it. Jim led the American League in hits once, RBI and slugging twice, and home runs three times. His lifetime batting average is .298. Jim was the American League MVP in 1978 and was selected to eight All-Star teams. Hall of Famers such as Reggie Jackson, Carl Yastrzemski, Tris Speaker, Billy Williams, Ernie Banks, and Al Kaline all have lower career slugging averages than Rice's .502. Jim wasn't Willie Mays in the outfield, but he wasn't a butcher, either. He caught nearly every ball he could reach. Until injuries took their toll, Rice had a strong accurate throwing arm. Yet, in the most recent Hall of Fame balloting, Rice received a mere 146 votes, less than one-third the total needed for enshrinement. And support for his candidacy appears to be dwindling.

Am I missing something here, or what?

In 1999, **Carlton Fisk,** the American League's best all-around catcher during the 1970s and 1980s, finished fourth in the

Hall of Fame balloting with a hefty 330 votes. **Gary Carter** finished back in the pack with only 168 ballots. I'm not sure what the writers are thinking about here. There wasn't a dime's worth of difference between these two strong-armed catchers defensively. Carter made ten All-Star squads, Fisk eleven. Fisk drove in 100 or more runs twice; Carter did it four times, including 1984, when he led the National League with 106 RBI. Gary's lifetime stats include 324 home runs, 1,225 RBI, a .262 batting average, and a .439 slugging percentage. Fisk's numbers—representing over 800 more at-bats—in the same categories: 376 homers, 1,330 RBI, .269, and .457. Fisk aged better than Carter, so perhaps he is remembered more favorably by the younger electors. However, as Johnny Bench—everyone's all-time All-Star catcher—recently pointed out to me, these two were essentially the same player. They should make the Hall as an entry.

Jim Kaat's 283 career victories include three seasons of 20 or more wins. He was probably the greatest fielding pitcher of all time; "Kitty" won 16 consecutive Gold Gloves from 1962 to 1977. **Bert Blyleven's** mound artillery featured what was probably the best right-handed curveball of the past quarter-century. He won 287 games despite pitching for mediocre clubs much of his career. Bob Lemon, Don Drysdale, Jim Bunning, Hal Newhouser, Catfish Hunter, Dazzy Vance, and Dizzy Dean are just some of the Hall of Famers who have fewer career wins than either Kaat or Blyleven.

Neither **Curt Flood** nor **Marvin Miller** has a résumé filled with gaudy statistics to recommend their inductions into the Hall. We should, however, honor both men with plaques for the off-the-field impact they had on baseball. Curt sacrificed a lucrative playing career to mount a legal challenge against the Reserve Clause, which kept players bound to their teams for life. Flood lost the case, but he ignited a cause. Other players, inspired by his fight, mounted challenges of their own until an arbitrator abolished the clause.

Though I think we should honor Curt for his accomplishment away from the diamond, we shouldn't forget that he was also a fine player. A seven-time Gold Glove winner, Flood was the second-best defensive centerfielder of the sixties (only Willie Mays was better). He was nearly as impressive on offense. Curt's career batting average was .293 and he drove in a lot of runs for a hitter who often batted second. He was a central figure on three pennant-winning St. Louis Cardinal teams.

As the activist president of the Players' Association, **Marvin Miller** led his rank and file into the twentieth century. Players won the right to negate trades, arbitrate salary disputes, and negotiate their contracts under free-market conditions. Marvin set the tone and directed the strategies that brought about these landmark changes. He also made the game on the field better. The padding you see on the outfield walls in parks throughout the country is a result of his intervention. That innovation and other improvements in playing conditions negotiated by Marvin dramatically reduced player injuries. Hank Aaron recently said, "Marvin Miller is as important to baseball history as Jackie Robinson." I agree, which is why I think Marvin should share digs in that same house in Cooperstown where Jackie now resides.

That brings us to one final suggestion concerning the Hall. Too many of our African-American alumni and players pass up opportunities to visit Cooperstown; that bothers me. They should go there to gain an appreciation of how we have woven ourselves into the fabric of baseball history.

After all, if someone deliberately denied us access to the place, Jesse Jackson and I would be up there with them picketing.

And the Winners Are...

I'd like to see the Baseball Writers Association of America change the qualifications for its major prizes. This may betray a former hitter's bias, but I don't think pitchers should win the Most Valuable Player Award. The best starter can only help his team in 30 or so games; a position player can help his club win in 140 or more games. Players like Ken Griffey Jr. might go 0-for-6, yet still preserve a victory with a dazzling catch. If a starter fails in his primary function, there's not much else he can contribute, particularly if he plays in the American League, where pitchers never hit. Pitchers already have the Cy Young Award (more about that later); let's leave the MVP Award for everyday players.

Starters, on the other hand, should be the sole candidates for the Cy Young Award. At the close of the 1998 season, many writers heavily touted San Diego reliever Trevor Hoffman as a Young candidate because he saved 52 games. Closers these days usually need to get only one to three outs in a ballgame to earn a save. That's not a lot of heavy lifting. You just can't compare what a closer does to the work of a stud like Roger Clemens, who protects his team's lead for seven or more innings every fifth game. Since their assignments are so different from that of starters, relievers should have their own award.

Yes, I know baseball already has the Rolaids Fireman of the

Year Award. But that is given solely on the basis of statistics, which might not accurately measure a reliever's effectiveness. For example, according to the rules, Jeff Shaw of the Dodgers could earn 40 saves in a season without ever entering a game with the tying run on base or at the plate. John Franco of the Mets might have only 20 saves, but face the tying run in each of them. Whose performance meant more to his team? The BBWAA should establish a Hoyt Wilhelm Award in the American League and a Lee Smith Award in the National. Guidelines for both prizes should direct the electors to base their selections on the quality rather than the quantity of a pitcher's saves.

And while we're ranting, let's examine the save rule. Saves are much too easy to come by. What are you saving if you protect a three-run lead in the ninth with no one on? Do you know how often major-league teams surrender three-run leads in the last inning? The worst team in baseball won't do that more than three or four times in a season. You could have George Costanza on the mound and win those games. Let's award saves only if the closer comes in to face the tying or winning run.

Setup men—those relievers who fend off the opposition until the closer does his star turn—are starved for recognition. They are rarely in a position to earn a win or a save. I wouldn't make them eligible for the Wilhelm or Smith Award; we're reserving those awards for closers. But Jerome Holtzman, the esteemed Chicago baseball writer, has on numerous occasions proposed that any pitcher who comes into a game and maintains a lead should be awarded a hold. I'd like to see baseball adopt that rule, with this tightener: award holds only when a reliever maintains a lead of two or fewer runs, or keeps the opposition from scoring.

Finally, Marvin Miller and I have long campaigned for the establishment of the Curt Flood Award in both leagues. It should be given annually to that player whose behavior best embodies the principles of fair play. Let's not have the writers vote for that one. The players should form the electorate so they can continually remind themselves of the debt they owe to one of the game's most courageous athletes.

Preserving the Great Masters

Shortly after retiring from baseball, I wrote a letter to Bob Howsam, former general manager of the Cincinnati Reds, voicing my concern that "baseball is losing those special people who can impart certain skills to young players. We lose them because baseball isn't willing to pay for their expertise. Those who can teach go into other fields for better money. When this happens, the game suffers."

I could have written that letter today. Young players who are rushed into the majors need master teachers to show them how to play the game properly. It's a shame to see a Hall of Famer like Detroit Tiger great Al Kaline working as a broadcaster. Kaline was one of the most fundamentally sound players of his generation. Everything he did on the field was out of a baseball textbook— from how he lined up to get off a perfect throw while catching a fly ball to the way he constantly worked the pitcher into a good hitter's count. Kaline was expert in every facet of the game. But instead of tutoring the Tigers' young talent throughout the season, Al is broadcasting, because he can make three or four times more money in the booth. Who can blame him? Teams must reexamine their priorities. They should invest the extra dollars it takes to persuade former elite players like Kaline, Carl Yastrezmski, Juan Marichal, and Warren Spahn to remain close to the diamond. Craftsmen such as these can push players to the next level.

Even specialists like Rico Carty have something to contribute to a franchise. Mr. Carty, an outfielder and designated hitter for 15 major-league seasons, had no speed to speak of. He ran the bases like a man carrying all of his life's possessions on his back. To say Rico had little range in the outfield would be a mistake, since it implies that he had any range at all. He wore a glove in the outfield only because it was fashionable. But, man, could he hit. As ungainly as he was on the basepaths, he was positively graceful at the plate. And he knew how to explain the rudiments of hitting to others. You couldn't talk to Rico for five minutes without coming away with something valuable. He should be spreading his gospel throughout some organization's minor-league system. In Japan, the government designates certain artisans as national treasures; it pays them handsomely to pass on their skills to others. This practice ensures that professions and crafts can maintain high standards. The accumulated knowledge of a lifetime devoted to excellence is valued rather than discarded. Baseball would be a better game if it treated its own treasures with the same reverence.

Big Mac and the Andro Hype

There was a mild controversy during the 1998 season when a nosey reporter spied into Mark McGwire's locker and discovered the slugger was taking androstenedione. This dietary supplement, which helps build muscle mass, is sold over the counter in U.S.

health-food stores and over the Internet. Many people wondered if the drug gave McGwire an unfair advantage in his quest for Roger Maris's record. After all, the International Olympic Committee bans the use of andro by its athletes because the committee considers it a performance-enhancing drug. Now major-league baseball has commissioned a Harvard study to determine whether it, too, should outlaw andro.

I don't see what all the fuss is about. Androstenedione is a performance-enhancing drug if you're competing in a Mr. Universe contest. But the supplement won't help anyone hit a baseball. After ingesting andro before hitting the weight room, Mark can do more reps with more weight while requiring less rest between sets. It's not a magic pill that instantly transforms you into another Arnold Schwarzenegger. Mark can't build bulk unless he has the discipline to do his work. The drug doesn't sharpen his batting eye or quicken his bat. Perhaps—and there's no way of proving this—McGwire's additional bulk adds another 10 feet to his homers. The way he hits them, what difference does that make? Whether his dingers soar 470 feet out of the yard or only 460, they're still home runs.

Anyone who claims that bulk gave Mark an edge doesn't understand hitting. Muscles do not necessarily make for slugging. Ken Griffey Jr. hits his fifty or more a year, and he doesn't touch weights. Mickey Mantle, Ralph Kiner, Willie Mays, Hank Aaron—nearly all the great home-run hitters of the past actually believed that weightlifting could hurt hitters by robbing them of their flexibility. It's bat speed, not size, that matters.

The Players' Association would have to ratify any ban before it could take effect. Gene Orza, the union's associate counsel, doesn't sound as if he thinks Mark will be switching to creatine anytime soon. "No one," says Orza, "should expect that the Harvard study is going to resolve the question that has to be answered: Does a perfectly legal, over-the-counter product such as androstenedione give a player a competitive advantage? If it doesn't, we don't care what the Olympic Committee thinks."

I'm with Gene. As long as they are openly selling this item in stores, players should have the right to use it. I do have some reservations on a personal level, though. I like Mark McGwire a lot; he's one of the best guys in baseball. Andro hasn't been tested enough for anyone to predict its long-term effects. In fact, there have been hardly any human studies done involving this hormone. I'd hate to find out 20 years from now that the supplement caused internal damage with continual use. Doctors suspect that excess testosterone, which andro triggers, might have implications in prostate cancer. And androstenedione can mask an athlete's use of steroids, the dangers of which are already known. For those reasons, I'd rather see players use muscle builders with lengthier track records. Maybe Mark should have another talk with Sammy Sosa. Sammy takes only one supplement to pump his bulging biceps—Flintstones Vitamins. He says he likes the Dino shapes best.

The Long and Short of It

Sportswriters, fans, announcers, players, and owners all sound the alarms whenever it takes two sides more than three hours to complete nine innings. It seems as if everybody thinks baseball games have gotten too long. The commissioner's office assigned a committee headed by Frank Robinson to uncover ways to accelerate games without being intrusive. Frank and his colleagues spent the entire 1998 season reviewing the problem and formulating solutions. I want to turn the floor over to him, so he can share his panel's findings:

"Baseball has a rhythm that is part of its appeal. So the trick is to shave time from the game without interrupting its flow. We watched teams play with the idea of cutting the fat from the steak. What we learned was that there are many minutes wasted during a game. Eliminate those elements and you can speed up the game without affecting play on the field. For example, here are some of the things baseball can do to lose its dead time:

"Get each half-inning started at regular intervals. As soon as the last out of an inning is recorded, the next half-inning should start within two minutes and five seconds. For a nationally televised game that features more advertising, the maximum would be two minutes and twenty seconds. In 1998, I watched a game between the Cubs and the Pirates. If they had started each half-inning as I described, which they didn't, they would have saved eight full minutes.

"Hitters should stay near the batter's box until the conclusion of their at-bat. Don't wander back to the dugout in between pitches. You probably don't notice this, but hitters no longer keep their extra bats out on deck, maybe because the dugouts are so much closer to the field. When a hitter breaks a bat, he will go all the way back to the dugout and down the tunnel to get his bat. He should instead prepare several game bats and keep them handy. If one cracks, wait at home plate for the bat boy to bring you a spare. We'd save about a minute and a half per broken bat if batters would just stay put.

"Managers should get into the habit of calling for relievers as they leave the dugout, rather than waiting until they reach the mound. Skippers should also give pinch-hitters as much advance notice as possible. When I played, managers would tell me before an inning started, "Frank, get ready, I might need you soon." That gave me time to find my helmet, make sure my bat was ready, and stretch while my teammates were up. So I was ready to hit as soon as my turn came. Today, many managers wait until the last minute to pick a pinch-hitter. Everybody has to wait while they go though their preparations. That wastes time.

"Once the hitter is in the batter's box, the pitcher has twenty seconds to deliver the ball, provided no one is on base. That rule is rarely enforced, and it should be. But hitters don't take advantage of it because they step out of the box. I tell them, 'If you know a pitcher who stalls when he gets the ball back from the catcher, why don't you stay in the batter's box? If you do, it's a ball.' You get enough hitters to follow that advice, and pretty soon pitchers are going to work faster."

The teams that followed the committee's recommendations last year played their games in 2 hours and 35 minutes. Teams that didn't played games that averaged close to three hours or more. Since shorter games will probably attract more fans, particularly young one who have to get to bed early, the owners should implement the suggestions made by Frank's committee. I especially like the fact that these proposals cut away time that no one will miss.

However, I've always felt that it's the quality of the game, not its length, that determines whether fans leave the ballpark satisfied. I've seen games played in just over two hours that were real yawners. On the other hand, I participated in the now-famous sixth game of the 1975 World Series. Each of its 12 innings was a virtual baseball highlight film, crammed with dazzling plays and clutch hits. Carlton Fisk ended the affair with a dramatic home run to left that came within inches of going foul. That contest is on everyone's short list of the greatest games ever played; many people even rate it number one. It took four hours and one minute to complete.

I don't recall anyone asking for their money back.

That Game in Cuba: What Television Didn't Show You

On March 28, 1999, the Baltimore Orioles traveled to Havana to play a game against a team of Cuban All-Stars. It was the first time an American major-league club had visited Cuba since Fidel Castro led the Communists to power in 1959. ESPN asked Jon Miller and me to broadcast this historic contest.

At first, I wasn't sure I would go. The game was not part of my regular ESPN contract, and I had mixed feelings about the event. As a baseball fan, I wanted to see the great Cuban players in action. But as someone who has read history and has many Cuban friends, I was aware of the repressive society Castro has forced on his people. The last thing I wanted was to give this dictator a public-relations opportunity at a time when he is hoping that the United States will legitimatize his world standing.

I discussed my dilemma with several Cuban friends (I can't mention their names because they all have families in Cuba and fear repercussions). Despite their own misgivings about the game, they encouraged me to go. The consensus was the event was going to take place anyway, so they wanted someone in the broadcast booth whom they trusted, someone who would represent their side.

Their interests were very much on my mind when I took part in an ESPN conference call to plan the broadcast. One of the producers suggested that Castro, accompanied by an interpreter, could come up to the booth so that we could interview him during the game. I refused to give this despot a forum for his oppressive policies. "You can invite him into the booth," I told them, "but I won't be there." My employers respected my wishes on this matter, even though having Castro on would have been a newsbreaking coup for them. Fidel never came near our microphones.

I didn't know what to expect when we arrived in Havana. However, I was intent on seeing all of Cuba, not just some sanitized version of the island that the Communists wanted to present. As it turned out, you don't have to do any excavating to explore every strata of Cuban society. You merely have to keep your eyes open. For example, our party stayed at the Melia Habana, a luxurious hotel where we were catered to as if we were royalty. Just beyond this near-palatial setting, only 100 feet or so from the swimming pool, you saw soul-withering squalor. People were living in slum conditions that may be familiar only to the poorest of Americans. And these were not the unemployed or disenfranchised. These were your average Cubans struggling to get by in a society that kills initiative and hope.

I was privileged to speak to many of them and was touched by their unconquerable zest for living. Life, for them, is a continual struggle, yet they embrace it with both hands. I have rarely met a friendlier, more passionate people. Castro may have stripped them of nearly everything else, but their dignity remains intact.

It may be a cliché to say we Americans take many of our liberties for granted. But I know I came away with a greater appreciation of our way of life when I saw the plight of the Cuban people. I saw soldiers arrest some Cubans just for speaking with Americans. Those who did talk to me often requested anonymity because they were afraid the authorities would punish them. I can tell you that I never met a more devout group of baseball fans. Hundreds of them gather in a section of a park called Equina Caliente, "The Hot Corner," to talk about their national game and our game in the United States (yes, they know who Ken Griffey Jr. is over there). They meet every day and talk baseball from dawn to dusk. At one point, I stood in the midst of a group of fans and, with the help of my interpreter, had a round-robin discussion that covered nearly every aspect of the sport. I couldn't help but be moved by the Cuban people's intense feeling for the game. I thought to myself, "These people may love baseball even more than I do."

You can see that in the way they cheer on their heroes. Those of you who saw the game between the Orioles and Cuban All-Stars in the comfort of your homes didn't get a chance to see the real Cuban baseball fans. Most of the people who attended that televised game were there by invitation only. Castro's people screened most of the invitees so that they presented a sober, almost antiseptic picture of Cuban baseball to the American viewing audience. It was largely a staged event. I got a taste of the real deal the evening before when I attended the Cuban World Series. This was not a baseball game, it was a party. American baseball owners could learn a thing or two about marketing from the Cuban teams. Throughout the stadium, there were bands playing festive Cuban music, and cheerleaders were dancing on the dugout. The fans danced, too, and they were roaring their team on from the very first pitch. It was electrifying.

It bothered me that none of you ever got to see any of that. Something else about the event you did see also disturbed me. Just before the game between the Orioles and All-Stars began, a ceremony took place at the middle of the diamond. Baltimore left-fielder B. J. Surhoff carried the American flag to point behind the mound as the Orioles followed. Cuban third baseman Omar Linares led his team out while carrying their country's flag. A band played the Cuban national anthem. Both the U.S. and Cuban players stood with their hats on their hearts throughout the anthem. But when the American anthem was played, only the Orioles kept their hats in place. The Cuban players removed their caps from their hearts. Where, I wondered, was the mutual respect between opponents that is the basis of all sports? I was steamed, but someone later told me the players were afraid to reciprocate the American gesture because of Castro's presence.

The game was an exciting pitcher's duel that the O's won, 3–2. The Cuban players were somewhat impressive, but the reports that Linares is the best player in the world and that Cuba could field a major-league juggernaut if given the opportunity are pure hyperbole. Linares is a good athlete, but he's more on the order of a Scott Rolen (which isn't exactly chopped liver) than a Ken Griffey Jr. or Barry Bonds. With just a little more seasoning, the two shortstops I saw, German Mesa and Marty Parct, could be big-leaguers. Cuba's outfielders, though, lack power and they don't seem particularly quick. The rest of the regulars looked like a good bunch of High Double A or Low Triple A prospects. However, two pitchers did impress me. Jose Ibar, a top Cuban hurler, doesn't throw hard enough to win as a starter in the States. He's a trick pitcher who relies on pinpoint control, but he could earn a spot on a major-league roster as a long reliever. Jose Contrares, however, has great stuff and showed real mound smarts. Had the Cubans started him, they very well may have won the game. Contrares could pitch and win in the majors right now.

Despite my initial misgivings, I'm glad I made the trip. It was an eye-opener to see the real Cuba, a place where surgeons are living in slum conditions. It gave me a greater appreciation for what we have here, not the material things, but the freedom to make better lives for ourselves. I will never forget the exuberant warmth, innate melancholy, and stoic courage of the Cuban people. They made me feel like family and reminded me that, at its best, this great game can remove many of the barriers that divide us from the rest of humankind. And if that sounds like a bit much, you should have been there.

10

Showdown

On April 5, 1998, Jon Miller and I were broadcasting a game between the San Francisco Giants and the Arizona Diamondbacks on ESPN. In the third inning we learned that the Oakland A's had just beaten the New York Yankees. When Jon noted that New York, which most pre-season polls had picked to run away with their division, was now 0–3, I replied, "I guess that means they're not going to win 162 games after all." I was right. Counting the regular season, the playoffs, and the World Series, the Bronx Bombers won only 125 games.

Don't tell me I'm not a prognosticator.

Nearly 2,000 major-league teams have taken the field in this century. If you count playoff and World Series victories, no club has ever won as many games as the 1998 New York Yankees. They didn't merely beat their competition, they flattened them. From April 4 to June 17 they won 24 straight series. New York finished 22 lengths ahead of the Boston Red Sox, the widest margin of victory in franchise history. Few teams have ever rolled through a season with such ease. And so, from the moment Yankee closer Mariano Rivera retired San Diego pinch hitter Mark Sweeney for the final out of the World Series, the Great Debate was on: Was this the greatest team of all time?

Hard question to answer. It has always been difficult to compare clubs and players across eras. How do you measure the Yankees' offense against a team like the 1906 Chicago Cubs, who hold the major-league record for most regular-season wins (116)? New York hit 207 home runs in 1998, a figure six other major league teams bested. In 1906, the deadball-era Cubs hit only 20 homers—and you can bet several of them were of the inside-the-park variety—*to finish second in the National League*. Chicago starters completed 125 games; New York's starters finished only 22 games. But the Yankee total was more than twice the American League average. Chicago's mark, believe it or not, was only slightly better than average for the times. Managers back then rarely called on their bullpens, which were largely composed of pitchers who weren't good enough to start. The Yankees stole 153 bases and were declared a team of roadrunners. The Cubs stole 283 bases and hardly anyone noticed. In 1906, 13 of the 16 major league teams swiped more bases than the '98 Yankees. When you look at those numbers, it's almost as if the New York and Chicago teams were playing different versions of the same sport.

You could say the same thing if you compared last season's Yankees to the 1909 Pirates, the 1927 Yankees, or almost any other club that enters the Greatest Team argument. So I don't see how we declare that one team was better than all the rest. But I do know of at least two opponents that would have given the Yankees a pretty good tussle. They didn't play in any bygone age, either.

The first team I would match against them, the 1975 Cincinnati Reds, won 108 games while finishing 20 games ahead of everyone else in the National League West. They swept a powerful Pittsburgh Pirates team in the National League Championship Playoffs, then triumphed over the Boston Red Sox in a life-and-death struggle that many have called the greatest World Series ever played. I was the second baseman on that club. We were the Big Red Machine, and we didn't believe that any team from any era could ever beat us.

Would the '98 Yankees have proven the exception? I don't how we can answer that to everyone's satisfaction. What do we do, buy the Strat-O-Matic cards for the 1975 and 1998 seasons so we can match the Reds and Yankees in a fantasy series? Run the statistics for both clubs through a computer to see who comes out on top? Have Joe Torre bring his Yankees to that ballpark in *Field of Dreams* and wait for the Reds in their prime to come charging out of the cornfield? Consult a Ouija board? I'm going to make my argument for the Reds the old-fashioned way, like some kid on the corner explaining why his favorite team is better than yours. Let's compare these two fabulous clubs, position by position:

Catcher: Not much of a comparison here. Johnny Bench was, quite simply, the greatest all-around catcher ever to don a face mask. For those of you who never saw him play, imagine a catcher with the defensive skills of Charles Johnson who could hit the ball as hard as Mike Piazza. That was Bench. From the moment he entered the league, he was the best defensive receiver in the game. He won ten consecutive Gold Gloves (1968–77), two MVP awards, and the Rookie of the Year award, and he was a first-ballot

Hall of Famer. Johnny was still at his peak in 1975. He batted .283 while slugging .510 with 39 doubles, 110 ribbies, and 83 runs scored. He even threw in 11 stolen bases (without being caught).

Bench was the National League's All-Star catcher in '75 and finished fourth in that season's MVP balloting. Base stealers never took liberties with him. Johnny had the quickest, strongest, and most accurate throwing arm of any catcher I've ever seen. Only Mike Scioscia, the Dodger receiver during the 1980s, could block the plate better than John.

The Yankees divided their catching chores between Jorge Posada and Joe Girardi. Posada is a promising but unfinished catcher. Though he possesses a strong arm, it's nothing like the cannon that Bench carried into battle. Jorge, who was playing his first full season in '98, is still learning how to call games.

Of the two, Girardi is the superior defensive catcher. He's a master at calling pitches, and knows how to get his hurlers through their assignments, even when they don't have their best stuff. That's a valuable skill. Yankee pitchers aren't timid about throwing hard-to-hit breaking balls low in the strike zone with runners on third, because they know Girardi will block those pitches if they skip in the dirt. As good as he is, though, he doesn't do anything defensively better or even as well as Bench did. And Girardi's arm is weak. He barely threw out 20 percent of the runners who tried to steal against him in 1998.

Joe has little power, but he can be a dangerous hitter in the clutch. Posada has the potential to hit 25 to 30 home runs if he ever gets 500 plate appearances; he swatted 17 in only 358 at-bats during 1998. If you combine Girardi and Posada's production last season, however, the two of them together didn't outperform the 1975 Johnny Bench in a single important offensive category. Neither Girardi nor Posada have ever won a Gold Glove, and I don't see either of them as a future Hall of Famer (though I think Posada has All-Star potential).

Advantage: Reds by a large margin.

First Base: On the surface, this appears to be a close match-up. New York's Tino Martinez has been one of the most productive hitters in baseball over the past five seasons. In 1998 he batted .281 with 28 home runs and 123 RBI. Tony Perez's offensive line for our Big Red Machine: .282, 20 home runs, 109 ribbies. So you might give a slight edge to Martinez. Except that home runs and RBI are much easier to come by today. Forty-four major leaguers drove in 100 or more runs last season. Martinez finished sixth among the American League leaders. Only 13 players hit the century mark in RBI during the 1975 season. Perez's total placed him third *among all major-leaguers.* Since fewer runs were produced back then, Perez's ribbies had a greater value than Tino's, because it didn't take as many runs to win the average game.

Defensively, you could flip a coin between them; they were both solid fielders. Perez would catch nearly any ball thrown in his vicinity. He saved his fellow infielders more than a few throwing errors. Martinez has demonstrated the same skill. Neither of them had the great range of a Don Mattingly or a Keith Hernandez, but they positioned themselves well and moved quickly for big men.

Tony was one of the great clutch hitters of his era. There was no teammate I would rather see stroll to the plate in the ninth with the winning run on second. You just knew that runner was as good as home. Tino, on the other hand, has come up short in some of the biggest games of his career during post-season play. I doubt that trend will continue. Tino's a fine hitter, and the tie-breaking grand slam he swatted against San Diego in the first game of the 1998 World Series may be just the thing he needed to end his October funk. Until Martinez establishes himself as a big-game player, however, I have to give Tony the edge here.

Advantage: Reds.

Second Base: Oh, do I hate indulging in what Norman Mailer refers to as "advertisements for myself." So let's just make a statistical comparison between the Yankees' Chuck Knoblauch and the Reds' second baseman:

	AB	Runs	Hits	D	T	HR	RBI	BB	AVG	SLG	OBP	SB
Knoblauch	603	117	160	25	4	17	64	76	.265	.405	.361	31
Reds 2b	498	107	163	30	5	27	94	132	.327	.508	.471	55

That guy playing for the Reds led the National League in walks, on-base percentage, and stolen bases. Chuck didn't lead his league in anything. The Reds' second baseman won the National League's MVP Award and a Gold Glove. Knoblauch wasn't a serious candidate for either prize (though he has won a Gold Glove in the past, and could very well earn a few more before he finishes playing). I've always enjoyed watching Chuck in action. At his best, he sets the table for his teammates by constantly working pitchers deep into the count, runs the bases smartly, and knows how to do all the little things that contribute to winning. He also has some power, though, as you all know by now, I prefer to see him rapping line-drive doubles and triples rather than lofting the ball for home runs. In many ways, he reminds me of that Reds second baseman, but . . .

Advantage: Okay, you don't have to twist my arm. I'm going with Cincinnati again. I'll let you decide by how much.

Shortstop: Here's an interesting donnybrook. New York's Derek Jeter finished third in the American League MVP voting. Davey Concepcion didn't get an MVP vote in 1975. Jeter has demonstrated more leadership qualities and has flashed more power than Concepcion. Derek slugged .481 in '98; Davey's 1975 slugging percentage was only .353 (though I believe the deceptively strong Davey would have slugged closer to .450 if he were playing with today's juiced baseball). It's obvious that Jeter is a more patient, better all-around hitter than Concepcion was. And Derek is probably three or four years away from his offensive prime.

Defensively, however, Concepcion has him in almost every department. The 1975 Concepcion had more range, softer hands, and better positioning than Jeter has shown us in his brief career. As I noted in an earlier chapter, he was the second-best fielding shortstop I've ever played with or against; only Ozzie Smith was better with the glove. Derek improves in the field every year, however, and he possesses a stronger arm than Davey ever had. It may be, in fact, the best throwing arm I've yet seen on any shortstop.

I've long said that Concepcion belongs in the Hall of Fame. Derek is putting together a Cooperstown career. So how do you choose between them?

Advantage: Yankees, in a squeaker. Though not Davey's equal on defense, Derek is a superb shortstop whose powerful bat gives him the better all around game.

Third Base: We have to weigh some intangibles here. Yankee third baseman Scott Brosius had a career year in 1998: .300, 19 homers, and 98 RBI. Pete Rose hit .323 for us, with a league-leading 215 hits, 42 doubles, and 130 runs scored. Both third basemen were World Series MVPs. Brosius showed a tad more power than Pete (a .472 slugging average, against Rose's .450); Pete got on base and put himself into scoring position more often than Scott.

Though Rose had been an infielder earlier in his career, in 1975 he was an outfielder playing out of position at third. Pete did a competent job, but he was merely average in the field. Brosius committed 22 errors, but he covered more ground than Pete, and had the better arm. There's not all that much difference between these two, if we are just comparing single-season stats; you might even pick Scott over Pete because of his defense. But you have to ignore numbers when you evaluate Rose. The thing that made him a great player was his intensity. He played every game as if it were the seventh game of the World Series. It was his focus rather than his talent that separated him from everybody else. For sheer skill, Pete wasn't the best hitter I ever saw. But he's baseball's all-time hit king. He wasn't fast, yet few players could match his base-running instincts. You rarely saw him get thrown out while trying to take an extra base. Pete was one of the rare players who could reach inside himself to draw out whatever it took to win. Brosius seems to be a hard-nosed player, but he hasn't consistently shown that quality yet. (If he can repeat last season's World Series performance, I might have to reassess my opinion.)

Advantage: Reds.

Left Field: George Foster played only 134 games for us in '75. He hit .300, with 23 home runs, while slugging .518. Had he played an entire season, George would have hit 30 or more homers and notched 100 ribbies. And if he, Bench, and Perez were hitting today with the rabbit ball and smaller ballparks, they would each hit between 45 and 50 big flies every year.

The Yankees used three leftfielders for most of 1998. Curtis was excellent defensively, but he slumped badly at the plate after a terrific start. From June on, Chad looked as if he were trying to slug every pitch out of the ballpark, which is never good policy for a hitter. Darryl Strawberry supplied New York with megawatt power, but he was shaky in the field. Tim Raines hit whenever he played, but he's never been a defensive standout. He was nimble on the bases, though. At 38, Raines could still scoot, though he didn't try to steal as often as in the past.

Once our manager, Sparky Anderson, gave George the left-field job in early May, he didn't have to share it with anyone. George could do it all. He had power and speed, hit for average, and was a good glove man. Foster had so much range he could have been a centerfielder.

Advantage: Reds. The Yankees needed three guys to cover left; we needed only one. The '75 George could outhit and outrun the '98 Raines, was a better fielder than Curtis, and could match Strawberry homer for homer.

Center Field: If I were to rate the all-time defensive centerfielders, Willie Mays would be 1-A, Curt Flood would be 1-B, and my former teammate Cesar Geronimo would be 1-C. And Geronimo had the best arm of the three. Only Roberto Clemente had a stronger, more accurate rifle. Cesar knew where to play every hitter depending on how our pitcher was throwing that day. That's why he always got a good jump on the ball. He was nearly as fast as anyone on our team, so, during those rare times when he misjudged a fly ball, he could often outrun his mistakes. Cesar won four consecutive Gold Glove awards, including one in '75.

New York's Bernie Williams has won two Gold Gloves, but I think of him as a good but not great centerfielder. Unlike Cesar, Bernie misjudges a lot of fly balls. He doesn't always position himself properly, though he compensates for that with his speed. His arm is strong but nothing special, and he doesn't come in for balls as well as Geronimo did.

Bernie has a huge edge over Cesar at the plate, however. Geronimo was mostly a singles hitter; he had only 36 extra-base hits in 1975, which was high for him. Despite playing only 128 games in 1998, Bernie nearly matched that number just in doubles (30). As a switch-hitter, Williams is a threat from both sides of the plate. He has been particularly devastating batting right-handed. He is also one of the swiftest players in the league. So I find it strange that the only thing Bernie doesn't do well on offense is steal bases; he was caught nine times in 24 stolen-base attempts, a terrible percentage. Williams is a batting champion (he led the American League at .339 in '98) with 30-home-run power. Cesar could never match his varied arsenal of offensive weapons.

Advantage: Yankees, by a wide margin.

Right Field: The Yankees' Paul O'Neill continues to be one of the most underrated players in baseball. O'Neill is an accomplished clutch hitter who always seems to work the pitcher into a good hitter's count (2–0, 2–1, 3–1). He rarely gets himself out by swinging at bad pitches. When Paul makes contact, which is often, he usually hits the ball with authority somewhere. They don't keep stats on this, but if they did, I'd bet he would be among the league leaders in hard-hit outs every year.

Paul approaches every at-bat with a Rose-like intensity. One of the things I love most about him is that he doesn't wait for someone else to get the offense going. O'Neill is a player who can pull rather than push the wagon. When his team is down, he'll take it upon himself to kick things into gear. (By contrast, Bernie Williams, as talented as he is, is at his best when no one expects him to be "The Man." That's why he's a perfect fit for the Yankees. When he was testing the free-agent market, speculation had him going to Arizona. Good thing he stayed in New York. With the Diamondbacks, Bernie would have been expected to lead the club, and that would have hurt him. Had he signed with Arizona and they didn't play well, I'm not sure you would ever have heard of him again.)

On defense, O'Neill is probably the best slow outfielder in baseball. He makes up for what he lacks in speed with perfect positioning. You will rarely see Paul make an error. His arm is powerful, though he will occasionally overthrow his target; you don't see too many runners trying to take the extra base on him. Despite his lack of speed, he's a crafty base runner who usually wins when he challenges an opposing outfielder's arm.

Cincinnati's Ken Griffey Sr. had a set of skills different from O'Neill's. Kenny didn't have quite as much power as Paul O'Neill, who regularly tops the 20-home-run mark, while Kenny never hit more than 14. But Griffey was one of the fastest men ever to play the game. An adept bat handler, he could have bunted .300. Though Kenny didn't hit the ball out of the park very often, he was strong enough to drive pitches into the farthest reaches of the outfield for doubles.

Griffey worked hard to turn himself into an outstanding rightfielder. Sparky Anderson once said he charged the ball as well as any outfielder of his day. Though O'Neill is a solid fielder, he just doesn't cover as much ground as Griffey did. Kenny's arm wasn't quite as strong as Paul's, but it was much more accurate. In the seven years we played together, I never saw him miss hitting the cut-off man.

We're comparing apples with oranges here. O'Neill hits third in the Yankee batting order. New York depends on him to drive runners in any way he can. Griffey batted second in our lineup. His job was to score runs or move Rose into scoring position with productive outs. Both men produced superbly in the roles they were given. Right field, however, is traditionally one of baseball's power positions, and O'Neill is clearly the winner in that department. So I reluctantly say . . .

Advantage: Yankees.

Bullpens: Throughout last season I heard many people say that the Yankees' pitching staff would have given them a huge advantage against us. Tim McCarver made that very point during the World Series. I beg to differ. A pitching staff is more than just your starters. You also have to consider the bullpen, and I think we could give New York quite a fight there. Both of our teams could provide their starters with deep relief.

Our closer, Rawly Eastwick, and the Yankees' Mariano Rivera were practically carbon copies of each other. Both threw hard and were difficult to hit up in the strike zone, but the 1975 Eastwick may have had a little more zip on his ball than Rivera did in 1998. Mariano had been a power pitcher during his two previous seasons, but last year he started to mix in more breaking balls and sinkers. As a consequence, his strikeout ratio tumbled. Rivera was one of the guys who struck out nearly a man an inning. In 1998 he struck out only 36 batters in 61 frames. Rawly had a better ratio with 61 K's in 90 innings. He also induced many batters to hit weak pop-ups; I know because I caught my share of them.

Rivera had more saves than Eastwick, 36 to 22, but we have to consider those numbers in the context of the times. In 1998, ten relievers, five in each league, had more saves than Mariano. In 1975, Eastwick led the National League in this category while posting the third-highest save total in the majors. Closers back then were more versatile than they are today. Eastwick would enter a game in non-save situations to retire some tough righty batters. Modern managers rarely use their closers unless a save is on the table. Working under those conditions, Rivera had more save opportunities than Eastwick. But, as we pointed out, Rawly was the most productive reliever in his league, while Rivera didn't even qualify for the top five. So I'm going to give a tissue-thin edge to my teammate in this match-up.

New York's Mike Stanton and Cincinnati's Will McEnaney acted as their clubs' left-handed setup men. Both could also close games. Stanton picked up six saves, and had as many as 27 with the Braves in 1993; McEnaney saved 15 for us. Stanton throws harder. He struck out nearly a man an inning in '98, but was erratic throughout the season. Mike would be unhittable for four or five appearances, then he'd get racked. McEnaney was steady throughout 1975. This difference in their consistency is reflected in their earned run averages: McEnaney 2.47, Stanton 5.47. Mike doesn't have much of a breaking pitch, so he's not especially effective against lefties. Will had a terrific curve, and his fastball darted all over the strike zone. Lefties just couldn't touch him. I'd take him over Stanton for that reason alone.

Pedro Borbon and Clay Carroll were our right-handed setup men, but they could also close. Blessed with a rubber arm, Borbon was capable of pitching nearly every day (he threw 125 innings in '75). Sparky would often leave him in a game though the sixth, seventh, *and* eighth. The Yankees didn't have anyone quite like him, although Ramiro Mendoza's arm was resilient enough to make him a jack-of-all-trades in '98. He started 14 games and relieved in 27 others. Mendoza could certainly give the Yankees three strong innings from time to time, but I doubt he could pitch as frequently as Borbon did (Mendoza threw more innings than Borbon only because Pedro never started).

Both pitchers threw sinkerball strikes. Pedro walked only 29 in 125 innings, Mendoza just 30 in 130. As you can see, this is another tight match-up. But Borbon, unlike Mendoza, was a proven closer who saved ten or more games four times in his career. He could take the ball in the ninth against right-handers when Eastwick wasn't available. I have to give him the nod because of that and his durability.

Jeff Nelson, New York's primary right-handed setup man, was hurt for part of '98, so his numbers (5–3, 3 saves, 3.79 in 40 innings) weren't the equal of Clay Carroll's (7–5, 7 saves, 2.62 in 98 innings). Nelson frequently pitched less than an inning; Clay often appeared for two innings or more. He was another Red reliever with a closer's mentality. For a while, the 37 saves he notched in 1972 were the major-league record.

Graeme Lloyd gave the 1998 Yankees something we lacked: a reliable southpaw specialist who could retire a lefty or two in the early or middle innings. But I think we more than make up for that with a bullpen stacked with four relief aces who could function in any role on any given night. Our guys were at least as talented as their bullpen brethren in New York, and far more flexible.

Advantage: Reds.

Starters: Now it gets interesting. There is no question that the '98 Yankees had better starting pitching than the '75 Reds, but I feel that our lineup, which was man-for-man better than New York's, would have eliminated that advantage in any series we played against them. We've all heard that baseball adage, "Good pitching stops good hitting." But it doesn't stop *great* hitting, and that's exactly what the Big Red Machine featured. For example, in the 1975 National League playoffs, we played the Pittsburgh

Pirates, the club with the second-lowest team ERA (3.01) in the major leagues. We swept them three straight (we played best-of-five series back then), and outscored them 19–7.

Take a good look at those seven runs allowed. That was a fearsome lineup the Pirates had. In 1975 they led the National League in home runs and slugging. Six Pittsburgh regulars hit .280 or better. Yet our starters held them in check throughout the playoffs. So, while they weren't a dominating bunch, I don't believe they would have been intimidated by the Yankee lineup.

That's not to say the Yankee hurlers would be cowering on the mound as we strode to the plate, either. David Cone (20–7, 3.55), for one, would be awfully tough against us if his arm was at its best (Coney was a bit rundown going into the '98 post-season). The Big Red Machine would devour any pitcher who relied solely on heat. Cone, though, is a hard thrower who mixes up his pitches and his arm angles. He has an excellent slider and change that he can throw for strikes anywhere in the count. David also changes speeds well, so he would be difficult to time.

David Wells (18–4, 3.49) has proven to be a big-game winner in the post-season. He's 8–1 in the playoffs and the World Series. That's a record worthy of respect. Though Wells is undoubtedly talented, he essentially has only two pitches—a fastball and a hard curve. There's not much difference in velocity between them. Wells relies on movement and location to get hitters out. Against a lineup like ours, that just wouldn't be enough. Rose, Perez, Griffey, Bench, and Foster could all adjust quickly to a pitcher. To keep them off the scoreboard, a hurler needed at least three pitches and more than two speeds. Wells might get through our lineup once, but after a few innings we would gauge the southpaw's limited repertoire. And then he'd be ours.

Andy Pettite, another Yankee left-hander (16–11, 4.24), would have an even more difficult time against us. Andy relies on a fastball, a cutter, and a curve, though his change is getting better each season. There isn't enough difference in speeds between his cutter and his fastball to throw off our timing. He doesn't throw as hard as Wells, so I think we'd get to him even sooner.

In fact, the Yankees would surrender much of the advantage their starting pitching represents if they let both Wells and Pettite face us in a series. Our lineup murdered left-handed pitching. Many right-handed batters don't hit lefties well, because they can't handle the ball running away from them. But our hitters were expert at pounding that pitch to the opposite field. Rose and Griffey were the kind of contact hitters who didn't care what arm you threw with. When they were on, they were going to get their knocks. There wasn't a lefty in either league who had a pitch that could consistently bother our right-handed sluggers Bench, Perez, and Foster. And though I'm left-handed, I usually hit southpaws better than right-handers.

I know Wells and Pettite are fine pitchers, and I don't want it to sound as if I'm dismissing their abilities. But it's hard for me to envision any southpaw giving us a hard time. After all, we used to torch Phillies ace Steve Carlton, who was one of the three or four best left-handers in baseball history. In the 1976 playoffs, for example, we scored six runs off him in seven innings. Carlton is a Hall of Famer who won four Cy Young Awards. He was an awesome pitcher, but not when he faced us. Is there anyone out there who wants to argue that either Pettite or Wells is in Carlton's class?

For the Yankees to have their best shot against our team, Orlando Hernandez (12–4, 3.13) would have to be one of their three starters. He would give us fits. Hernandez has all those different pitches, arm angles, and mound gyrations, and he never throws at the same speed twice in a row. Luis Tiant was the Red Sox ace when we played them in the '75 World Series. He beat us twice, including a shutout in the opening game. Hernandez, as I stated earlier, is Tiant redux. He might be the toughest pitcher on either side.

Hideki Irabu probably wouldn't start in a series against us, but he certainly gives the Yankee rotation a better fifth arm than anyone we could run out there. After a lackluster major-league rookie season, the Japanese righty tightened his motion in 1998 and put together a good year (13–9, 4.06). Irabu's fastball had more movement, and he demonstrated much better control with his curve. But again, with only two pitches—Irabu is still developing a proper off-speed pitch—he couldn't hold us for more than a few innings.

From our side of the mound, I must admit the Yankee lineup would stack up nicely against our starters. Gary Nolan (15–9, 3.16) had a weakness against teams that ran as well as the '98 Yankees did; he didn't hold runners well at all. Bench could compensate for some of that with his powerful arm. I doubt guys like O'Neill, Brosius, Williams, or Curtis would challenge Johnny often (and we would steal against Girardi and Posada almost at will). But Nolan's Achilles' heel would present a problem, especially if Jeter and Knoblauch got on base.

Nolan, who threw hard when he first came up in 1967, was pretty much a control pitcher by '75. He worked the corners and induced hitters to swing at a lot of bad pitches. There is hardly a batter in the Yankee lineup who hacks at anything out of the strike zone. They would make Nolan come to them, and I don't think Gary was fast enough to win that war.

Don Gullett (15–4, 2.42 in an injury-marred season) was the sort of heat-throwing lefty who gives the Yankees problems. When Gullett was healthy, he was as overpowering as Tom Seaver, Steve Carlton, Ferguson Jenkins, or any other power pitcher this side of Nolan Ryan. Fastball, curve, slider, change, Don had all the pitches. His ball had great movement, and he could throw strikes any time in the count. The Yankees couldn't simply sit back and wait for Don to go 2–0 or 3–1 against them. They would have to come out swinging—not their long suit—or he'd take them apart.

Jack Billingham (15–11, 4.11) would probably be the key to our starting pitching despite his relatively high ERA. Billingham, like David Wells, was at his best in big games. He pitched 25⅓ innings for us in three World Series and surrendered only one run. Jack had a great sinking fastball that hitters found difficult to elevate. He mixed it with a slider, change, and curve, and threw all four pitches for strikes. He's another starter whose stuff the Yankees couldn't sit on. If he was on, Jack could make them hit his pitch and you'd see a lot of ground-ball outs.

Left handed Fred Norman (12–4, 3.73) was our fourth starter. He had three good pitches—fastball, screwball, and change—and an outstanding pick-off move. The Yankees would not be able to steal a base against the Norman-Bench combination. But Freddie was erratic. He walked too many hitters, which would be fatal against New York's highly disciplined batting order. Pat Darcy (11–5, 3.57) was a good pitcher in '75, but he didn't have a pitch to frighten the Yankees.

Advantage: Yankees, but not by as much as everyone thinks.

Okay, so how do I think it would all shake out? Our two clubs would play six or seven tight ballgames. The Yankee hitters would score against our starters early; we would adjust to their pitchers to put the tying runs on the scoreboard in the middle innings. After that, it would come down to relief pitching and defense. I think our bullpen, laden as it was with closers, would have withstood the pressure better. And New York just couldn't match us on defense. In 1998, Bernie Williams was the only Yankee fielder to win a Gold Glove. In 1975, Cincinnati not only won four Gold Gloves, but won them at baseball's most important defensive positions: catcher, shortstop, center field, and second base. The only position where New York would rate an edge was third base, not exactly a critical spot. Our edge in fielding would have made the difference. In the late innings, we would have punched through their defense to score; they'd grow old waiting for that to happen against us.

So the winner is . . . Reds in six. Unless Cone was in top form. Then we'd stay with him in a seventh game and beat their bullpen.

All right, perhaps this hasn't been the most dispassionate evaluation you'll ever read. Yankee fans among you are free to disagree with my conclusions. But while you're preparing your rebuttals, allow me to give you one last thing to consider. The 1975 Big Red Machine was no one-trick pony. The scary thing about our club is that we were even better in 1976. Our offensive statistics might not have seemed as impressive; '76 was a pitcher's year, and hitting was way down in both leagues. However, the 1975 Reds led the National League in only three offensive categories: runs scored, stolen bases, and walks. The 1976 model topped both leagues in every major hitting category except stolen bases (we finished third with 210, although we did lead the majors in stolen-base percentage). Our defense, starting pitching, and bench were also stronger. Only our bullpen dropped back a notch from the previous season. We made a mistake in trading Clay Carroll, whom we never quite replaced, and McEnaney had a bad year. Lefties, though, still found Will unhittable, and he was good enough to earn two saves in the World Series.

McEnaney wasn't the only player on our team who turned it up a notch that October. We beat the Philadelphia Phillies in three straight before sweeping the Yankees in the Fall Classic. Since the playoffs were introduced in 1969, no club has gone undefeated in the post-season.

Power, hitting, defense, speed, and pitching—our '76 club had it all. And I doubt you'll ever see a smarter bunch of players. We would go three weeks at a time without making a mental error such as throwing to the wrong base or forgetting the number of outs. It's rare for a team today to play three games without some-one on the field suffering a brain cramp. The '98 Yankees were also a sharp group. One of the many things I admired about them was how they rarely beat themselves. But I think our dugout housed a few more players with Ph.D.'s from Doubleday U. Everyone on our roster knew how to play the game.

Which is a big reason why we got fitted for rings in '75 and '76. That's no small accomplishment. As hard as it is to win a World Series, it's even harder to repeat. Every team is taking dead aim at you, and it's difficult to maintain your drive after you've won baseball's ultimate prize. So before we start arguing over which club is the greatest of all time, I'd like to issue a little chal-lenge to the current Bronx Bombers: If you want a crack at the title, let's see *you* do two in a row. Then we can talk.

Baseball Brainstorming

No one has granted me the patent on good ideas, so I've asked some of baseball's movers and shakers to share their recommendations for upgrading the game. Each of these contributors will, in some way, help shape the direction baseball will take over the next ten years. I might not agree with all their suggestions, but they certainly are thought-provoking. It will be interesting to see how many of our ideas actually get implemented.

Donald Fehr (president, Players' Association): "Baseball must do a number of things if it is to build on last year's spectacular season. In general, we need to do a lot more fan outreach. And that starts with identifying all those things we can do that will attract and interest fans. How do we provide them with a better experience when they come to the park or watch on TV? We have to continually remind people of our message: 'We want you to come to our baseball games because, if you do, you will get to see these superb athletes quite literally do something no one else in the world can do.' And that is special.

"We must also find ways to draw new fans, which may mean staging promotions that go beyond the realm of the game itself. For example, we had Beanie Baby giveaways throughout the majors in 1998. Now, in many respects that may seem silly. What does a Beanie Baby have to do with baseball? But those promotions brought a lot of people out to games who would not have come otherwise. They got to see baseball live, many of them for the first time. And if you got your Beanie Baby in Yankee Stadium last May 17, you also got to see a perfect game. Wasn't that a nice coincidence?

"If those new fans pay attention, they can grasp that they are watching a subtle, complex game that requires consummate skill. They'll see what it means to field a ball in the hole and nip the runner at first, how difficult it is to hit a pitcher who is throwing four different pitches from four different angles at four different speeds. Or see exactly how much ground Ken Griffey has to cover before making some breathtaking catch. That dash for the ball is as remarkable as the play itself. You can't quite catch that on television. At the ballpark, they'll see the game played in a defining context.

"I'm not saying you can't become a devout fan by following the game on TV, but I do think coming out to the park is a special experience. Let's say you have a crucial situation, late innings of a ballgame, the tying runs get on and the manager comes out for a meeting at the mound with his pitcher, catcher, and shortstop. If you're at home, TV cuts to a commercial.

But when you're in the stadium, you see the entire drama unfold before you. You'll have a tendency—particularly if you're accompanied by someone who's knowledgeable—to ponder and discuss all the options they're considering. You begin to appreciate the ebb and flow of the game.

"To look at outreach in another sense, I also believe that baseball has an obligation to expand to as many cities as we can, so that the major-league game becomes more readily accessible to more fans as a general proposition. The time has come to consider—although I recognize that there are tremendous difficulties with this—expanding to non-U.S. and Canadian cities. However, until we see how any owner-proposed revenue-sharing plans work and what our next agreement (between labor and management) looks like, it would be difficult to seriously consider expansion. It may be three or four years before we deal with that issue.

"I think we also have to take a look at scheduling and ask whether a balanced schedule makes any sense, or should we go for a more unbalanced schedule that provides more games between teams that are reasonably close by. I'm not necessarily talking about teams with so-called natural rivalries. Many rivalries are simply a function of who's hot at the moment. You know, the old Cardinals-Cubs rivalry was tremendous at one time, but when the Mets were a power, both St. Louis and Chicago had rivalries with them that were just as strong. I'm thinking more of arranging it so that, whenever teams are reasonably close, the fans from one city can follow their club to another city more often. That's what matters."

Joe's Comment: I agree with much of what Don says, except when it comes to expansion. When Don looks at expansion, he sees jobs for players. The owners see a chance to rake in those megabuck franchise fees. I see a further dilution of the talent pool. Any question of expansion should be put aside until the baseball pipeline is once again overflowing with top drawer players.

Jon Miller (the announcer for the San Francisco Giants is also Joe Morgan's broadcasting partner for ESPN Baseball): "I believe in the principle that the game itself is always enough. It is so exciting, entertaining, and compelling on so many different levels that, when allowed to unfold unencumbered, it can attract all the fans it needs. Why change much of anything? Fans are turning out in record numbers. They are investing more money in the game than at any time in history. So I would table all this talk about realignment, increased interleague play, and any other radical changes. Instead, let's maximize the things fans enjoy about the game.

"For instance, this talk that teams which share a close proximity should be playing each other in the same league is a good notion, but we can do it without any realignment of the two leagues. Let's look at the Dodgers and Giants. They are part of the longest, most ferocious rivalry in baseball. But last season the Giants played the Dodgers twelve times. That's as often as they played the St. Louis Cardinals. And San Francisco also played the Texas Rangers, the Anaheim Mariners, and the Seattle Mariners. There were no compelling reasons for San Francisco to play any of those American League clubs. And it was the same for much of interleague play. I mean, whose heart starts palpitating when the Detroit Tigers play the Pittsburgh Pirates? The fans of those respective teams couldn't care less about those games.

"But they do care about baseball's natural rivalries, and owners should take advantage of those. For instance, the Giants should play the four other teams in the National League West 17 times, for a total of 68 games. Then they should play the other National League clubs 11 times each. That would leave six games—three at home and three away—with their most obvious interleague rivals, the Oakland Athletics.

"Now, what have we accomplished with this setup? We've extracted the best aspect from interleague play, which, in its present form, is the tail wagging the dog. Because the reason the Yankees and Red Sox, Dodgers and Giants only play against each other 12 times a season is interleague competition. It's driving the rest of the schedule, as well as driving the notion that radical realignment is necessary. That's totally backwards. There is a demand for Yankees-Mets, Cubs–White Sox, Giants-A's, Houston-Texas. You can find a natural interleague rival for almost every club. Leave interleague play to that, limit it to six games, and you can schedule more games between the teams that are battling each other for the division. You end up nurturing rivalries. That's all the tweaking the game on the field might need. The rest of it has to come on the business end between the owners and players. My advice to both sides is that all of that should be straightened out behind closed doors. Baseball fans don't need to hear about it."

Joe: Jon and I often disagree, but we have one thing in common: We both love the game and want to see it flourish. Here, though, we have some matters of divergence. Things go in cycles, Jon. There is no way of guaranteeing perfect matchups every year, even among geographical rivals. And your interleague play plan threatens the integrity of the races. For example, suppose the Mets and Braves are locked in a pennant race. Requiring the Mets to meet the powerhouse Yankees while the Braves played six games against some American League turkey would grant Atlanta a tremendous advantage. The only fair way to work this is to have every team in a division play the same opponents an equal number of times.

Tom Reich (a players' agent, he numbers Cubs rightfielder Sammy Sosa among his clients): "The biggest problem in the game is clearly the economic disparity between the high-end and low-end teams. It starts with revenues; everybody focuses on payrolls, but the payroll is a function of revenue limitations. Small-market teams reason, 'We can afford to spend $30 million on player salaries, but why do it when we still won't be able to compete with teams spending $60 million, $70 million, or more?' So they accept their plight and slash their payrolls to $20 million or less. At the same time they receive revenue sharing, or subsidies if you will, from the large-market teams. Only they're not spending the money on salaries as they should to improve their product. They pocket it as profit. The Montreal Expos are a good example of this. Now, I do agree there has to be even greater revenue sharing to the bottom teams. However, baseball must impose a requirement that the money be spent on players so that franchises become more competitive. If a team fails to spend the money, baseball should reduce its entitlement in the future, dollar for dollar.

"Many of these low-end teams wouldn't need these subsidies if they could move into new venues. Why? Because it's revenue, not market size, that is operative here. Cutting-edge stadiums can generate big revenues in supposedly small markets. Look at Cleveland, Texas, and Baltimore. They were considered small-market teams while they were stuck in horrible ballparks. Now all three are among baseball's high rollers. The population of those towns didn't change significantly, so what happened? Both teams moved into beautiful new ballparks, and the fans responded by coming out in record numbers.

"There has to be a hands-on, coordinated effort between major-league baseball and the Players' Association to establish a committee that can assist any team with a stadium problem, franchises like Montreal and Pittsburgh. This isn't to say these franchises are inept, its just an attempt to have some of the brightest minds in the game augment their efforts. If, after a period of time, they can't come up with a solution to the venue problem, then that team probably has to be moved.

"I'm a Pittsburgher, and I am intimately familiar with the problems the Pirates have encountered. They had a stadium approved. Now they're having difficulty getting the additional approvals they need at the state level. It was butchered by legislative incompetence. Pittsburgh is a legendary franchise with a solid baseball fan base, even though it is a football town. The plans for the new ballpark are first-rate, the location couldn't be better. The Pirates would flourish there. Pittsburgh might not become a big-revenue franchise, but it would move to the middle of the pack. From there, it could be competitive. So here is a situation where a franchise sorely needs baseball to put the full weight of the institution behind a coordinated appeal to the legislature.

"These efforts would be supported by additional subsidies from major-league baseball, such as interest-free loans to help finance construction. One of the trip cords in getting approval from the politicians and the taxpayers is the dollar difference between how much the franchise will pay to finance the venue and how much of the bill the public will have to pick up. If major-league baseball can augment a franchise's contribution, it can mean the difference between getting approval and not."

Joe: I agree with Tom, but baseball cannot expect municipalities to give any team a free ride on stadiums. Franchises and cities must enter into partnerships that spell out the advantages to both parties. If you want the local politicians to cooperate, you have to give them something to entice the voters. Demonstrate what keeping the ball club will mean to the city in terms of jobs, taxes, and other revenues. For some time now, there has been talk about building a new Yankee Stadium on Manhattan's West Side. Everyone argues the advantages or disadvantages of the move, but I've yet to seen any concrete figures on what the public will gain if it helps George Steinbrenner finance his new home. Voters need to know that. Once a venue is built, a city should retain some dates for itself so it can make additional revenues by renting it out for concerts and other events.

Peter Pascarelli (a veteran baseball beat writer and columnist, currently director of information for ESPN): "I know the owners want expansion because it generates a quick buck for them in franchise fees. The Players' Association supports expansion, since it means more jobs for its membership. But neither agenda has anything to do with the good of the game. Colorado has been a great market. Arizona was good for one year, but let's see what happens down the road. The Tampa Bay Devil Rays and Florida Marlins were just disastrous mistakes. If baseball was going to go anywhere in Florida, it should have looked toward Orlando.

"Perhaps it was good for the game to go to Arizona and get some kind of foothold in Florida. But I don't think it would injure baseball's future if Montreal or Minnesota lost their franchises. I'm not talking about moving those clubs, either. I'm talking about contraction as opposed to expansion. Let the major leagues buy back those franchises and enter their players into a dispersal draft. Baseball officially denies this, but executives have told me that there is an emergency mechanism in both leagues' by-laws that would allow such a thing. It was put there in case some franchise went bankrupt. Disperse the talent of two teams among both leagues, and you would immediately improve the quality of play.

"Instead, the owners are talking about expanding to two more cities in the near future. Where can they go to next? Charlotte may be one spot, but many people have questions about its viability. The Orioles would likely block a Northern Virginia bid in court. Las Vegas is another possibility; it's a fast-growing metropolitan area. But would baseball, with its gambling sensitivities, really want to do that? Plus I don't know if Las Vegas's gaming enterprises—the real power in that town—would want baseball to come in. They'd have to take baseball games off their betting boards, and they're not going to find that palatable. New Orleans is often mentioned as a candidate. Unfortunately, it's not a good sports town.

"I think baseball can expand in other ways, such as a World Baseball Cup, which is something I think you'll see in the next five years or so. Countries from all over the world would field teams, just as they do in soccer's World Cup. You could have it in February or March, around spring training time, so the players would be conditioning themselves for their regular season while playing for their national teams. Start with several best-of-three elimination rounds, go to a best-of-five semifinals, then, ultimately a seven-game series for the cup. Schedule the games in sites all over the world. It would be a festival of baseball. You just know there would be huge worldwide interest here, in the Far East, Australia, and Latin America. It would be a fabulous marketing tool."

Joe: Great idea, a World Cup. Getting the entire planet focused on the game for a specific period would be the most exciting thing that could happen to the sport. I just don't know how feasible it would be in terms of timing. Because the major-league season is so long (from mid-February to late October, if you count spring training and the post-season), there is only a narrow window left open for scheduling any World Cup competition. Since conditions vary so widely from country to country—it may be warm in some countries while it is positively frosty here—weather would have a tremendous impact on where the games were played in the United States.

Dusty Baker (the manager of the San Francisco Giants, and a two-time winner of the National League's Manager of the Year Award): "Players can promote our game better by giving the fans more access. Sign autographs, be more personable. The guys on my team are pretty good at that, but I'd like to see more of it throughout both leagues. When I was a player with the Dodgers (1976–83), we had official autograph days. Half the team would go one Sunday, the other half would show up the next Sunday. You came to the park twice, you could get Steve Garvey's autograph, Fernando Valenzuela's, Ron Cey's. The entire club.

"Now I hear they have to pay the players to do that. And if a guy doesn't want to go, you can't make him. Some people think its weird that I sign so many autographs, especially for kids. But the importance of doing that kind of thing was passed on to me by other players. And that's something baseball can do better. It's not very good at passing on its history.

"From the time a franchise signs a young player, it should start acquainting him with the game's traditions. Don't just teach that young man how to play, teach him what the game means. And the way to do that is to surround him with the sport's legends. I played with Henry Aaron in Atlanta; he was my role model. One day I asked him who he talked to whenever he had a baseball problem or went into a slump. He said he could always turn to Stan Musial. That floored me.

"With the Dodgers, I would find myself sitting next to Duke Snider one day, Don Newcombe the next. Pee Wee Reese would come into the clubhouse. They made the game's history come alive for me. We're trying to do that with the Giants. Willie Mays, Orlando Cepeda, Jim Ray Hart, Mike McCormick—we bring all those guys around for spring training. They can show our young players how to act like major-leaguers. Few organizations have done this. And the teams that do bring in their greatest names don't want them talking too much to the players. They're afraid the coaches will be intimidated by their presence.

"Well, as far as I'm concerned, Hall of Famers like Lou Brock, Bob Gibson, Warren Spahn, and Ernie Banks can come to my players and say anything they want to them. They can't do anything but help us. Sandy Koufax visited me one day a couple of seasons back, and the whole team came around. When he started talking about pitching, it was like Moses had just come down from the mountaintop. Managers and teams should be encouraging that kind of participation."

Joe: I think players should sign, but fans also have to be sensitive about encroaching on an athlete's time. A player can sign a hundred autographs as he leaves the stadium, but if he doesn't sign that hundred and first, he's a bad guy. That's not fair. Fans also have to understand that players are human. If an athlete has just spent three hours playing a game his team lost, and he went 0-4 with a couple of K's, it's probably not a good idea to approach him for a signature. Fans also shouldn't expect players to sign multiple autographs. One to a customer is plenty. People often send me entire collections to sign—bats, balls, scorecards, books. These aren't real fans, they're traders trying to make money off my signature. I'll sign one item and send the rest back.

Mike Veeck (senior vice president and director of marketing for the Tampa Bay Devil Rays, and owner of several minor-league ball clubs): "So-called baseball purists always say, "The game is enough to bring fans out to the park. It doesn't need embellishing.' Well, those people never owned a ball club. If you catered only to the purists, 75 percent of your seats would remain empty. When people come the ballpark, we should celebrate the three hours that we have them. We have to make them laugh, because life outside of the stadium is very serious. That's what the owners forget. For years the owners said, 'Hey, Veeck will play in the minor leagues, but his act doesn't work in the majors.' Now think about that. Descartes obviously isn't hanging around with these people, because the logic of this situation must escape them. Is there a difference between major-league laughter and the minor-league version? The owners and general managers have to under-stand that we're not making bombs here; this is a game. Bill Veeck would play better today than he did in the forties and fifties because, among most owners, fun and joy are in such short supply.

"I own one of the most successful teams in minor-league his-tory, the St. Paul Saints. One month before our season starts, we will sell every seat for every game. It's not because I'm a smart dude. We sell out because we have created a relationship between the team and the community. And it's built on laughter. We'll do anything to keep people entertained. On *M*A*S*H* Night, we gave away baseballs bearing camouflage patterns. Chia Pet Night was a huge draw. We honored great American inventors like Ron Popeil for his Veg-O-Matic. Whoopee Cushion Night is another huge success. It featured the world's largest Bronx salute. We just did silly things and the fans loved it. Did we violate taste once in a while? Sure, but we never sacrificed our PG rating.

"Vasectomy Night in Charleston might have been pushing the envelope a bit, though. But if you're looking to make a splash in the press, what better place to do something like that than the Bible Belt? Actually, the way it happened was that Father's Day was coming up. The finest vasectomy surgeon in the world works at the Medical University of South Carolina. He had perfected the technique and wanted to do a giveaway. Sounded good to me! I thought everyone would laugh, which they did. But then they pre-tended to be horrified.

"A little more than an hour after I announced it, the archdio-cese rose up to murder me, the media took after me. Some people were confused. Did you come to the park if you *had* a vasectomy or to *get* one? Bud Selig called the president of the National Asso-ciation and said, 'This is a disgrace, we've got to get Mike to call it off.' Eventually, I referred all the calls to my mother. Funny thing about the press. None of the female reporters got on my case. They all thought it was a great idea. But the male writers got their pants in a wedgie.

"Obviously I believe we have to take more chances to connect with the fans. Make decisions based on the heart rather than the pocketbook. Use your club as a platform for things you believe in. My father did that while never forgetting to have fun. When you behave decently with the fans, when they sense your sincerity, they pay you back to the nines. So the first thing we must do is become method actors. You know the method philosophy, you cannot *pretend,* you must *be.* We have to prove that what happened in 1998 to produce so much goodwill—the McGwire-and-Sosa love fest—wasn't a fluke, an accident, or just a lot of hype; it's who baseball is."

Joe: I think baseball must market itself more creatively, especially with the youth market. Anyone who thinks otherwise just isn't facing the reality of the times. But Vasectomy Night? Makes me wince just to think about it.

Jerry Colangelo (owner, Arizona Diamondbacks): "We must continually remind the public of the unique thing we have to sell. Of the major sports, we still have the best ticket prices. The average ticket price in the NFL, NBA, and NHL is anywhere between $35 and $50. In baseball, it's something like $14. We can appeal to more of a mass market than the other three sports. Baseball also must encourage young people in this country to participate in the game. We should be building ballfields, supplying equipment for young players. That's how you grow fans. We need formal programs to do this big job. And that's not only from a league standpoint. Individual teams should get out in their local markets to establish a prominent role for baseball.

"In my opinion, you won't have major-league franchises per se in other countries for at least a decade. But baseball is global, and we mustn't forget that. Look at how many foreign-born players are on our rosters. Their numbers will continue to rise. Baseball has developed pretty well in Japan, Korea, and Australia. There is a lot of work to be done, however, in Europe. First we must expose the people over there to the game via radio and television. Now you're creating interest. Then we can put on clinics and start leagues. This is a long, long pull, but that's what a grassroots global approach is all about."

Joe: One vehicle we can use to reach young fans is the World Series. Presently, every Series game is scheduled at night so that TV can maximize its advertising revenues. That's putting short-term profits over long-term growth. Young fans are often tuning out on the Series in midgame because they have to go to bed early. Let's give them an opportunity to see some games played in their entirety. Baseball should schedule any World Series games played on Saturday or Sunday for the afternoon.

John Hart (general manager, Cleveland Indians): "There are markets that are having difficulty drawing fans, and seem unable to persuade their communities to help them acquire new stadiums. If all else fails, we may have to move those teams. But when you look at the shrinking pool of viable franchise cities, you realize we should at least consider expanding internationally. As a first step, there is talk of letting our better minor-leaguers participate in the Olympics. If it's done right, I could support something like that.

"I agree that new stadiums will help franchises that are currently hurting at the box office, but they aren't panaceas in and of themselves. Just because you build it, doesn't mean anyone will come. You can put a bad ball club in the Taj Mahal and it won't draw. Our stadium helped us turn around the franchises, but front offices also have to be creative in signing and deploying talent.

"One thing that should not and will not happen is the abandonment of the minor leagues by major-league baseball. Every so often you hear someone suggest that the colleges can now do the work of the low minors in developing talent at no cost or a negligible cost to us. But it is the minor leagues that separate us from the other major sports.

"These clubs are, for the most part, operated extremely well by independent operators. They are fabulous marketers who live and die on community outreach; that's why the players down there are so accessible. Our minor-league outposts represent our grass roots; they not only build ballplayers, they create fans who flow up to our big-league game. That's invaluable, and something college baseball simply cannot provide. We fund a lot of the expenses for minor-league clubs and will continue to do so. They can help us grow. Baseball might talk about cutting the number of minor-league teams, but it will never happen. We need that pipeline to be continually filled with young talent, especially now, when the younger players help balance our payroll.

"However, the recent dramatic escalation of the bonuses paid to college players entering the minors or, in some cases, coming directly to the majors, is a concern. J. D. Drew gets $7 million from the Cardinals, players like [Philadelphia Phillies number-one draft pick] Pat Burrell are getting four or five million or more. Such contracts are becoming prohibitive for most clubs. You know, the purpose of the college draft is to permit the worst teams to improve themselves by getting that first crack at college talent. These huge signing bonuses undermine that goal. If a small-market team like the Pirates knows some elite—but, by our standards, still unproven—college player wants $5 million to sign, they'll pass on him to take an inferior talent. We need to do something to discourage this.

"International signings also place a burden on small-market teams. You only have a certain number of clubs that can compete for those foreign players. I think it's great that clubs are signing foreign-born talent as the Yankees have with Orlando Hernandez or the Dodgers with Chan Ho Park. But we have no system in place to control the influx of these players. So the richest clubs grab the best talent. I think we have to consider counting these foreign signings against a club's picks in the college draft. For instance, if you sign an Orlando Hernandez for $6.6 million, perhaps he should count as your first- or second-round pick."

Joe: To John's point about the high price of college talent: Years ago, we had something called the Bonus Baby rule. If you signed a player out of college or high school for an amount beyond a set maximum, he had to stay on your 25-man major-league roster for an entire year; if you sent him to the minors, another team could draft him. We could restore some of the competitive balance John talks about by reinstating that rule.

David Cone (New York Yankees pitcher): "I believe Commissioner Selig's chief assistant Paul Beeston [formerly the president/CEO of the Toronto Blue Jays] should and will play a pivotal role in the talks between the Players' Union and management. He has the respect of the players, Don Fehr, and the commissioner. We've never had that kind of key player involved in these conversations from a power position. If we can resolve any differences we might have, management can then start marketing the players. That's something the owners have been reluctant to do in the past because, some people think, of the past labor struggles. Management got into the rut of trashing its own product—and a large part of that is the players—rather than building it up.

"I know some people are saying that the owners will try to impose the kind of salary caps that restrict players' revenues in the NBA. Whether the majority of the owners will advocate a salary cap remains to be seen, but I hope that's not the case. The NBA is not a valid model for comparison. Baseball has the minor leagues; basketball doesn't. Baseball teams have the potential to completely control a player's contract for 12 years, 6 in the minors and 6 in the majors. The top college basketball players also, by and large, receive much bigger signing bonuses than college baseball players.

"We've taken some steps in fan outreach besides signing more autographs and being more accessible. The union has established the Players' Trust Fund and other charitable activities that reach out to the communities. In 1998 we established grants in Mark McGwire's and Sammy Sosa's names to build ballfields in the communities of their choice. We need to do more of those kinds of things.

"On the field, I don't think we need to do to much tinkering with the game itself. I know when the mound was lowered in 1969, arm injuries and ERAs rose. I can't prove a correlation, but if someone wanted to raise the pitcher's mound another five inches, I wouldn't exactly object . . ."

Joe: Baseball owners took note of the way the basketball players caved in on the salary cap issue. I think they were heartened by the success of NBA commissioner David Stern's hard-line stance. Coney and his fellow members should be prepared for the owners to insist on a salary cap, drawn along the lines of the NBA model, during the next round of negotiations. My guess is the owners will be willing to fight a long war, no matter how ultimately self-destructive it may be, to limit salaries in some fashion. If I were the players, I'd start digging the trenches now.

Bud Selig (Major League Baseball Commissioner): "One problem we must address is the schedule. We have significant scheduling problems. We hear the grumbling from all sources, but, frankly, the only way to solve those problems is to have some realignment between the leagues, something more modest than I suggested a year or so ago, but realignment none the less. This will also let us expand on our geographical rivalries while assisting our marketing endeavors. For the next phase of this, I see two to five teams crossing over both ways. The format isn't set yet, but it would be done geographically for the most part. However, there could be some others [who realign] to solve some of the structural problems we have. We also have a mission to grow the game internationally. You may be seeing a team like the Seattle Mariners playing a series against an American League rival in Japan sometime soon."

Joe: Hey, Bud, let's do some math. If five teams cross over both ways, that's ten teams switching, exactly one-third of all major-league clubs. That's not radical? If you're going to start doing that, why not just abolish both leagues and lump all the franchises together? I also notice you said the "next phase of this." So how many more realignments are we looking at? Let's keep the National and American League rivalries intact; they lend spice to the game. As for the schedule, there is always someone complaining about it, but baseball has survived. Besides, you can adjust the schedule without restructuring. Simply have clubs play more games against opponents within their division. And one more thing—if Cincinnati, the oldest franchise in professional baseball, ever switches to the American League, I'm out of here!

Andrew Levy (president of Wish You Were Here Productions, a marketing agent who has worked with such players as David Cone, Tino Martinez, and John Franco): "On-the-field is always going to be baseball's number-one priority, but it must give more focus to building the game off the field. I'd like to see the major league teams reach the younger market through school programs that will educate kids about baseball. Have players visit schools to explain how the game works. On the surface, this is a simple sport, but it has a lot of complexities. The more you understand them, the better a fan you'll be.

"This is important because baseball does a good job with the 18-to-54-year-old groups, but it's missing the young people that it can build on for the future. Teams should bring 100 kids out to every game. Have them arrive two or three hours early so they can meet the players for photos and autographs. Then give them the game, a free drink, and a hot dog. Make it a memorable outing and you'll create fans for life.

"The game also needs more of a Saturday-morning programming presence. You see NBA and NHL stars doing endorsements during that children's prime time. Because the players have to go through Major League Properties, the licensing arm of baseball, it makes it difficult for sponsors to get the Jeters, the A-Rods, and the Garciaparras. That system needs to be streamlined for greater accessibility.

"I know it sounds corny, but it means so much for younger fans to hear from their idols. Unfortunately, most players don't have the time to answer all their requests. You come home from a road trip, there can be 200 or more pieces of mail waiting for you. If a player tackles this himself, he's going to miss important things like the letter from some child who is gravely ill. So they should consider fan-mail services. The one we started for David Cone scans the mail and picks out the most important requests. We have personal postcards that David signs and sends back to fans. It's just another way of ensuring outreach."

Joe: I love the idea of teaching fans the nuances of the game. Beside school programs that reach only the kids, I think baseball should offer interactive tutorials through the Web sites of each major-league team for fans in general. Then you could plug into, say, the San Diego Padres site and hear Tony Gwynn talk about the mechanics of hitting while demonstrating via slow-motion video every element of his swing.

Bob Costas (sports announcer, NBC Sports): "While what happened in 1998 was wonderful, it only temporarily disguises the fundamental problem that baseball has. Baseball has to do what basketball just did. At any short-term cost, the owners and players must remake their economic system. If that means shutting the game down for as long as it takes to get it done, then that is what they have to do.

"Just as you wouldn't let one team put ten players on the field to your nine, or allow them to have four outs an inning to your three, neither should one team enter a season with a $20 million payroll while another has an $80 million payroll. It's ridiculous. Baseball needs comprehensive revenue sharing coupled with salary caps and maximum salaries for individuals. This can only work if the owners agree to commit a minimum amount of money that would go to the players in general. If that minimum isn't met through salaries, then baseball as an industry makes up the difference and turns it over to the Players' Association, which can distribute the money any way it wants.

"My idea for revenue sharing would call for each team to keep half of its revenues while donating the other half to the league. This is on the theory that the other team is always half of the attraction. For example, the Yankees get $50 million a year in local broadcast revenue, and the Brewers get $3 million. New York kicks $25 million into the pool, the Brewers put in a million and a half. Then all that money is redistributed in a weighted system that balances it between the smaller markets and the larger. Steinbrenner and Rupert Murdoch will get payments, but it's a trickle to them, while a major amount goes to the Brewers and Royals.

"To make this work fairly, the teams would have to agree to maintain a payroll range with minimums as well as maximums, which you could not exceed or fall beneath. This system would also grant exceptions that would allow teams to hold on to their star players, just as the NBA does with the now modified 'Larry Bird Rule.' Seattle could offer Ken Griffey more money than any other team could, but Griffey would still have the freedom to go to another club. The top amount Seattle would be permitted to pay Griffey would not be unlimited. There would be a maximum, but it would be a generous maximum.

"That's the main thing that has to happen. Marvin Miller and Don Fehr have always made the point that during post–free agency, more different teams won or contended than in baseball's earlier eras. They claimed that free agency was not only good for the players' pocketbooks, it also invigorated the game. They were correct. But now the thing has extended out to a point of distortion. Their arguments no longer hold.

"If I were a player, salary would not be my sole concern. I would be more concerned with working conditions, one of which would be that every player has at least a chance to play on a club that can win. George Brett just went into the Hall of Fame. He was a Kansas City Royal all his life, Mr. Kansas City. But if his career began now, he'd couldn't stay with that franchise. Not out of greed, although someone would pay him a lot of money. He'd have to get off the Royals so he would have a chance to win. Is that good for the game? What kind of a crazy situation is that?

"The other thing baseball must do is take a clear look at its competitive structure. Baseball's wild-card system is the stupidest thing in history. What amazes me is not that the cynical owners would do it for more television revenue; I put nothing past them. What astounds me is how much of the baseball press can't put two and two together on this one. They argue that it gives more teams a chance. A chance at what? Certainly not a pennant race, because if you have a wild card, you can't have a pennant race. All the urgency and drama of the 162-game season has been diminished.

"Here's what they should do. Eliminate the wild card. Of the three division champions, give the team with the best record a bye for the first round of post-season play. Now you've replaced this side race for the mediocrity of the wild card—something no one understands, since you can be in first place by three games in your own division, but two games behind in the wild-card chase—with a race for excellence. And everyone can grasp it at a glance: "Hey, we're five up in the Central Division, but two games in back of the leader in the East for the best record in the league. So even though we've clinched our division, we're still chasing till the end of the year for that first-round bye."

"Now you've restored the integrity of the pennant race. If the team that gets the bye wins the LCS, they are clearly the best team in the league. If the other team beats the club with the bye, it had to go the harder route of an extra series and have, at the very least, won its own division. You cannot have a World Series participant under this system that isn't vetted in a way that makes sense. And that's important because, more than the other major sports, which are slam-bam action affairs, baseball is dependent upon context. That's why it matters to the fan that the teams that play in the World Series belong in the World Series."

Joe: Over the last few years, I've come to think of Bob as the voice and conscience of baseball's fans. And I know he's speaking for a lot of them when he voices these concerns. Like Jon Miller, he truly loves this great game. But I have to disagree with him on a number of issues. Bob and Jon often talk about how the wild card destroys pennant races. When did we ever have pennant races every year? If it weren't for the wild card in 1998, the teams chasing the Yankees and Braves in their respective divisions would have been packing their tents in May. The wild card all but guarantees that there will be at least one race for the post-season in each league every season. I don't think it's hard to follow, either. We explain it on every ESPN broadcast, and you can decipher it with one glance at the wild-card standings that most newspapers carry daily.

The wild card also ensures that the two best teams in each league will be in the playoffs, even if they happen to play in the same division. Under Bob's three-division setup, a league's second-best team can still miss the post-season. In 1993, Atlanta won the National League West with 104 victories while second-place San Francisco won 103. Philadelphia won the NL East by winning 97 games. Yet the Giants sat home while a team with a lesser record met Atlanta in the playoffs. Was that good for baseball or fair to San Francisco? The wild card also inspires more late-season transactions, many of them involving baseball's biggest names. Those deals grab headlines while energizing fans.

I don't thinking granting a bye to a team is a good idea at all. Instead of rewarding it, you'd put the club with the best record at a disadvantage. Baseball is a game of skill, timing, and feel. A weeks' rust could kill a team. Finally, there is no way baseball can survive another shutdown. And if the owners try to enforce a salary cap without making a compelling case to the players, that's exactly what we could be headed for.

12

Fifty Plus Two

I played second base because that was Jackie Robinson's position. Jackie was my boyhood hero; he made it possible for me to live out my version of the American dream on major-league dia-monds throughout the country. I owe him a lot, but I'm certainly not the only one in his debt. When Jackie broke the color line in 1947, baseball made a vow to him: "Succeed, and we will open the game to other African-Americans." Jackie surpassed every expectation. For nearly a decade he was the National League's most dominant force. Rookie of the Year, MVP, perennial All-Star, Hall of Famer, Jackie more than upheld his end of the bargain. Baseball, however, has kept only half of its promise. While current major-league rosters may appear to be integrated, there still exists in baseball a color line that deprives the sport of precious talent.

To see what I'm talking about, just thumb through a media guide for any major-league team. You will notice few black faces among the executives and scouts. Then go to the various publica-tions that every year list baseball's top 100 movers and shakers.

The only African-Americans you'll find among that prestigious group are National League president Len Coleman, Seattle Mariners superstar Ken Griffey Jr., and a meager handful of other black players.

There are currently no black or Hispanic general managers, and few African-Americans, Latinos, or women holding genuine decision-making positions on any big-league clubs. You often hear of how someone started out keeping statistics for a club before working his way up into a front-office position. Minorities rarely get those entry-level jobs, and when they do, they don't lead anywhere. As we write this, there are only two African-American managers—Dusty Baker of the San Francisco Giants and Jerry Manuel of the Chicago White Sox—and one Latino skipper, Felipe Alou of the Montreal Expos.

If Jackie were alive today, he'd be charging at this issue with spikes raised high.

In 1997, in the midst of the fiftieth-anniversary celebration of Jackie's major-league debut, baseball's Executive Council, in the person of its then president, Bud Selig, promised to address this inequity in the executive suites and dugouts. During the past two years—as the player agent Tom Reich puts it, fifty plus two from the time Jackie broke the color line—teams have hired six general managers and nine managers. Four of the five highest-ranking positions in the commissioner's office have also been filled. Of those twenty hires, only one, Jerry Manuel, was a minority member. The number of minorities in positions of authority has actually regressed since the Robinson gala. One black general manager, Bob Watson, resigned his position with the New York Yankees shortly after the 1997 season ended; two black managers,

Cito Gaston and Don Baylor, were fired. Whites succeeded all three; minorities weren't even given the opportunity to interview for any of the positions. If you go back to 1993, the numbers are even worse. Major-league teams have named 35 managers since then, but Manuel has been the only minority hired.

On one level, this shouldn't surprise anyone. Baseball, like most businesses, takes its lead from the CEO. The owners elected Bud Selig commissioner of baseball in July 1997. When it came time to fill executive positions in his own office, Selig first enlisted Paul Beeston, former president of the Toronto Blue Jays and one of the ablest men in the game, to serve as major-league baseball's president and chief operating officer. Selig and Beeston then hired Sandy Alderson, a former president and general manager with the Oakland A's, as executive vice-president of baseball operations, Robert Manfred as executive vice-president for human resources and labor relations, and Bob DuPuy as executive vice-president for administration. Selig didn't invite applications from any minority candidates.

Not long after the hirings were announced, Bob Watson said, "The commissioner's office made promises during the Jackie Robinson ceremonies that there were going to be minorities hired. Well, now they're 0-for-3." Watson had good reason to take umbrage over the hirings; there had been much media speculation that Watson was a strong candidate for the job, which eventually went to Alderson. The commissioner's office did nothing to quell that public perception, but the reality is Watson never officially interviewed for the position. "I did talk to Paul Beeston in the middle of last summer [1998]," Watson later said, "and he told me they were thinking of restructuring. He said they would include my name on a short list. That's the last I heard of it until the news came out that Sandy was their guy." (Funny thing about those hirings. When the position Alderson was hired for was discussed with Watson, a salary in the range of $400,000 to $500,000 was mentioned. The commissioner agreed to pay Sandy at least $1 million a year. Afterward, Bob was informally approached about accepting a position as one of Alderson's assistants. He was told the job paid $100,000. However, when a Caucasian was hired for that spot, the salary suddenly jumped to $250,000. Do you detect a pattern here?)

Now let me throw a trivia question at you: Who was the only general manager to have two teams reach post-season play in 1998? The answer is Mr. Watson. Both the New York Yankees and Houston Astros were largely his creations. The Yankee club he assembled has won two world championships in the past three seasons. Watson has demonstrated administrative skills and a baseball acumen second to none. Yet he didn't even rate the courtesy of a phone call to inform him he was out of the running for a job he coveted. One has to wonder if anyone ever seriously considered his candidacy.

Commissioner Selig defended his choices by saying, "We hired two people who had a combined 20 years' experience in front offices in Paul and Sandy. You can't replicate that kind of experience." Well, Bob Watson has been in baseball *for over 30 years,* thank you very much. Having been a player as well as an executive, he has a greater breadth of experience than any of the commissioner's recent hirings.

Baseball needs men like Watson, particularly now. The game's immediate future could well hinge on the negotiations that will take place between the owners and players starting in 2000. Watson has viewed baseball's ongoing labor wars from the perspective of a player and a member of management. His presence would be immensely valuable to both sides at the bargaining table. But instead of helping to ensure a vibrant future for the sport he cherishes, Bob is currently working with his son in Watson and Co., a firm specializing in entertainment finance. What a waste for the sport! No one can duplicate what someone like Bob Watson carries in his heart and head. When he is forced to leave the game to seek employment in another industry, baseball loses.

The recent appalling treatment of Watson and other qualified blacks is nothing new. It reflects a condition that has existed for as long as I can remember. Retirement from baseball has always been far more traumatic for black players than for white players. When an African-American removes his uniform, it frequently means he has severed all ties to the game. If he desires to stay in baseball, he quickly discovers there are few jobs of consequence open to him.

For example, when Paul Molitor, a white player, announced that his playing days were over, the Minnesota Twins offered him his pick of jobs. Paul had an opportunity to coach, work in the front office, or assume the team's public face as a broadcaster (he decided to broadcast while working as a part-time coach). At the time of his retirement, Molitor had been with the Twins all of three seasons. Minnesota played below .500 throughout his tenure with the club.

Kirby Puckett, an African-American, spent his entire 14-year playing career with the Twins. His achievements had earned him the status of local icon. Puckett helped lead Minnesota to two world championships. When glaucoma forced Kirby to retire, the Twins gave him a job. In the public-relations department. Minnesota didn't offer Kirby, one of the game's brightest players, a decision-making role as it had Molitor. I have nothing against Paul. A pro's pro, Molitor is precisely the sort of individual baseball should keep in the game after he departs from the playing field. But I just have to wonder why the Twins didn't give Kirby the same range of choices they offered Molitor.

Then again, at least the Twins offered Puckett a position. Jackie Robinson was the first to discover how baseball would discard African-Americans once they could no longer produce between the lines. He learned how the owners could wring every last run from your body then show you the door. His wife, Rachel, has told me on several occasions how badly Jackie wanted to stay in baseball after he retired as a player. He yearned to be baseball's first black manager. No one would give him a job.

Think about that. Here was a fiery, inspirational leader, one of the smartest ballplayers ever to grace a diamond. Everyone acknowledges that it was Robinson who taught the Dodgers how to win. Even his opponents respected his competitive spirit. As Leo Durocher, a bitter Robinson rival, once said, "You want guys on your team who come to play. Robinson never comes to play. He comes to beat ya. He comes to take the bat and ram it up your ass sideways." Pardon me, but isn't that the kind of personality you would want leading your team? Yet baseball couldn't find a spot for Jackie in any of its dugouts. Forget manager. No one even offered him a coaching position. So he went to work as a vice-president for Chock Full O' Nuts. What's your definition of a tragedy? I just gave you mine. Baseball suffered immeasurably the day it let all that knowledge, courage, and class walk out the clubhouse door. The owners' indifference to Robinson's hopes set a tone that continues to this day.

For years, many front offices claimed the reason there weren't more African-American managers was because they wouldn't return to the minors to learn their trade. That was, and remains, nothing more than a pathetic excuse. I don't know of a single black ballplayer who ever refused a managing apprenticeship in the minor leagues. Although if one had, I wouldn't have blamed him. Joe Torre, Pete Rose, Lou Piniella, Larry Dierker, and countless other white former players became managers without spending a day in the minors. Jack McKeon hadn't managed a major-league team in seven years when the Cincinnati Reds tapped him as skipper in 1998. Larry Dierker came out of a broadcast booth to manage; he hadn't worn a uniform in nearly twenty years. Dierker, it should be mentioned, wasn't the first to take over a club after such a long hiatus from the field. In 1980 the San Diego Padres named its announcer, Jerry Coleman, as manager. Coleman had last played in 1957 and had no managing experience whatsoever.

Yet baseball forced Frank Robinson, a Hall of Famer, to spend several years managing in the Puerto Rican Winter League to prove he could handle the job in a major-league dugout. Why did he have to do that? Didn't anyone in a major-league front office ever see Frank play? It was obvious there wasn't anything he didn't know about the game. And he was not just a leader, but THE leader on every ball club that ever employed him. What did he have to prove to anybody?

Frank finally got his shot with the Cleveland Indians in 1974. But little has changed since he became baseball's first black manager. African-Americans are still overlooked when teams hire skippers. "Let's face it," one American League official who wished to remain anonymous told us, "blacks still have to prove they're better just to get considered for a job."

And sometimes being better isn't enough. Cito Gaston is the only American League manager in the last 26 years to guide his club to two consecutive world championships. Since Toronto fired him on September 24, 1997, baseball has hired nine managers. No one called Cito for any of those jobs. When we mentioned this lack of interest in Gaston, one National League executive said, "Hey, look at Bill Russell. He got fired by the Dodgers and took a job managing in Double-A ball (for the Tampa Bay Devil Rays). He's working his way back up. Cito hasn't managed for two years now; he should do the same thing. You know, out of sight, out of mind."

All I could think when I heard his response was "Bill Russell? Bill Russell! Bill Russell managed the Dodgers for less than one season. He's never won anything. How can anyone compare his record to Cito Gaston's?" When you have to listen to nonsense like this, your first impulse is to reach out, reach out and strangle someone. However, after cooling off and giving the matter some thought, I had to admit this executive had a point, though it wasn't the one he thought he was making. Cito had been out of the game for two years. A white manager with Gaston's record would not have been kept unemployed for that long. Some team would have hired him by now, and no one would have required him to work his way back up through the minors.

For an example of the double standard baseball applies to African-Americans, just compare Cito's status to Davey Johnson's. I have the highest regard for Davey's ability; he is unquestionably one of the best baseball managers of the last quarter-century. But he has only one world championship on his résumé to Cito's two. Davey has taken two sabbaticals from baseball in the last four years. Both times he came back to plum jobs, with the Baltimore Orioles in 1996 and the Los Angeles Dodgers during the off-season in 1998. Joe Torre had been a broadcaster for five seasons when the St. Louis Cardinals brought him back to the dugout in 1990. No one asked either of them to return to the bush leagues to prove they hadn't forgotten how to manage a baseball team. So why would anyone ask that of Cito? "Owners," says Frank Robinson, "should be breaking this guy's door down. He is a proven commodity. Wouldn't you think an expansion team like the Tampa Bay Devil Rays would bring someone like this, a proven winner and recognizable personality, on board?"

We have had several successful black managers—Gaston, Robinson, Don Baylor, and Dusty Baker have all won Manager of the Year awards (Dusty's done it twice)—yet this has not initiated a hiring trend, which is downright unusual for baseball, where success usually engenders imitation. Every season you hear of a number of African-Americans who are supposedly being considered for managerial positions. Teams circulate a different set of names every few years. The current crop includes Davey Lopes, a coach with the San Diego Padres, along with two New York Yankee coaches, Willie Randolph and Chris Chambliss. They seem to be on every club's short list of managerial candidates, but apparently that's just for public consumption. As Bob Watson recently pointed out, "People are under the impression that these guys are being interviewed, and that is not the fact. Their names are brought up by the media relentlessly. I can tell you that when I was the Yankees' general manager [1995–97], nobody ever asked for permission to talk to either Willie or Chris [as baseball's rules against employee tampering require]."

Frank Robinson tells a similar story: "Teams used to throw my name out as a managerial candidate all the time. But when it came time for an interview, I never got a call. Baseball is good at throwing names out without acting on them. Like with Bob and the commissioner's office. Even I thought Watson had been interviewed for a job. So when he didn't get it I thought, 'Well, all right, at least he was interviewed.' When I found out he wasn't, I was upset. But that's how they operate."

I know about baseball's list of usual suspects, because I was on it for a while. To be fair, I must admit some teams even offered me jobs that I wasn't prepared to accept. So they used me as a kind of cover. Once I turned them down, general managers could declare, "Well, we asked Joe, but he wasn't interested," and then hire some white candidate. I would later discover that they hadn't approached any other African-Americans. Those offers always left me with ambiguous feelings. I was flattered that my name kept coming up, but I was also offended that the owners seemed to think that I was the only black man in America who could manage a baseball team.

What kept me from managing? Timing and economics. The Houston Astros wanted me as their skipper in 1983. The idea of returning to my first major-league club as its manager was tempting. In fact, I went to sleep certain I would take the position. I woke up certain I had lost my mind. Having just come off a good year with the San Francisco Giants, I still wanted to play.

After I finally retired in 1984, Houston approached me once

again. This time I barely considered it. I knew that all managers were hired to be fired; I needed some financial security for my family. My plan was to establish a business or two, then pursue managing. Before I could implement my plan, television called and I realized I would be more at home in front of a microphone than behind a manager's desk. I also thought that since there were few black voices representing baseball, I could do another kind of trailblazing off the field.

I was more fortunate than most black players, because the offers that came my way were legitimate. When teams do interview African-Americans for managing jobs, the process is often a sham. One black coach told me he sat through a session in which the interviewee hardly asked him a single question. Instead, this executive spent most of the time complaining about another African-American candidate who had preceded the coach.

Frank Robinson has sat through a number of these pseudo-interviews. He tells us, "It doesn't take long to figure out if a club is sincerely interested in you. Just listen to the questions they ask you. In a serious interview, clubs want to discover what you know about their entire organization, not just the major-league roster. They'll ask your opinions on their minor-league prospects, perhaps as far down as the Rookie League. Many of them will describe hypothetical situations to get some idea of how you would handle ballplayers. You get in-depth questions such as who you would want on your coaching staff.

"If they really don't intend to hire you, they ask a lot of generalities. And sometimes they don't ask much of anything. In 1996, I sat through the strangest interview; the team didn't ask me a single baseball question. Instead they had me listen to some tape describing math problems. I was supposed to answer questions based on that tape. I told them, 'I've been in this game for over forty years. What does this have to do with managing a team?' They couldn't answer me. So I just filled in the blanks without really reading the thing. I mean, why should I go through that to manage a ball club?

"The identity of the interviewer also tells you how serious the club is. If you are not talking to the very top of senior management, say the general manager, you have almost no chance. When they just bring you in for window dressing, you end up talking to the head of player development or scouting. The GM might make a brief appearance, but then he has to leave to take a phone call. When I left the last two interviews I've had, I knew they weren't serious. I knew I didn't have a prayer."

Even when an African-American has a genuine shot at managing, front offices will search for reasons not to hire him. Shortly after Tony LaRussa left the Oakland A's in 1995, Chris Chambliss, not yet a Yankee coach, interviewed for the job. One of Oakland's owners told me Chambliss couldn't have created a better impression. Had this gentleman been calling the shots, he would have hired Chris in a New York minute.

Unfortunately, the decision wasn't his. Sandy Alderson did Oakland's hiring and firing; he chose Art Howe. The A's told Chris that they had opted to go with a more experienced manager because they felt they needed someone who could work with their young players. Well, minor-league teams are composed of nothing but young players; Chris did such a horrendous job of handling them, he had been named minor-league manager of the year twice.

When you mention the disparity between white and black hirings in baseball's upper echelons to the commissioner, he responds with the same tired mantra: "We know," Bud Selig recently told Jon Heyman, a baseball writer with *New York Newsday,* "that we have to do better. We've made some meaningful appointments, and we're going to continue to work on it. No question, at the managerial and general managerial levels, we have to do better."

Nice words, but why is it taking baseball so long to put an aggressive hiring plan into action? It certainly moves quickly when it wants to. For example, in 1993, a wrongful dismissal suit accused Marge Schott, owner of the Cincinnati Reds, of having referred to Dave Parker and Eric Davis, two well-paid black players, as "my million-dollar niggers." She also allegedly made other, more scathing racist comments. Blacks weren't her only targets. When it came to bigotry, Ms. Schott was an equal-opportunity employer. She called Jews "money grubbers" and "Jew bastards," Hitler someone who "had the right idea about them [the Jews], but went too far," and men who wore earrings "fruits."

When Schott's repugnant characterizations raised public ire across the country, her fellow owners didn't sit on their hands wondering what to do. They fined her $25,000 and suspended her from running the Reds for a year. The owners allowed her to return from her suspension a few months early, but only after she completed several rounds of diversity training. Whoever worked with her in that program failed to make a lasting impression. After Schott made further ethnic deprecations, major-league baseball punished her with an indefinite suspension that continues to this day.

With Schott on the sidelines, owners proactively altered the makeup of her organization. They put Len Coleman, the National League's president and an African-American, in charge of the franchise. At the time of Schott's first suspension, only one of Cincinnati's forty-five front-office employees was a member of a minority group, a low even for baseball. Today, under Coleman's stewardship, the Reds have what is arguably the most racially and ethnically diverse organization in the major leagues. Cincinnati's chief financial officer, assistant general manager, head of scouting, and head of player development are all minorities. This is a direct result of a program the owners implemented in response to the media furor over Schott's remarks. So, you see, when a probing spotlight forces baseball to take action, it can expeditiously address the issue of employment inequality. One has to wonder, then, why it can't apply some of the same remedies it used in the Schott affair to other teams across the board? I can only surmise it is because the people in power choose not to do so.

Almost every time the commissioner claims baseball is doing better on the race issue (and it is, if you're comparing conditions to 1946, the year before Jackie broke the color line), his representatives trot out statistics supporting his claim that minority hirings throughout baseball are on the rise. They never break down those stats by ethnic group, gender, or job description. "Those numbers," says Frank Robinson, currently an assistant in the commissioner's office, "aren't what they appear to be. A lot of the jobs they represent belong to secretaries and janitors. Now, I'm not knocking them; I have great respect for anyone who holds a job. But many of these good people are not in jobs with any power.

"The minorities who hold positions with any meaning at all

are almost all assistants; those jobs are overrated. What I mean by that is the opportunity is not there to move up. You are never considered for the next step. Look around. How many assistant general managers who are members of minorities have moved up? None. How many have even interviewed for general manager's jobs? Very few. If you are a minority assistant general manager for a team, your club will hire a white executive from another team when your boss's job opens up." Baseball also pads those numbers by including Japanese and Latino scouts working in their own countries as minority employees. Will you explain to me how you can count someone employed in his native land as a minority?

While African-Americans do find more opportunities on the diamond than in the boardroom, the playing field has also never been quite as level as it may seem to the casual observer. When I joined professional baseball, most coaches, managers, and execs were Southerners, many of whom helped perpetuate racial biases and stereotypes. They considered African-American players to be physically gifted but mentally deficient. Few teams had black second baseman, shortstops, catchers, or pitchers, a trend that continues to this day; it's no coincidence that baseball people consider those spots "thinking man's positions." No matter what position you played when you signed, clubs would try to fit an outfielder's glove on you if you were black.

The Houston Astros wanted me to switch to the outfield after I signed with them, even though it was obvious I didn't have a strong enough arm to play there. They only dropped the idea when I threatened to go home. Had I agreed to their plan, I might never have made it to the majors. And if I had, I doubt I would have won two MVP awards or made the Hall of Fame. My power, speed, and production stood out at second base; most of the second basemen who played in my era were singles-hitting glove men. As an out-fielder, my numbers would have appeared less impressive.

Think that doesn't go on today? When the Arizona Diamond-backs acquired second baseman Tony Womack, an African-American base-stealing champion, from the Pirates this spring, they immediately announced he would switch to right field. The fact that Womack lacked the strong arm or power bat traditionally associated with right field didn't seem to trouble anyone. Tony was injured during spring training, and it was only while he was on the disabled list that somebody in the Diamondbacks organi-zation realized that if Womack was going to play the outfield at all, he was better suited for left. But I still have to question why they wanted to move him off second (the Pirates, by the way, were con-templating the same switch). Womack has played only two full major-league seasons. He was just coming into his own at second. Tony wasn't a Gold Glover, by all measures, but the defensive rat-ings annually published by Stats, Inc., had him in the middle of the pack among second baseman. In their Zone Ratings, which measure a player's range, Womack scored higher than such highly regarded glove men as Bret Boone and Chuck Knoblauch. Do you see anybody moving *them* to the outfield?

Unless you experience it, you have no idea what it is like to have people form an opinion of you based solely on your skin color. After turning professional, I was fortunate not to encounter much racism on the part of my teammates, managers, or coaches. I did see examples of it in the minor leagues, though. My first road trip with the Durham Bulls was an eye-opener. Our bus pulled alongside a motel in Winston-Salem. I started off the bus with the rest of the players when the driver, the only other black person in our organization, called me back.

"We don't stay there," he explained, "we stay somewhere else."

I had to leave my teammates to register in a motel located in the town's "black section." That night at the ballpark, as I started for the field, I noticed signs that read COLORED DRINKING FOUNTAIN and WHITE DRINKING FOUNTAIN, and finally one that read COLORED BATHROOM. I immediately went numb.

When I joined my teammates for warmups, I noticed a section of the right-field grandstand fenced in like a cage. The black section. The fans there rose to cheer as I stepped to the plate for batting practice. They were trying to show their support for me; I was so stunned I couldn't acknowledge them.

You see, I had been raised in Oakland, a melting-pot community where diversity was treasured. We believed each race or nationality brought different strengths to the table. Half of my friends were white, and we were all color-blind; I had never been forced to confront such overt bigotry. It ate at me throughout the game. I not only felt that these conditions were intolerable, I also felt I was giving them my tacit approval by staying on the field. After the game, back at the motel, I decided to quit baseball.

The bus driver tried to dissuade me, but I wouldn't listen. I was ready to book my plane reservations when I started to imagine what it would be like to return home to my parents as a quitter. That brought me up short. It shamed me so, I decided I had to stay. The next afternoon our manager, Billy Goodman, took me aside. The bus driver had told him what had happened. Referring to those offensive signs, Billy said, "Joe, there are people in this world who think this way [about blacks], but your teammates don't."

I had to admit the truth in that. From the time I had joined the Bulls, no one connected to the team had expressed any hostility toward me. And I didn't see much of it as I moved up to the big leagues. My first managers with Houston, Lum Harris and Grady Hatton, didn't care what color you were as long as you could deliver on the field.

Harry Walker was another story. He succeeded Hatton as the Astros' manager in 1968 and was, without question, the most blatant racist I have ever met in baseball. I doubt this guy even owned a pair of black shoes. From the moment he donned an Astros uniform in 1968, Harry began targeting black players. He constantly deprecated my roommate Jimmy Wynn, who was only the best player on our club. If Jimmy jogged the last couple of steps into second base on a double, Harry would grouse, "I'm tired of that shit. He never hustles." Then he'd fine Jimmy. But Harry kept his mouth shut whenever white teammates like Rusty Staub or Denis Menke did the same thing.

During the early seventies, our two best minor-league prospects were Bob Watson (yes, that Bob Watson) and John Mayberry, both black. Watson, known as "The Bull," was six feet two, 220 pounds; Mayberry was six feet four and weighed around 240. These guys were built for power, but Harry tried to ruin their careers by transforming them into dainty singles hitters. If Watson, a right-handed hitter, drove the ball down the left-field line for a booming double, Harry would fine him for not slapping the pitch the other way. He even demoted Watson to the minors because he wouldn't stop pulling the ball. (When Bob returned, the front office told him to ignore Harry and use the hitting style that had made him a minor-league sensation. Bob would go on to play 19 years in the majors while hitting .295 with power.) When Mayberry refused to heed Walker, the manager traded John to the Kansas City Royals (for a reliever we did not need) where he became a slugging All-Star.

Harry spent a lot of time trying to pit black against white. We had a white outfielder, Curt Blefary, who got along famously with Don Wilson, a black pitcher. After they became baseball's first integrated roommates, Harry started picking on Blefary as if he were a black player; Walker eventually traded Blef to the Yankees for Joe Pepitone. Walker rode Wilson so badly, Don literally tried to strangle him on at least one occasion.

If a black player made a mistake, Harry blasted him. He would reserve any constructive criticism for the white players. I never let him rattle me. He would tell me to bunt in obviously inappropriate situations. At times when a stolen base could help the club, Harry often flashed the "do not steal" sign to me or Jimmy Wynn, even though we were the team's best base thieves. One day I went 4-for-4 with a home run against Mets left-hander Tug McGraw. Walker sent Jimmy Wynn to pinch-hit for me in the ninth inning, even though McGraw was still pitching. When the beat writers asked me how I felt about Harry's "strategy," I just smiled and said, "He's the manager."

I would, however, challenge Harry whenever he tried to humiliate me. For example, during one team meeting he said, "Everybody here does what I ask him to except for Joe." I stood up and said, "Harry, name one time when I haven't done something you asked. You're just upset because you can't get under my skin. And do you know why? Because I play for my family first, my teammates second, and this organization third. You're not even on the list. I don't play for you." That ended that meeting.

Fortunately, Harry was a baseball aberration. Most coaches and managers encouraged you to succeed no matter what your race or nationality. They had to; players were their bread and butter. Throughout my career, however, I have noticed that African-Americans had to be vastly superior to their white counterparts if they were to hold their places on a major-league roster. Hank Aaron, Willie Mays, Lou Brock, Billy Williams, and Ernie Banks had no trouble finding playing time. But there were few jobs available if you were a black, middle-tier talent.

In his 1970 best-seller, *Ball Four*, Jim Bouton wrote about Ike Brown, an African-American third baseman who had been stuck in the Detroit Tigers minor-league system for years despite an outstanding hitting record. Brown could play several positions and, at the very least, would have been an ideal addition to the Tiger bench. Mike Marshall, the ace reliever whom I briefly played with on the Astros, suggested to Bouton that color was the reason Brown's career was stalled: "How many Negroes on the Detroit club? Earl Wilson, Gates Brown, and Willie Horton. Two stars, and Brown is the best pinch-hitter in the business." When I read that, I immediately understood Marshall's point. While there were many black regulars in both leagues, there were few utility men or role players.

A study done in 1967 by Aaron Rosenblatt, author of *Negroes in Baseball: The Failure of Success*, supported this observation. Rosenblatt found that among players with batting averages below .250, the proportion of black players steadily declined. Rosenblatt concluded, "The undistinguished Negro player is less likely to play in the major leagues than the equally undistinguished white player." Other studies published around the same time reported similar findings. Which meant that we didn't have any black versions of players like Ducky Schofield, who sat on the bench for most of his 19-year career, or Phil Gagliano, who played a dozen years in the majors without once holding a regular position.

We still don't. You could compile a long list of utility ball players who spent five years or more in the big leagues: I guarantee you won't find many African-Americans among them. The only current black utility player I can think of is Lenny Harris, who hits around .270 every season, can play six different positions, and has to fight for a spot on someone's roster nearly every spring. (I don't count guys like Tony Phillips or Bip Roberts, who are really semi-regulars.) For every Lenny Harris, there are twenty Tim Bogars. Houston recently gave Bogar, a white utility infielder who hit about a buck-fifty last year, a two-year, $1.5 million contract. I'm happy for Tim and his family. But you don't see teams making deals like that with Lenny Harris, and Lenny's a better ballplayer.

A few years back, the Yankee starting shortstop was Bobby Meacham. Though not a star, Meacham had displayed excellent range at short, second, and third. He was a switch-hitter who could produce some runs despite his mediocre batting average. Bobby had some occasional pop in his bat, knew how to work a pitcher for a walk, ran the bases well, and was an excellent base stealer. In other words, he had all the talents you look for in a bench player. As soon as it became apparent, however, that Bobby could not start for New York, he was not only off the team, but out of baseball.

When you see countless examples of this sort of thing, baseball's message becomes clear: If you're black, we'll keep you on the roster only if you're so talented you can't be ignored. A manager has no choice but to play a Ken Griffey Jr., but when skippers have the discretion to fill those two or three key auxiliary roles on their ball clubs—positions that few outside the ball club pay any attention to—they will usually choose a white player over an African-American.

Why is this important? Because utility ballplayers often continue in baseball as coaches or even managers in the minor and major leagues. They flow into the talent pipeline that leads to the manager's chair or front office. That's not to say many of them reach the top positions, but at least they have a chance for consideration. The winnowing of black ballplayers from major-league benches denies them that chance.

I had hoped that baseball's newest franchises might bring with them some fresh ideas that would alter the status quo, but I haven't seen much evidence that this will happen. When ESPN covered the 1997 expansion draft, I saw the Arizona Diamondbacks' "war room," where they kept track of all the talent available that day.

Nearly the entire organization was present; none of them minorities or women. It looked like your typical old white boy's network. When I talked to them about their player preferences, they all used the same buzzword: *character*. The Diamondbacks wanted players who demonstrated character as well as talent. No one could define what they meant by that word. So I closely watched how they drafted; most of the players they picked were Caucasian. One of the few African-American players they chose, centerfielder Devon White, was their best player in 1998. He led the Diamondbacks in batting average, slugging percentage, runs scored, RBI, doubles, and stolen bases, and he tied first baseman Travis Lee for the team lead in home runs. White is a Gold Glove–quality outfielder who has played on three world championship clubs. There isn't anything he doesn't know about chasing a fly ball; having Devon in center is like having an extra coach in your lineup. In other words, he's precisely the kind of presence any front office should want on a fledgling major-league team.

So of course, as soon as the season ended, Arizona allowed White to sign with the Los Angeles Dodgers as a free agent. The club didn't even present Devon with a serious offer. When asked why he hadn't retained White, Diamondbacks general manager Joe Garagiola Jr. replied that they just couldn't afford to pay him. Within weeks, Arizona signed San Diego Padre centerfielder Steve Finley as White's replacement.

For twice the money White had been asking for.

I'm not saying Arizona preferred Steve over Devon because Finley is white. The team's actions do raise my suspicions, though. Steve's been a fine player, one of those guys who give you everything he's got in every game. He's also been in a batting slump for about year and a half. In 1998, White hit more than Finley, showed greater power, and was a better base stealer. He has always been the superior centerfielder. Couldn't afford him? When you compare both players for production on the dollar, White was a steal.

What is most disturbing about baseball's not-so-subtle racism is how it damages the game on the field. As a result of expansion, nearly every current major-league roster carries two or three players who, under pre-expansion conditions, would still be in the minors. There simply aren't enough skilled ballplayers to go around. And now the owners and the players' union are actively discussing adding two more teams in the next five years. If it doesn't want the quality of its product to diminish any further, baseball must expand its talent pool. Unfortunately, it is currently all but ignoring what was once a rich source of gifted players.

Since 1981, African-American participation in this country's other two major sports, basketball and football, has increased by over 10 percent while decreasing in baseball by about one-third. "Baseball," Bob Watson has repeatedly said, "has to examine how it's going to get the stud player back. You don't see the stud players coming out of the inner city anymore. Eric Davis and Darryl Strawberry were the last of that stud group. If Darryl Strawberry were coming up today, it would be as a basketball player."

Scouting—or the lack of it—is the primary reason baseball is losing the Michael Jordans and Randy Mosses to basketball and football. (Michael has told me more than once how he dearly wanted to play baseball as a youngster, but basketball pursued him more aggressively. And let me tell you, based on what I saw, he could have played if someone had gotten hold of him twenty years ago. Michael had enough natural ability to be a baseball superstar.) Baseball employs few black scouts. The African-American bird dogs who first touted players like Dusty Baker, Curt Flood, Vada Pinson, Tommy Harper, and me to white scouts are no longer scouring America's inner cities for talent.

This is a matter of economics as much as of race. Some years back, the owners collectively decided to cut expenses by slashing their scouting staffs. They chose instead to rely on a scouting combine that furnishes reports on prospects to all the major-league teams. Many of the scouts they released were black.

Since the scouting combine came into existence, African-American signings have plummeted. Combine scouts rarely venture into the inner-city neighborhoods where the preponderance of minority athletic talent resides. College has become the primary showcase for young baseball players; over 80 percent of the draftees signed in the last decade came up through the collegiate ranks. For a variety of sociological and economic reasons, college attendees make up a smaller percentage of the African-American population than the white. Those African-Americans who do attend colleges often can't afford to go to those big-name schools that regularly attract baseball scouts to their games. Therefore, many potential star players never get seen. I am a Hall of Famer, but if I were 18 years old today, I probably wouldn't get the chance to play pro ball.

John Young, a former scouting director for the Detroit Tigers, conducted a study some years back that graphically illustrates how difficult it is for African-Americans to enter baseball. He found that over 40 percent of the players drafted came from colleges in Southern California. Barely 2 percent of those players were African-American. In 1998 there wasn't a single African-American on the U.S. National Baseball Team. I cover the College World Series for ESPN every year. The overwhelming majority of the players I watch are Caucasian. Out of every 100 players drafted, only 5 or 6 have a legitimate chance to make it to the big leagues. But the other 95 at least get the opportunity to fail. That's not the case for African-Americans. The only ones who get signed are the "absolutely can't miss" prospects.

While baseball has been turning away from black talent, Latino participation in professional baseball has been on the upswing for the last twenty years. There are now more Hispanics than African-Americans playing major-league ball. Once again, dollars are dictating signing policies. Forget the large bonuses and contracts that baseball rewards to high-profile imports like Orlando and Livan Hernandez. Teams view Latino players as cheap labor. Many Hispanic players agree to come to the United States for little more than the price of a plane ticket. Their bonuses are far below what we pay white American kids (which continues another baseball tradition in minority hirings: black players almost always receive smaller bonuses than their Caucasian counterparts).

Basketball attracts inner-city talent by setting up camps where young players can hone and showcase their skills. Baseball does not have an equivalent program in the United States. It does, however, run baseball academies in Latin American countries, a leading factor in the recent rise of major-league baseball's Hispanic population. As one baseball executive recently told us, those academies are often used to stash away underage Latino ballplayers. "It's against the rules to sign a player until he's 16. So teams take these 14- and 15-year-olds in their academies, get them under contract as soon as they hit 16, then bring them over here for pennies. You couldn't get away with that in the U.S., so they don't bother building academies."

Which is exactly what it should be doing. I think everyone should have a chance to play major-league baseball, no matter where he or she is born. However, we should pursue talent in this country at least as fervently as we pursue it overseas. Baseball would be a better game if it explored all of its options. This isn't just about race—I would be nearly as upset if baseball was signing nothing but African-American players—but about making the greatest game in the world better.

And it's also about making the sport more financially sound. A few years ago, Jesse Jackson and some other African-American leaders threatened to lead a black boycott of major-league baseball unless teams hired more minorities in decision-making roles. Hardly anyone noticed, and for good reason. Blacks have been boycotting baseball for the past 25 years.

According to a study by the Simmons Market Research Bureau in 1988, the last time anyone broke down ticket sales by race, African-Americans represented only 7.5 percent of major-league baseball's attendance (and National League president Leonard Coleman tells us, "That seems generous; I doubt the percentage is that high today"). Black attendance in the NBA is more than twice that. The average baseball fan spends $35 whenever he or she comes out to the stadium. If baseball could match basketball's African-American attendance figures, it would be pulling another 4 to 5 million people to its games. That's a lot of money being left outside the till, and it doesn't include revenues generated by ancillary items purchased away from the stadiums.

You would think baseball would be desperate to close this attendance gap, and perhaps it is. But it doesn't seem to know how. Unless it takes aggressive action soon, the numbers are going to worsen. Many inner-city kids barely know who Greg Maddux, Barry Bonds, or Mark McGwire is. But they can recite Charles Barkley's statistics by heart. They are playing hoops instead of stickball. When they grow up, these youngsters will be standing in line to watch the action on the hard courts instead of the diamonds.

I contend that baseball cannot realize its full potential on the field or in the box office without reaching out to the African-American population. Black executives and managers like Frank Robinson, Bob Watson, and Cito Gaston can only enrich the game with their knowledge and experience. Increasing the player talent pool will elevate the standard of play on the field. Broadening the African-American fan base will elevate revenues throughout the major leagues.

Okay, now that I've outlined the problems, let's look at a few solutions. To increase minority participation on every level, baseball should take the following steps:

Get Out of Denial. When ESPN held its first town meeting on the subject of sports and race, baseball refused to send a representative. However, John Moores, the owner of the San Diego Padres, did attend our second televised gathering. John was relatively new to baseball. When I asked him some questions concerning minority employment on his team, he said, "I won't lie to you, I don't know the answers, but I'll look into this and get back to you." Which he did. He sent me a breakdown of the entire organization, including how many black scouts they had. The moment John looked at the numbers, he saw the racial imbalance on his own payroll. Now he has an opportunity to do something about it. You can't come up with any solutions until you acknowledge there is a problem. Ninety percent of baseball's hierarchy seems unable to recognize the inequality of its employment practices.

Commissioner Selig must provide leadership on this issue. He can start by radically altering the hiring policies within his own office. I don't have much hope that this will happen anytime soon. Selig—who I suspect is a decent man at heart—just doesn't seem to get it. On April 15, 1997, Jackie Robinson Day throughout major-league baseball, I asked him, "Are we going to do anything about the African-American problem?" He replied, "Joe, we're making that a priority. You will be very pleased with what you will see the remainder of the year. You are going to see a real change." But, as we've documented here, the only change was for the worse.

Nearly two years later, in February 1999, my collaborator on this book, Richard Lally, interviewed Commissioner Selig. Toward the end of their dialogue, they had this exchange:

LALLY: You're aware of Joe's concerns regarding the hiring of African-Americans as managers and in the front office. Do you share these concerns, and will baseball take steps to change its hiring practices?

COMMISSIONER SELIG: Yes, I share Joe's concerns. Baseball has made progress, but we need to do better. And you will see positive changes over the next one to two years.

If that strikes a familiar chord, just reread what Bud told me on Jackie Robinson Day. Once again, the commissioner gives us yet another vague, open-ended promise. Bud's proclamations are starting to read like one of those five-year plans the Chinese Communists kept implementing every two years—you know, the ones that never yielded any crops. If we take Selig at his word, the modifications that were supposed to take place in 1997 have now apparently been put off to 2000 or beyond. Is it any wonder that baseball has so alienated its African-American constituency?

On April 13, 1999, the commissioner did convene a meeting to address the issue of minority hirings. National League president Len Coleman, Henry Aaron, Frank Robinson, and I were among the attendees. We all discussed the problem and some possible solutions. At the conclusion of this session, the commissioner promised to work aggressively to address the imbalance. He mentioned a letter that he later sent to all the major-league owners. It asked them to send a list of all candidates for any top positions that opened on their clubs and threatened them with a punitive response if minorities were not included in the hiring process. It was a good first step. Now we have to see if the commissioner and owners will back these words with actions.

Hire More African-American Scouts. A key step. Black scouts in urban areas traditionally do more than just uncover talent. They act as baseball ambassadors, speaking at Hot Stove League dinners, running clinics, talking up the game with players. When a scout signs a player, nearly everybody in that young man's neighborhood starts following his progress as well as his team's. Fans are born every time a local sandlot or high school star puts his name on a major-league contract. Baseball can make significant inroads with the African-American fan base if it hires personnel that can deliver black talent.

Why is it important to send black scouts into the inner cities? For the same reason teams send Hispanic scouts to South America and Japanese scouts to Japan. They know the territory. Many white scouts are reluctant to enter black communities, but black scouts can speak the language of urban youth. They are aware of a whole range of issues specific to the inner city. They can anticipate and address these concerns in a way that will raise the comfort level for the player and his family.

Go to the Source: Baseball must also build academies and camps in urban centers. If an academy were opened near Los

Angeles or Oakland, we could stock it full of inner-city prospects. And not just black kids. You would attract urban whites, Hispanics, Asians, and other ethnic groups. Many of these would be kids from lower-income families who wouldn't otherwise have a chance to strut their stuff for major-league scouts.

There is a program in place that encourages urban kids of all races to participate in baseball. National League president Leonard Coleman currently runs Reviving Baseball in the Inner Cities (RBI), an organization founded by John Young in 1989, out of his New York City offices. RBI sponsors leagues, clinics, and a World Series in over 100 U.S. neighborhoods. More than 100,000 youngsters, both boys and girls, participated in the program in 1998.

RBI could produce a treasure trove of future players and fans. But the program cannot thrive unless major-league baseball, the owners and players, lend it greater support. As Leonard Coleman observes, "The best marketing strategy this game could adopt would be to make sure that every kid in America is playing baseball again. RBI has gone from 2 cities to 121 in only a few years, but we've made all that progress on a shoestring. This is where we should be investing more marketing dollars. If you play baseball as a kid, you'll get your parents to take you to games and you'll take your own children when you grow up. So there is an economic benefit for the teams.

"When we get more kids playing, we expand the athletic talent pool. And baseball is at its best when it transcends the playing field to have an impact on society. Baseball teaches values of leadership and teamwork. Kids learn how to perform under pressure. A number of teams currently sponsor our program in big-league cities. For example, Philadelphia has a great program. But we need increased resources from the major-league central office so we can reach into Des Moines, New Orleans, Rochester, and other cities that don't have big-league teams. Among the players, Kevin Brown, Eric Davis, Cecil Fielder, Heathcliff Slocumb, and Eddie Murray have all been generous with their money and involvement. Kevin Brown just pledged $1 million to start an RBI academy near Los Angeles. We need more of that kind of thing."

Organize a Network: During the late 1980s a group of former African-American players founded the Baseball Network, which supplied teams with lists of qualified minority candidates whenever job opportunities arose. The group met on several occasions with the commissioner and major-league owners to cross-reference information and help formulate policy. Its efforts opened up interviews to candidates who were formerly excluded from the process. Unfortunately, the organization fell apart when its director, Ben Moore, died in an automobile accident. This network should be revived to act as both guide and watchdog. It could provide baseball with a database of minority job candidates, and call for accountability if its suggestions are ignored.

Until then, any black player with aspirations of coaching, managing, or working in some team's front office should seek out Frank Robinson, Bob Watson, Davey Lopes, and others who can tell him how the process works (and how it doesn't work). They should also look for mentors within their own organizations. When I played for Houston, I would visit our vice-president, Tal Smith, during the off-season to watch how the front office functioned. He would explain how he evaluated talent and negotiated trades. I drank it all up, though I was only 22. I didn't become a baseball executive, but I believe the insights I gained in Tal's office have made me a better, more well-rounded baseball analyst. They helped prepare me for a career I wasn't even thinking about back then. Which is why I counsel all players, regardless of color, to broaden their baseball education whenever they can. As that commercial for the New York State Lottery says, "Hey, you never know."

Make African-American Fans Feel Welcome: All of the above suggestions will go a long way toward accomplishing this goal, but baseball should hire marketing agencies that know how to specifically target African-American consumers.

African-Americans in baseball must also take some responsibility if they want to effect genuine change. Players should start holding their teams accountable. They should demand to know why there aren't more African-Americans working in their team's front office. When a manager's position opens, they should ask to see a list of African-American candidates for that job. If the game's elite black talents people like Junior Griffey, Frank Thomas, and Barry Bonds—stand up on this issue, their organizations won't dare tell them to go away. Owners and general managers will have to respond or risk antagonizing their biggest stars.

Ideally, no one would have to pressure the owners to do the right thing. They would see on their own that there are at least three compelling reasons why they should alter their hiring practices. First, diversification will strengthen the game by multiplying its sources of talent, revenues, and ideas. Second, they still have to close the books on their debt to Jackie Robinson. Third, and most important, the owners should change the status quo because it is the decent thing to do. You wouldn't think I'd be writing this 50 years after the game's color line supposedly came down, 40 years after Rosa Parks, 35 years after Birmingham and Martin. I am not unappreciative of the progress the game has made in matters of race, but it needs to do more. It needs to open its eyes. When I think about the conditions that many of baseball's African-Americans must currently endure, I am reminded of what Ralph Ellison wrote in his brilliant 1952 novel, *Invisible Man:* "I am a man of substance, of flesh and bone, fiber and liquids—and I might even be said to possess a mind. I am invisible, understand, simply because people refuse to see me."

Athletes can withstand the disappointment of rejection; even the best hitters come away from the plate empty-handed more often than not. But it is quite another, far more painful thing to be ignored. This great game should never turn its back on men who have dedicated their lives to it just because they were not born white. We call ourselves the National Pastime; we are supposed to be better than that. Let's complete what Jackie started. I want baseball to become a land of the color-blind, where excellence is prized no matter what neighborhood it comes from, a place where Davey Lopes, Cito Gaston, Bob Watson, and others equally gifted are invisible men no more.

Index

Index

Index

Index

Index

Index

Index